THEORIZING SEXUALITY

THEORIZING **SOCIETY**
Series editor: Larry Ray

Published titles:
Mary Evans: *Gender and Social Theory*
Stevi Jackson and Sue Scott: *Theorizing Sexuality*
Michael Marinetto: *Social Theory, the State and Modern Society*
Barbara Misztal: *Theories of Social Remembering*
Barry Smart: *Culture and Society*

THEORIZING SEXUALITY

Stevi Jackson and Sue Scott

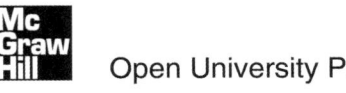
Open University Press

The views expressed in this publication are those of the authors and do not necessarily represent the decisions or the stated policy of the Institute of Education.

Open University Press
McGraw-Hill Education
McGraw-Hill House
Shoppenhangers Road
Maidenhead
Berkshire
England
SL6 2QL

email: enquiries@openup.co.uk
world wide web: www.openup.co.uk

and Two Penn Plaza, New York, NY 10121—2289, USA

Copyright © Stevi Jackson and Sue Scott 2010.

All rights reserved. Except for the quotation of short passages for the purpose of criticism and review, no part of this publication may reproduced, stored in a retrieval system, or transmitted, in any form or by any means, electronic, mechanical, photocopying, recording or otherwise, without the prior written permission of the publisher or a licence from the Copyright Licensing Agency Limited. Details of such licences (for reprographic reproduction) may be obtained from the Copyright Licensing Agency Ltd of Saffron House, 6–10 Kirby Street, London, EC1N 8TS.

A catalogue record of this book is available from the British Library

ISBN-13: 978-0-33-521824-0 (pb) 978-0-33-521825-7 (hb)
ISBN-10: 0-33-521824-5 (pb) 0-33-521825-3 (hb)

Typeset by Kerrypress, Luton, Bedfordshire
Printed and bound in the UK by Bell and Bain Ltd, Glasgow.

Fictitious names of companies, products, people, characters and/or data that may be used herein (in case studies or in examples) are not intended to represent any real individual, company, product or event.

Mixed Sources
Product group from well-managed
forests and other controlled sources
www.fsc.org Cert no. TT-COC-002769
© 1996 Forest Stewardship Council

This book is dedicated to the memory of Anne Witz (1952–2006),
a sociologist, a feminist, an excellent colleague and a very dear friend.

CONTENTS

	Series editor's foreword	*ix*
	Acknowledgements	*xiii*
	Publishers' acknowledgements	*xv*
	Introduction: the case for the sociality of sexuality	1
1	Conceptualizing sexuality: from Kinsey to queer and beyond	5
2	Feminist engagements: politicizing the personal and engendering theory	24
3	Modernity and its discontents	50
4	Is heterosexuality still compulsory?	74
5	Risk, governance and surveillance: the boundaries of childhood	101
6	The sexual self in late modernity	121
7	Embodied practices and sexual pleasure	139
8	Concluding thoughts on ordinary sexuality	161
	References	167
	Index	185

SERIES EDITOR'S FOREWORD

Sociology is reflexively engaged with the object of its study, society. In the wake of the rapid and profound social changes of the later twentieth century, there is extensive debate as to whether our theoretical frames of reference are appropriate for novel configurations of culture, economy and society. Sociology is further confronted with the question of whether recent theoretical preoccupations – for example, with the 'cultural turn', post-modernism, deconstruction, globalization and identity – adequately grasp social processes in the twenty-first century. An important issue here is the relationship between contemporary social problems and theories on the one hand and the classical heritage of Marx, Durkheim, Weber and Simmel on the other. Sociology is still reluctant to forget its founders and the continuing relevance of the classical tradition is both powerful and problematic. It is powerful because the classics constitute a rich source of insights, concepts and analyses that can be deployed and reinterpreted to analyse current problems. But it is problematic because the social world of the classics is largely that of industrial, patriarchal, imperial and high bourgeois European societies prior to the First World War. How do we begin to relate the concepts formed in this milieu to the concerns of the globalized social world that is post-colonial, post-industrial and has seen the rise and collapse of Soviet socialism? Social theory in the twenty-first Century faces the challenge of grasping the fateful contemporary paradox that resurgent nationalism and religious attachments, exposing the fractured and dispersed basis of intolerance, accompany the growth of globalized culture, politics and economies. How does sociology reconfigure the understandings of identity, culture, history and society in appropriate ways? These are some of the major challenges for sociology that this series, *Theorizing Society*, aims to address.

This series intends to map out the ways in which social theory is being transformed and how contemporary issues have emerged. Each book in the series offers a concise and up-to-date overview of the principal ideas, innovations and theoretical concepts in relation to its topic. The series is designed to provide a review of recent developments in social theory, offering a comprehensive collection of introductions to major theoretical issues. The focus of individual books is organized around topics which reflect the major areas of teaching and research in contemporary social theory, including modernity, post-modernism, structuralism and post-structuralism; culture and economy; globalization; feminism and sexuality; memory, identity and social solidarity. While being accessible to undergraduates, these books allow authors to develop personal and programmatic statements about the state and future development of theoretically defined fields.

Theorizing Sexuality is situated directly within these debates and develops a specifically sociological approach that emphasizes the centrality of the social in relation to sexuality. To this end Jackson and Scott counterbalance the influence of some recent theoretical trends found in cultural, literary and philosophical approaches. They further argue for the continued importance of gender in understanding contemporary patterns of sexual life and emphasize those aspects of the social construction of sexuality that affect everyday sexual lives in contemporary Western societies. Sexuality is here not limited to 'sex acts' or to sexual identities but involves feelings and relationships – the ways in which, they say, we are or are not defined as sexual by others along with the ways in which we define ourselves. Jackson and Scott note the growing social influence of biological determinism, especially in evolutionary psychology, and the failure of sociologists of sexuality effectively to challenge it. They argue that sexuality is not biologically given; it isn't even foundational to the human condition or social order. Their critique of socio-biology, which has re-emerged as a popular evolutionary psychology, is an important contribution to an issue likely to assume increasing importance in the immediate future. Eschewing the view that sexuality is the 'inner truth of our being or source of life's most meaningful experiences', they want to locate it within the mundane actualities of social life. In this context Jackson and Scott further engage with and critique the limitations of psychoanalytical theories of sexuality. They argue that sociological accounts of sexuality must *make sense* of everyday experience if they are to have an impact on the public imagination. To this end they have returned to the conceptualization of the social self developed by George Herbert Mead. They offer a nuanced rereading of Mead that provides the basis for a sophisticated and flexible theory of human agency that takes account of the variable ways of becoming and being gendered. Their use of Mead engages with the sociological dilemmas of late modernity and they argue that for Mead the self, and the reflexivity that makes selfhood possible, are anchored in sociality. This is in contrast to concepts of late modernity that envisage the self as cast adrift from traditional cultural expectations, from habitual taken-for-granted ways of being.

Jackson and Scott argue that Mead offers a processual and contingent perspective on how people assimilate new ways of living, how they enact them, and how life choices change the self. This symbolic interactionist approach is melded with critical analysis of more recent sociologies of intimacy in, for example, Beck, Giddens, and Butler along with theories of the self, the body and embodiment. Jackson and Scott develop a critical analysis of current theoretical debates on late modernity. Their emphasis on reflexivity develops into theorizing the self as always 'in process', rather than a fixed structure and by virtue of its constant reflexivity, in dialogue between self as subject and as object. The sexual self is then viewed as a product of socially located biographies and of ongoing interaction between self and others and is temporally located through the interpretive interplay between past and present. The self is not separate from the social but is a dimension of it, since it is the possession of reflexive selves, our ability to locate ourselves in relation to others, which makes sociality possible.

This theorization enables the authors to think about the ways in which sexuality has become a contested site of reflexive self-construction. They develop a nuanced understanding of the sociality of the body as objectified embodiment. In relation to sexuality this does not mean seeing bodies as sexual objects; rather it involves recognition that bodies can be perceived as objects of desire and can also be acted upon sexually. This is an important theorization of sexualities of everyday life which foregrounds the richness of a sociological approach while engaging with feminist and cultural theories.

Larry Ray
Professor of Sociology
University of Kent

ACKNOWLEDGEMENTS

The ideas in this book have had a long gestation period and a number of scholars have influenced and inspired us as sociologists and feminists, most significantly: John Gagnon and the late William Simon, Liz Stanley, Sue Wise, Dorothy Smith, Christine Delphy, Ken Plummer, Steven Seidman. Many colleagues have listened to us present, or read drafts of, the papers we have produced in the process of writing the book and have made valuable comments or engaged in productive debate with us and we are grateful for their contribution. These include Momin Rahman, Diane Richardson, Liz Stanley, Alan Warde and Anne Witz. Anne was our best critic; we miss her and wish she were still around to continue the debate. Finally, we would like to thank our immediate colleagues for their support and, in particular, Petra Nordqvist for her invaluable help in compiling the bibliography.

PUBLISHERS' ACKNOWLEDGEMENTS

The publishers wish to thank the following publishers for permission to reproduce revised parts of the following in *Theorizing Sexuality*.

Jackson, S. (2006) Heterosexuality, Sexuality and Gender: Re-thinking the Intersections, in D. Richardson, M. Casey and J. McLaughlin (eds) *Intersections between Feminist and Queer Theory*. London: Palgrave. *Reproduced with permission of Palgrave Macmillan.*

Jackson, S. and Scott, S. (2001) Putting the Body's Feet on the Ground: Towards a Reconceptualisation of Gendered and Sexual Embodiment, in K. Backett-Milburn and L. McKie (eds) *Constructing Gendered Bodies*. London: Palgrave. *Reproduced with permission of Palgrave Macmillan.*

Jackson, S. and Scott, S. (1997) Gut Reactions to Matters of the Heart: Reflections on Rationality, Irrationality and Sexuality, *Sociological Review* 45(4): 551–575. *Reproduced with permission of Sociological Review.*

Jackson, S. (2006) Gender, Sexuality and Heterosexuality: The Complexity (and Limits) of Heteronormativity, *Feminist Theory*, 7(1):105–121. *Reprinted with permission of Sage Publications.*

Jackson, S. and Scott, S. (2004) Sexual Antinomies in Late Modernity, *Sexualities*, 7(2): 241–256. *Reprinted with permission of Sage Publications.*

Jackson, S. and Scott, S (2007) Faking Like a Woman? Towards an Interpretaive Theorization of Sexual Pleasure, *Body & Society*, 13(2): 95–116. *Reprinted with permission of Sage Publications.*

INTRODUCTION: THE CASE FOR THE SOCIALITY OF SEXUALITY

This book is the culmination of collaborative work that began in the early 1990s. It was always our intention to work towards a full-length book on theorizing sexuality and the articles we published along the way were seen as contributing to this final aim – though it has taken us a great deal longer than we expected. The book, then, draws upon and extends our previously published work, but reworks and reshapes it, weaving it in with new and unpublished material.[1] This brief introduction serves as a statement of where we stand and the form of theorizing we seek to advance.

We are motivated by the need to develop a distinctively sociological approach to sexuality in order to emphasize the centrality of the social in relation to sexuality and to counterbalance the influence of more cultural, literary and philosophical theory in this field. Sociologists were originally highly influential in the development of radical theories of sexuality and, in particular, in challenging essentialist understandings of sexuality. These earlier arguments for the social construction of sexuality have, however, been eclipsed by the influence of more culturally inflected poststructuralist and queer theories. These newer contributions do offer some new analytical tools, but much has also been lost as a result of forgetting earlier insights, in particular means of theorizing everyday sexuality and of locating sexuality within wider patterns of sociality (see Chapter 1). The work of theory, for us, is to make sense of ordinary, quotidian sexuality and it must therefore be congruent with what is empirically known about it, and serve as a guide to what might be empirically knowable. We therefore eschew forms of theory that operate at high levels of abstraction and have no connection with everyday life.

We do not see sexuality as in any way foundational to the human condition or social order. Rather than seeing sexuality as the inner truth of our being or as source of life's most meaningful experiences, we want to locate it within the mundane actualities of social life. One of our central concerns, then, is to challenge the 'specialness' of sexuality, the ways in which it is set apart from routine sociality. But what do we mean by sexuality? For us sexuality does not denote a pre-given entity; it is a product of the social definition and ordering of erotic life, encompassing all desires, practices and identities deemed to be erotic. This does not mean that it is not 'real'; it is very much a part of our social landscape. Yet the concept of sexuality remains rather slippery and fluid because what is deemed erotic and hence sexual is by no means fixed. Moreover sexuality is not limited to 'sex acts' or to sexual identities but involves feelings and relationships, the ways in which we are or are not defined as sexual by others and the ways in which we so define ourselves.

We prefer to use the terms sex and sexual only in the context of sexuality and not in the sense of sex differences or distinctions; gender then refers to all aspects of the division and difference between women and men. We are thus making an analytical distinction between gender and sexuality, but see them as empirically interrelated; elucidating that interrelationship is central to our project. As feminists we are concerned with the continued inequalities of gender, evident in relation to sexuality as in relation to every other aspect of sociality. We see gender as fundamental to the social ordering of sexuality while recognizing that sexuality has effects on, and implications for, gender as well as vice versa. Yet mapping these interconnections is no easy task, since gender and sexuality are phenomena of a rather different order: gender is a fundamental social division and cultural distinction whereas sexuality is a sphere of social life. Where gender and sexuality most obviously intersect is in the institution and practice of heterosexuality. One of the main contributions of feminism and queer theory has been to bring heterosexuality into question as both a normative form of sexuality and a gendered institution. In the latter sense heterosexuality is not only about sexual relations, but also entails a wider set of gendered social relations and practices and is thus the paradigmatic case for considering how sexuality is embedded in non-sexual aspects of social life.

Throughout the book, we refer to sexuality more often in the singular, rather than the currently more fashionable plural form, sexualities. We do so in order to emphasize our commitment to treating sexuality as a sphere of human, social activity and a field of sociological inquiry. The term 'sexualities' has its place: it is useful when referring to individual sexual practices, lifestyles or identities and in highlighting their diversity. It is this emphasis on diversity that accounts for the popularity of the plural form. But attending only to sexualities in the plural, while demonstrating and validating the multiplicity of forms that human sexual life can take, limits us to issues of practice and identity. This in turn can divert attention away from exploring the wider social ordering of sexuality, in particular the centrality of gender and institutionalized heterosexuality as axes around which sexual lives are ordered and which connect sexuality with non-sexual aspects of sociality.

Our approach to theorizing these issues is eclectic. We both came to the study of sexuality through the interpretive sociological tradition and in particular the pioneering work of John Gagnon and William Simon (1974). We have also been strongly influenced by materialist feminism which 'combines a radically anti-essentialist approach to gender and sexuality with a socio structural analysis informed by Marxism' (Brickell 2006: 88). We owe particular intellectual debts to Christine Delphy and also to Dorothy Smith, who has long been working on synthesizing insights for Marxism and phenomenological and interactionist sociology. We do not see any necessary contradiction between a materialist position and the utilization of interpretive sociologies since they illuminate different dimensions of sociality and both address the actualities of social life, the former at the macro-social level and the latter in terms of everyday social practices. We are not attempting a synthesis here, but rather establishing a fully sociological approach by recognizing that the social is multifaceted or multidimensional (Jackson 2006a, 2006b). What can be seen from one perspective is often obscured from another and we therefore need to be able to view the social from multiple directions (see especially Chapter 4). From the vantage point of structures we can see patterns of inequality and the social ordering of institutions, but miss much of what goes on in daily social interaction; in focusing only on interaction and practices we can miss the ways in which structures both constrain and enable those practices. It is also crucially important to understand the meanings of sexual life and its subjective import and to be able to think about how these relate to the patterns of sociality within which we live as gendered, sexual beings.

In addressing these multiple dimensions of the sociality of sexuality (structure, practice, meaning, subjectivity), we are engaging in *theorizing* rather than constructing a definitive theory. We do, however, have some clear aims. First, we wish to recover and develop some of the lost insights of interactionist sociology and to demonstrate their continued relevance for feminist and sociological analysis. Second, we argue for the continued salience of gender in understanding contemporary patterns of sexual life. Finally, we are all too aware of the growing social influence of biological determinism, especially evolutionary psychology, and the failure of sociologists of sexuality effectively to challenge it (see Jackson and Rees 2007). We maintain that sociological accounts of sexuality cannot have any purchase on the public imagination unless they *make sense* of everyday experience.

The contents of the book are guided by these interests. Chapters 1–4 engage with major areas of debate on sexuality, the first two charting the development of sociological and feminist thought before moving on to the theme of modernity and the central issue of heterosexuality. We then take up themes that we see as particularly significant in advancing the theorizing of sexuality and understanding its contemporary forms: the ways in which the boundaries between childhood and adulthood are implicated in the ordering of sexual life (Chapter 5), the place of reflexive selfhood within contemporary sexual life (Chapter 6) and finally sexuality as embodied practice (Chapter 7). In Chapters 6 and 7 in particular we seek to challenge some of the dominant modes of thinking within current social and feminist theory and it is here that we make our strongest claims for the utility of the pragmatist and interactionist tradition in sociology. In Chapter 8 we conclude the book by arguing for a focus on the ordinary and everyday aspects of the sexual as central to the future of theorizing sexuality.

We have not attempted to cover all aspects of sexuality and have limited the range of substantive themes we discuss. Some might expect any attempt to theorize sexuality to pay more attention to its dissident or transgressive forms. Others might anticipate a greater emphasis on more central feminist concerns, such as commercial sex and sexual violence and abuse. These issues are not absent: we do attend to them in the context of wider discussions but have not made them organizing principles of the book. Our aim throughout is to emphasize those aspects of the social configuration of sexuality that impinge on everyday sexual lives in contemporary Western societies.

Note

1 Chapter 3 incorporates material from Jackson and Scott (1997) and introduces ideas from Jackson and Scott (2004); Chapter 4 draws, in part, on Jackson (2006a), (2006b); Chapter 5 includes a reworking and substantial updating of Jackson and Scott (1999); Chapter 6 develops ideas first aired in Jackson (2007), as well as in previously unpublished jointly authored conference papers; Chapter 7 synthesizes Jackson and Scott (2001a, 2007); Chapter 8 expands and develops an argument originally presented in Jackson (2008).

CHAPTER 1

CONCEPTUALIZING SEXUALITY: FROM KINSEY TO QUEER AND BEYOND

The explicit sociological theorizing of sexuality has a relatively short history, dating back to the late 1960s. It is not that sociologists had nothing to say about sexuality before that time: there had been some attention to the social ordering of sexual relations and a few empirical studies of sexual behaviour. Sexuality itself, however, was rarely questioned; indeed, it was treated largely as a given, something that could be regulated by social institutions and conventions, but was itself a pre-social fact. Radical stances on sexuality, which challenged prevailing cultural mores, tended to pose that challenge in terms of freeing our supposedly natural sexuality from socially imposed repression. Many sexual radicals framed their arguments in terms of the one coherent body of ideas that did exist: psychoanalytic theory. Psychoanalysis not only had a presence within academic circles, but also impacted on commonsense thinking. Concepts such as repression, sexual drives and the libido filtered into everyday language, and continue to reinforce the taken-for-granted assumption that sexuality is a natural force, albeit one constrained by social norms. Sociological theorizing, therefore, had to contend with the influence of psychoanalysis.

Rethinking sexuality as a social rather than a natural or psychological phenomenon emerged in the 1960s from social constructionist perspectives with their roots in phenomenological and interactionist sociology. One focus here was the sociology of deviance, where a generation of scholars began to question the ways in which the boundaries between deviant and conforming behaviour were drawn. Once illicit and dissident forms of sexuality were understood as a matter of social definition, it was but a short step to thinking of sexuality itself as socially constructed. The first fully developed theory of the social construction of sexuality, from John Gagnon and William Simon ([1973] 1974), shared this interactionist orientation, but was concerned with ordinary everyday sexuality rather than the deviant or the transgressive.

The confluence of these new ideas with the emergent feminist and gay movements in the West created a climate in which social theories of sexuality became politically significant. The idea that sexuality was socially constructed undercut much of the ideology that legitimized women's subordination and defined homosexuality as illness or perversion. Many of the younger scholars who began to develop the sociology of sexuality in the 1970s – ourselves included – aligned themselves with these social movements. The radicalization of approaches to sexuality created a climate in which new theories could flourish and, over the succeeding decades, a number of competing perspectives emerged. Significant among these were new forms of psychoanalytic theory and Foucault's genealogical approach to the history of sexuality. Both of these were associated with the rise of poststructuralism and postmodernism which, by the 1990s, found expression in a new form of social constructionism: queer theory.

In this opening chapter we will map out these developments and outline the perspective that informs the arguments to be developed throughout the book. Beginning from some of the early pre-theoretical work on sexuality, moving on to the Freudian tradition, we will then elucidate the ways in which it was challenged by the earlier social constructionists before evaluating the contribution of Foucault and queer theory. In the course of these discussions we will begin to establish our own position.

Cataloguing sexual behaviour

While sexology dates back to the late nineteenth century, located within the medical and emerging psychological paradigms of the time, the debates with which we are engaging here have their origins in the mid-twentieth century when researchers began to map the social distribution of and variation in sexual practices.[1] The landmark studies marking this new departure were those of Alfred Kinsey and his colleagues: *Sexual Behaviour in the Human Male* (1948) and *Sexual Behaviour in the Human Female* (1953). Kinsey's background was in biology rather than in social science, but these were in many ways sociological studies based on interviews with 12,000 men and women – though only data from white men (around 5300) and women (5940) were analysed in the original studies (Kinsey et al. 1948: 7; 1953: 31). Kinsey's work was in many respects more radical than that of many of his contemporaries in that he emphasized the diversity of sexual practices and argued that much of what is seen as abnormal in human sexuality is actually quite common and therefore cannot, in scientific terms, reasonably be seen as deviant. Perhaps the best-known example of this is the 'Kinsey Scale',[2] which suggested that heterosexuality and homosexuality are located on a continuum rather than being binary opposites. This understanding grew out of findings which indicated that 'at least 37%' of men had had a 'homosexual' experience culminating in orgasm since the onset of adolescence (Kinsey et al. 1948: 623). Although Kinsey's team challenged the assumption that homosexuals constituted a discrete identifiable category, the volume on male sexuality remains, in many respects, wedded to the notion that sexuality was natural. This bias, as John Gagnon points out, suited Kinsey's ideological project 'to justify disapproved patterns of sexual conduct by an appeal to biological origins, to the power and wisdom of nature' (Gagnon, 2004: 92). However, the evidence for biology was not there since the 'facts' that Kinsey's team collected were sociological ones, concerning the influence of class, age, religion and marital status.

By the time the volume on women was written, Kinsey's 'sense of scientific and moral correctness' had become more muted (Gagnon 2004: 92). In recanting his previous assertions on the 'natural' differences between female and male sexuality, Kinsey gave more credence to social factors.

> We have perpetuated the age-old traditions concerning the slower respons[e]... of the female ... the idea that there are basic differences in the nature of orgasm among females and males, the greater emotional content of the female's sexual response and still other areas which are not based on scientifically accumulated data – and all of which now appear to be incorrect. ... It now appears that the very techniques which have been suggested in marriage manuals, both ancient and modern, have given rise to some of the differences that we have thought were inherent in females and males.
>
> (Kinsey et al. 1953, quoted in Gagnon 2004: 93)

Thus Kinsey's approach in this second volume can be read as being 'located within a framework in which sexual behaviour and sexual convention are treated as malleable, as the products of culture and history and circumstance' (Stanley 1995: 37). While Kinsey still held to the conviction that sexuality was at root natural, part of our mammalian heritage, he was closer to a social constructionist perspective than many of his contemporaries – most of the work on sexuality undertaken in the 1950s and 1960s continued to endorse a biologistic and/or psychologistic approach seeing it as an innate human proclivity. This was the case with most British empirical work on sexuality before 1970 (see e.g. Chesser 1949, 1965; Slater and Woodside 1951; Gorer 1971; Schofield 1965, 1973) as well as the Mass Observation 'Little Kinsey' (see Stanley 1995). This work was either apparently atheoretical or informed by psychoanalysis. Liz Stanley (1995) identifies a number of common assumptions underpinning this work:

- The definition of 'sex' is treated as quite unproblematic and equated with vaginal penetration; even those studies that record a variety of sexual practices, such as Schofield (1965, 1973), group everything other than intercourse as 'petting', which is then distinguished from 'sex'.

- 'Sex' is unproblematically defined as heterosexual, and that even when evidence of other forms of desire or practice is discovered, it is ignored.

- Sex is regarded as entirely natural and men and women regarded as 'naturally' different in their sexual desires and capacities – with men treated as the norm.

- A drive reduction model is assumed in which sex is an innate need or drive which must find an outlet. Social experience may shape or channel such drives, but the drives themselves are given by biology.

These assumptions, as Stanley (1995) points out, amount to an implicit theorization of sexuality even where it was not explicitly linked to a psychoanalytic framework. In some cases they persisted despite evidence that might have undermined them. For example, the report of the Mass Observation Study of 1949, because it draws on qualitative data, actually reveals considerable complexity and diversity in people's sexual lives, which was explained away. Thus women's dissatisfaction with heterosex, often articulated as discontent with narrowly genital sexual activity, devoid of sensuality or tenderness, could have brought the definition of 'sex as intercourse' into question, but instead is presented as a product of 'sexual conservatism' rather than of the social organization of sexuality (Stanley 1995).

This biologistic, drive reduction model of sexuality also informed more explicitly theoretical accounts of sexuality. One example is Kingsley Davis's functionalist account of prostitution, published somewhat earlier. Davis (1937) assumes that the demand for prostitution is 'the result of a simple biological appetite' by which he clearly means men's appetite. He goes on: 'When all other sources of gratification fail due to the defects of person or circumstance, prostitution can be relied upon to furnish relief' (Davis 1937: 753). He suggests that prostitution also provides for the gratification of perverse desires, which might be denied in marriage. While he does acknowledge the possibility of women seeking sexual gratification, in the final analysis it is male sexual needs, taken as given, which determine the functional necessity of prostitution:

> Enabling a small number of women to take care of the needs of a large number of men, it is the most convenient sexual outlet for an

army, and for the legions of strangers, perverts, and physically repulsive in our midst. It performs a function, apparently, which no other institution fully performs.

(Davis 1937: 755)

Here, as Mary McIntosh (1978) notes, no institutional arrangements are deemed necessary to satisfy any needs that women may have.

Although most social scientists failed to challenge the assumption that sexuality was part of human nature until the 1960s, anthropologists had for some time been gathering a wealth of evidence on the wide variety of sexual beliefs, attitudes and practices existing in diverse cultural settings. This was brought together by Ford and Beach (1952), who catalogued variations in, among other things, how human sexuality was understood, what was considered erotic in different cultures and how sexual acts were initiated and performed. They also drew attention to major differences in gendered patterns of sexual conduct, from societies in which men were sexual predators to those in which they were sexually timid; from societies where women were active initiators of and participants in sexual encounters, and where they regularly achieved orgasm, to those where they were sexually submissive and did not seem to experience orgasm. Ford and Beach's (1952) synthesis of the anthropological literature thus linked women's sexual satisfaction to their sexual and social autonomy. They also suggested that these differences were the product of culture rather than nature, that human sexuality was learned rather than innate behaviour. Anthropology thus provided empirical ammunition for later social constructionists, enabling them to counter both biological explanations and the universalizing claims of psychoanalysis.

Psychoanalysis

Much of the research on sexuality up to the 1960s was either implicitly or explicitly informed by psychoanalysis. While a number of competing schools of thought developed within psychoanalysis, the dominant reading of Freud until the 1970s was a literal one – a reading later to be challenged by Lacan (1977) and others. Since the post-Lacanian versions of Freud are now more widely known than the original, it is worth briefly summarizing Freud's central ideas on gender and sexuality as expressed in some of his most influential works (Freud 1905, 1925, 1931, 1933). The impression gained from these writings is of a tension between the biological and the cultural:[3] on the one hand, we have a narrative premised on innate sexual drives and the anatomical distinction between the sexes; on the other hand, sexual development is located in a particular social context, that of the family. Freud's use of such terms as repression and inhibition are ambiguous too, sometimes denoting forces external to the individual while at other times being characterized as inbuilt in our psyches. For example he conceptualizes inhibitions as 'dams … restricting the flow … of sexual development' and goes on to say:

> One gets the impression from civilised children that the construction of these dams is the product of education, and no doubt education has much to do with it. But in reality this development is organically determined and fixed by heredity. … Education [is] following the lines already laid down organically and … impressing them somewhat more clearly and deeply.
>
> (Freud 1905: 117–118)

At the same time, Freud did not envisage the sexual instinct, drive or libido as innately oriented towards procreative, genital heterosexuality, but rather towards polymorphous pleasures – and this is what is often now seen as a potentially radical view. A constant theme in his work is the tension between this pre-social sexuality and the requirements of civilization: our drives must be contained and channelled for civilization to exist, but this entails costs in the form of unhappiness and neurosis (see especially Freud, *Civilization and its Discontents*, 1930). This conception of what is necessary for civilization underpins his account of what must happen to a child to transform him or her into a functioning adult member of society.

Freud traces the vicissitudes of the libido through various stages that condition the form of our adult sexualities, subsuming our gender and effectively determining our psychic functioning. All this occurs in the context of family relationships, which, in psychoanalysis, are invested with profound emotional and erotic significance. In infancy, according to Freud, the 'sexual drives' are polymorphous and have, as yet, had no order imposed upon them: the infant is bisexual, or more accurately of neither sex. Infant pleasures progressively become ordered, though maternal care, around the oral, anal and genital organs. The last of these phases prepares the child for the castration complex, which is the point at which the paths of female and male development diverge.

Until that time children of both sexes are primarily oriented towards the mother: she is their primary (sexual) object. For both 'sexes' the discovery of anatomical sexual difference, that girls 'lack' a penis (as does the mother), is traumatic. For both it disrupts their relationship with their mother but with very different consequences; the boy sees the girl's missing organ as castration and fears that this punishment (from his father) will befall him as a consequence of desiring his mother. As Parveen Adams dramatically puts it, 'with the sword of Damocles hanging over his genitals, the boy has to make up his mind in a hurry' (Adams 1989: 248).

He gives up, represses his desire for his mother and identifies with his erstwhile castrator, his father, but in so doing retains women as his primary object choice. This resolution of the Oedipus complex is not available to girls. The little girl, on seeing the penis, wants one for herself, sees her own puny clitoris as inadequate, blames her mother for her 'lack' and transfers her object choice to her father. This penis envy marks her for life (for example, it is seen as the source of female vanity) and can be displaced only by desire for a child, particularly a male child who brings with him the penis for which she longs (Freud 1925, 1931, 1933). Because she is never forced to abandon her Oedipal desires for her father, a woman lacks the strong super-ego developed by the male as a consequence of Oedipal resolution and hence she is without the sense of justice possessed by the male. For both boys and girls, the genital trauma leads to a period of latency during which sexual desires are buried deep. At puberty boys experience an 'accession of the libido' which will be directed towards active heterosexual genital sexuality, while girls experience 'a fresh wave of repression' (Freud 1905: 220; see also Freud 1931, 1933) which leads to clitoral vaginal transference and an abandonment of active masculine sexuality in favour of passive feminine sexuality.

This account of Freud may seem overly bald and crude to those more used to the later Lacanian interpretation, but it is based on what Freud actually wrote. This was also how Freud was read up to the 1970s, although there were numerous modifications and revisions in circulation among psychoanalysts by this time. In addition, Freud was given a new twist by 'radical' writers such as Reich (1951) and Marcuse (1956, 1964). Where Freud saw repression as a prerequisite for civilization, the 'sexual radicals' saw it a product of capitalism, shackling us to the work ethic. Freeing human sexuality from repression was therefore seen as part of the political struggle against capitalist exploitation. This view nevertheless relied on a drive reduction model and failed to offer any real challenge to the Freudian framework. With the development of second wave feminism, Freud was subjected to far more critical scrutiny. Feminists objected to the obvious male bias in the over-valorization of the penis, the male-defined view of female sexuality and the conceptualization of the libido itself as a masculine force (see e.g. Millet 1971; Jackson 1978a). Alongside these critiques, however, the feminist rehabilitation of Freud was also underway (see Mitchell 1975). We will return to these alternative readings of Freud, briefly, later in this chapter and in the next, but for now we want to highlight the sociological alternative to psychoanalysis that developed in the 1960s and which, in our view, provides a far more satisfactory basis for theorizing sexuality.

The emergence of social constructionism

The sociological perspectives that were later grouped together under the heading of social constructionism derive from two distinct theoretical sources: the North American tradition of pragmatist philosophy and its sociological elaboration as symbolic interactionism (Mead 1934; Blumer 1969) and the European tradition of social phenomenology associated with the work of Alfred Schutz (1972). These traditions were famously brought together by Peter Berger and Thomas Luckmann in *The Social Construction of Reality* (1966), one of the earliest explicit uses of the term social construction. Notably Berger and Luckmann (1966: 67) use sexuality to demonstrate the plasticity of human conduct and culture, to suggest that 'man [sic] constructs his own nature'. Drawing on anthropological evidence of diverse patterns of sexual conduct in different cultures they argue that the 'empirical relativity of these configurations, their immense variety and luxurious inventiveness, indicate that they are the product of man's [sic] own socio-cultural formations rather than of a biologically fixed human nature' (Berger and Luckmann 1966: 67).

Interactionism and phenomenology provided the theoretical foundations for the 'new deviancy theories' that emerged in the 1960s, in which deviance as seen as a matter of social definition rather than a quality of particular acts or actors. Becoming and being deviant were conceived as interactional processes, an outcome of labelling (Becker 1963; Matza 1969). One early example of work on sexuality deriving, in part, from this approach is Mary McIntosh's (1968) analysis of the 'homosexual role'.[4] McIntosh draws on labelling theory to call into question 'the conception of homosexuality as a condition' (McIntosh 1968: 183) and to argue that although homosexual behaviour may occur in a variety of historical and cultural contexts, the modern Western idea of 'the homosexual', a role that can be inhabited, is historically and culturally specific. Other writers who came to play a significant part in the development of the sociology of sexuality, such as Ken Plummer (1975, 2003), were also influenced by these ideas, but more significantly by the pioneering work of Gagnon and Simon ([1973] 1974).

John Gagnon and William Simon had both been educated at the University of Chicago, the home of pragmatism and symbolic interactionism. Although this was not the dominant perspective at Chicago at the time they were students, Gagnon has made it clear in an interview that figures such at G.H. Mead, Howard Becker and Erving Goffman had a major impact on their sociology of sexuality (see Gagnon 2004). Gagnon emphasizes the significance of viewing non-occupational aspects of life as 'careers' (cf. Becker 1963; Goffman 1963a), which 'offered a processual and contingent perspective on how people assimilated new ways of living, how they enacted them, and how life choices changed the self' (Gagnon 2004: 272). They were also influenced by Kenneth Burke (1945), whose work on 'the grammar of motives' enabled them to ask new questions about the framing of human sexual conduct and whose emphasis on symbolic action and dramaturgical methodology parallels ideas emerging from the interactionism.[5] Gagnon and Simon began to apply these ideas to sexuality while working at the Kinsey Institute, continuing in the tradition, begun by Kinsey himself, of exploring the social sources of human sexual conduct. They published a number of articles in the 1960s, brought together in the path-breaking text, *Sexual Conduct*, first published in the USA in 1973 and in Britain a year later.

Gagnon and Simon 'were truly the first sociologists to radically question the biologism, the naturalism and the essentialism that pervaded most existing research and study' (Plummer 2001: 131). They did more than simply assert the pre-eminence of the social over the innate: in questioning the concept of repression they allowed for a positive conceptualization of the social – as *producing* sexuality rather than negatively moulding or modifying inborn drives. Here their argument not only presaged Foucault's critique of the repressive hypothesis, but also directly addressed the social construction of desire and of the sexual self. From our perspective as feminists this has distinct advantages: female sexuality cannot be seen as a repressed version of male sexuality and neither male sexuality nor heterosexuality can be taken as the norm of human sexual being.

Gagnon and Simon explicitly set up their argument against the received Freudian wisdom of 1960s sexology. While William Simon later effected a partial rapprochement with psychoanalysis, he continued to reiterate some of the key points of the original critique (Simon 1996). Gagnon and Simon (1974) challenged psychoanalysis on four main grounds. First, they questioned the notion of an innate sexual drive; second, and relatedly, they contested the idea of sexuality as an overwhelming force, instead insisting on locating it in the mundane actualities of everyday life; third, they argued against the psychoanalytic emphasis on infancy and childhood in the development of human sexuality; finally, they made an analytic distinction between gender and sexuality, in contradistinction to their conflation in psychoanalytic theory.

Gagnon and Simon challenge all forms of biological determinism, arguing that human sexual conduct is a social product rather than the result of civilization's repression of primordial drives. Contrary to the commonsense assumption that sexuality is the most natural of human proclivities, they see it as representing 'humanity at its most social' (Simon 1996: 154). 'The sexual area may be precisely that realm wherein the superordinate position of the sociocultural over the biological level is most complete' (Gagnon and Simon 1974: 15). They argue that psychoanalysts' 'unproven assumption' of a powerful, innate sexual drive is a major obstacle to understanding human sexuality (Gagnon and Simon 1974: 15). There is little evidence, they contend, that such a drive exists or that it finds expression in particular sexual acts: the empirical variability of human sexuality cannot be explained by the repression or modification of some innate natural urge, but must be understood as meaningful conduct. For Gagnon and Simon (1974), acts, feelings and body parts are not sexual in themselves, but become so only through the application of sociocultural scripts that imbue them with sexual significance.

Sexual conduct and the sexual self are fully social, embedded in wider patterns of sociality. One of Gagnon and Simon's most important critical insights was and is their emphasis on the everydayness of sexuality, forcing us to reflect on the importance accorded to sexuality in late modern societies, to question the idea of the sexual as a high intensity drive, to be aware that sexual conduct can be guided by non-sexual motives, that it occurs in the context of ordinary lives and is shaped by wider social relations. This view of sex is radical in that it runs counter to much commonsense thinking. Sex is usually seen as special, outside and apart from routine sociality, uniquely exciting and transforming, raising us above the mundane quotidian – or alternatively as a dangerous force with the power to undermine 'civilization' and reduce us to barbarism. We share Gagnon and Simon's opposition to 'traditions that stressed the power of the sexual for purposes of social change or appealing to sexuality as a source of political and personal redemption' (Gagnon 2004: 280). We have always been suspicious of inflated claims made about sexuality and continue to ask: 'What *is* so special about sex?' (Jackson and Scott 2004).

Interactionism has the edge over psychoanalysis, then, in conceptualizing sexuality as interwoven with the everyday social fabric of our past and present lives. Psychoanalysis, with its emphasis on the unknowable unconscious, says little about everyday sexuality and assumes that our sexual subjectivity is set on an irreversible course by the traumas of infancy so that adult sexual desires are unconsciously determined by a past inaccessible to consciousness. Gagnon and Simon directly contest this overemphasis on both early life and the unconscious, arguing that sexuality is constantly, reflexively, modified throughout our lives. Psychoanalytic reasoning rests on interpreting childhood experience through the filter of adult sexual understandings. Since nothing is sexual in itself, children do not begin to construct a sense of themselves as sexual beings until they have gained access to sexual scripts. Echoing G.H. Mead's *Philosophy of the Present* (1932), Gagnon and Simon suggest that rather than the past determining the present, 'the present significantly reshapes the past as we reconstruct our biographies to bring them into greater congruence with our current identities, roles, situations and available vocabularies' (Gagnon and Simon 1974: 13). Thus in place of the unconscious as the foundation of the psyche, we have the intrapsychic, 'a socially based form of mental life' (Gagnon 2004: 276). Gagnon and Simon's approach thus allows for agency and change in the constitution of the sexual self. Its changeability is not a consequence of unpredictable eruptions of the unconscious but is envisaged as an ongoing reflexive process. Sexual conduct entails actively 'doing sex', not only in terms of sexual acts, but also as making and modifying sexual meaning.

The way in which Gagnon and Simon theorized the construction of sexual selfhood has particular relevance for us as feminists. Rather than viewing sexuality and gender as inextricably interrelated, with sexual or affective desires and identifications determining gender, as is the case in psychoanalysis, they argue that the sexual self is developed on the basis of the prior construction of a gendered self. In refusing to abstract the sexual from its wider social context, they avoided the conflation of gender and sexuality thus providing a means of making an analytical distinction between them while exploring their interrelationship. How gender and sexuality are interrelated becomes, then, a matter for exploration rather than being decided in advance.

The concept of 'sexual scripts', so central to Gagnon and Simon's work can, unfortunately, too easily be interpreted as suggesting fixed, socially determined lines of conduct. Gagnon and Simon themselves note this potential limitation: while the dramaturgical analogy is appropriate for understanding human sexuality – we *act* sexually – 'the conventional dramatic form' is 'more often than not … inappropriate' (Gagnon and Simon 1974: 23). As they point out, even the most conventional of erotic sequences 'derives from a complicated set of layered symbolic meanings' which might not be the same even for participants in the same sexual 'drama' (1974: 23). Scripts are, therefore, fluid improvisations involving ongoing processes of interpretation and negotiation.

In *Sexual Conduct*, Gagnon and Simon focused on the interacting individual and, while they made generalizations about the processes of becoming and being sexual, did not attend to the wider cultural contexts in which sexual scripts were located. This left them open to the criticism of failing to address where scripts come from (see e.g. Walby 1990). Much of the discussion, moreover, was framed within the language of the socialization paradigm and thus too easily misread as a deterministic account (especially in relation to gender). These problems were overcome in later work when, separately and together, they introduced the idea of three analytically distinct but interrelated dimensions of scripting: the intrapsychic, the interpersonal and the cultural (Simon and Gagnon 1986; Laumann et al. 1994; Laumann and Gagnon 1995; Simon 1996), enabling distinctions between 'the agentic individual, the interactional situation, and the surrounding sociocultural order' (Gagnon 2004: 276). This permits a more nuanced analysis of how sexual scripts emerge, evolve and change and are sustained culturally, interpersonally and subjectively, and allows for individual agency and variation without assuming voluntarism.

Cultural scenarios are the 'cultural narratives' constructed around sexuality, 'what the intersubjective culture treats as sexuality' (Laumann et al. 1994: 6) and that also provide 'instructional guides' for sexual conduct (Simon 1996: 40). Cultural scenarios, the stuff of media representations, public debate and commonsense knowledge, provide a shared, or at least generally available, stock of cultural knowledge about sexuality. Cultural scenarios or scripts do not *determine* sexual conduct, but are resources that enable us to make sense of the sexual. In late modern societies, moreover, there are competing sexual scenarios available, and therefore multiple scripts on which social actors can draw.

Interpersonal scripting emerges from and is deployed within everyday interaction, not only in negotiating sexual activities but also in talking about sex with others. In negotiating sexual relationships and activities, wider cultural scenarios are interactively shaped 'into scripts for behaviour in specific contexts' (Simon 1996: 41). This is far from an automatic process since sexual partners may be mobilizing or drawing on different variants or forms of cultural scenarios; hence the co-construction of scripts within a given relationship entails active interpretation and negotiation as well as potential conflict. In heterosexual relationships this leaves room for unequal participation in any mutually agreed script: his definition of sexual reality may take precedence over hers. In practice, though, many such instances of everyday interpersonal scripting might involve little more than predictable variations on common cultural themes (see Simon 1996: 41), but they are, nonetheless, locally, interactively produced by the actors involved.

Intrapsychic scripting occurs at the level of our individual desires and thoughts, the internal reflexive processes of the self. Unlike the psychoanalytic psyche, where desires originate largely in our unconscious, intrapsychic scripting is a process through which we reflexively interpret material from cultural scenarios and interpersonal experience through internal conversations with ourselves. William Simon (1996) directly contests the Freudian notion of the 'id' as the 'embodiment of the sexual' therefore belonging in the realm of 'nature' held in check only by the civilized ego and super-ego. He argues that 'the problem of desire is not that of a conflict between nature and civilization: rather, it is a problem of the emergence of the intrapsychic as an autonomous domain following the experience of living in modern civilizations' (Simon 1996: 44). Intrapsychic scripting is the means by which we make sense of desires and practices and informs, and is informed by, our engagement with interpersonal scripting. It is through our inner, intrapsychic life that we experience desire, construct fantasies and reflect upon sexual experiences. This should not be taken to imply that the sexual self is stable and orderly, but rather that instability and disorder are social in origin rather than the consequence of 'primal chaos': it is 'the disorder of social life that creates the chaos of inner life' (Simon 1996: 44).

Foucault and the reorientation of social constructionism

For Gagnon and Simon the sexual is a matter of social definition, but they do not investigate how the idea of sexuality itself arose; this, however, was central to Foucault's project. In embarking on *the* history of sexuality he signalled a problematization of the concept of sexuality (Halperin 1995). He was not investigating a pre-given object but rather the historical emergence of the construct of sexuality. Sexuality came into being as an object of discourse, as an apparatus that ordered bodies and pleasures into what we know as 'sex'. Central to this endeavour and its starting point was Foucault's critique of the 'repressive hypothesis'. Like Gagnon and Simon, Foucault questioned the idea that sexuality was a pre-given object shaped by repressive forces, but he did so from a different perspective. In line with his previous elaboration of the idea that discourse produces its own objects (Foucault 1972) and his understanding of power as productive (Foucault 1979), Foucault sees sexuality as an *effect* of power: 'sexuality is not, in relation to power, an exterior domain to which power is applied ... on the contrary it is a result and an instrument of power's designs' (Foucault [1978] 1981: 152).

Foucault begins the first volume of *The History of Sexuality* by bringing into question the repressive hypothesis that had hitherto informed received wisdom about sexuality's past and present. In a brilliantly ironic tone Foucault sets out the familiar story of the Victorian age as one in which sexuality was repressed and silenced and reveals the ideological investments in this narrative: Marxists annexe it to 'the ceremonial history of the modes of production' (Foucault 1980: 5), sexual radicals can pride themselves on 'being subversive' (1980: 6) and psychoanalysts can profit from it. 'Ours is, after all, the only civilization in which officials are paid to listen to all and sundry impart the secrets of their sex' (Foucault 1981: 7). It is, then, this idea of repression that Foucault sets out to investigate:

> The question I would like to pose is not, why are we repressed? But rather, why do we say, with so much passion and so much resentment against our most recent past, against our present, and against ourselves, that we are repressed? ... What led us to show, ostentatiously, that sex is something we hide, to say it is something we silence? ... What paths have brought us to the point where we are 'at fault' with respect to our own sex? And how have we come to be a civilization so peculiar as to tell itself that, through an abuse of power which has not ended, it has long 'sinned' against sex?
>
> (Foucault 1981: 8–9)

Foucault raises three doubts about the repressive hypothesis, which he proceeds to address in the remainder of the volume. The first is whether the supposed repression beginning in the seventeenth century and culminating in the Victorian era is historically verifiable. The second doubt is whether power works primarily through repression. The third and final doubt is whether the critique of repression actually opposes the operation of power or is part of the very discourse it purports to oppose. He argues that historically we have not witnessed increasing repression from the seventeenth to the nineteenth century, but rather an incitement to discourse about sex from the Catholic confessional of the Counter-Reformation to the nineteenth-century science of sex and beyond. The operation of power through the deployment of these sexual discourses, far from repressing a pre-given sexuality, created new sexual subjects and new possibilities for subjectivity. A key example here is homosexuality. Rather than being a form of sexuality constant throughout history it is, for Foucault, a product of the nineteenth-century construction of the homosexual as a 'personage', which made it possible to *be* a homosexual:

> It was consubstantial with him less as a habitual sin than as a singular nature ... Homosexuality appeared as one of the forms of sexuality when it was transposed from the practice of sodomy onto a kind of interior androgyny, a hermaphrodism of the soul. The sodomite had been a temporary aberration; the homosexual was now a species.
>
> (Foucault 1981: 43)

The third doubt directly contests the position of those sexual radicals who sought to liberate us from the effects of repression. The idea that freeing ourselves from repression would also free us from domination, as expressed, for example, by Reich (1951), 'unfolded within the deployment of sexuality, and not outside or against it' (Foucault 1981: 131); it represented simply a tactical shift within the deployment and could not be expected to dismantle it. This anti-repressive struggle depended on the language of psychoanalysis which is also, for Foucault, a product of the historical deployment of sexuality, a particular regime of truth arising in particular circumstances.

There can be no notion of sex as an already existing sphere of human activities and attributes; rather sex is 'a complex idea which was formed inside the deployment of sexuality' (Foucault 1980: 152). Foucault argues that rather than sexuality being grafted onto sex, sexuality produced sex; thus both sex and sexuality are of relatively recent historical origin, speaking of how he came so see this he says:

> couldn't it be that sex – which seems to be an instance having its own laws and constraints, on the basis of which the masculine and feminine sexes are defined – be something which on the contrary is *produced* by the apparatus of sexuality? What this discourse of sexuality was initially applied to wasn't sex but the body, the sexual organs, pleasures, kinship relations, interpersonal relations.
>
> (Foucault 1980: 210, emphasis in original)

This 'heterogeneous ensemble', he maintains, was eventually 'completely overlaid by the apparatus of sexuality', which 'produced, as the keystone of its discourse and perhaps of its very functioning, the idea of sex' (Foucault 1980: 210). Thus Foucault's terminology does not permit a distinction between sex as erotic acts and sensations and sex as sex difference – what we would call gender. Both are subsumed under 'sex'; both are products of the apparatus of sexuality. The conflation of gender and sexuality, which Gagnon and Simon (1974) argued against, reappears with Foucault but as an effect of discourse and power rather than, as in psychoanalysis, as ontologically entwined in the human psyche.

We would prefer to maintain, along with Gagnon and Simon, the distinction between gender and sexuality while acknowledging, with Foucault, that they are commonly discursively conflated. Gagnon and Simon were motivated to make the gender–sexuality distinction in part because they sought to explain sexual selfhood and how we come to be sexual and, in so doing, to contest biological accounts of sexual being. Although Foucault does suggest that particular sexual subjectivities are discursive constructions, he was not particularly interested either in the question of where sexual desires come from or in contesting biological arguments about the origins of individual sexualities. When asked in an interview for his opinion on whether homosexuality was an innate predisposition or social in origin, he replied 'On this question I have absolutely nothing to say. "No comment"' (cited in Halperin 1995: 4). Thus while he is usually read as a social constructionist, what is being constructed, for Foucault, is not individual sexual subjectivity. His contribution has been to sensitize us to the discursive constitution of sexuality itself. Where Gagnon and Simon contested the inflated importance of sexuality in contemporary society, Foucault provides us with an account of how we came to understand sexuality as a fundamental 'truth' of our being.

Queer theory

Foucault's influence on studies of sexuality has arguably had its greatest impact through the development of queer theory, which has set much of the theoretical agenda in the field since the 1990s (see e.g. Gamson and Moon 2004). Queer theory is not a unified perspective and not easy to define since most of its founding canonical texts do not identify themselves as queer (see e.g. Butler 1990a; Dollimore 1991; Fuss 1991; Sedgwick 1991). It emerged as an approach to dissident sexualities framed within deconstructionist, poststructuralist or postmodern perspectives. Some have already declared its demise. Theresa de Lauretis, among those credited with originating the idea of queer theory, claimed that it had become 'a conceptually vacuous creature of the publishing industry' (de Lauretis 1994: 297). Queer theory, however, has refused to die; indeed, in some circles it has come to stand in for the entirety of critical studies of sexuality and has extended its influence to discussions of the broader sphere of intimate relations (Stacey 1996, 2004; Roseneil and Budgeon 2004). There are signs that it might outlive its postmodern parent, now arguably in decline (Matthewman and Hoey 2006).

Queer theory departs from earlier gay affirmative scholarship in that it seeks to destabilize all identities, challenging 'the assumption of a unified homosexual identity' (Seidman 1997: 93). Lesbian and gay identities can still be mobilized politically, but only on the understanding that they are provisional and contingent. As Judith Butler (1991) puts it:

> Identity categories tend to be instruments of regulatory regimes, whether as the normalizing categories of oppressive structures or as the rallying points for a liberatory contestation of that very oppression. This is not to say that I will not appear at political occasions under the sign of lesbian, *but that I would like to have it permanently unclear what precisely that sign signifies.*
>
> (Butler 1991: 13–14, our emphasis)

Queer theory de-essentializes identity (Halperin 1995) and destabilizes the binary divide of heterosexuality and homosexuality – and sometimes the gender binary. While Foucault may be a major theoretical influence, queer arguments also make use of Derridian deconstruction and Lacanian psychoanalysis. This appropriation of psychoanalysis may seem particularly inappropriate given Foucault's critique of its regulatory regime. What makes this even remotely possible is Lacan's rereading of Freud through structural linguistics, which, through its focus on the symbolic, is held to divest it of both essentialism and misogyny and to alert us to the precariousness of sexed identities (see Chapter 2). Foucault is kinder to this variant of psychoanalysis than to the cruder form lampooned in the opening chapter of *The History of Sexuality*. As he notes, more recent psychoanalytic theory does not assume a pre-existing desire held down by repression, but rather 'that the law is what constitutes both desire and the lack on which it is predicated' (Foucault 1981: 81),[6] so that power is implicated in bringing desire into being. Nonetheless, Foucault argues, the idea of the law as constitutive of desire still locates power as essentially negative and prescriptive, concerned with prohibition and censorship. We would add that, in addition, Lacanian psychoanalysis is as universalistic and ahistorical as more literal readings of Freud and makes claims to uncover the truth of our being, which sits uneasily alongside Foucault.

Many theorists of sexuality, however, draw on both Freud and Foucault while seeming to be oblivious to the contradictions inherent in so doing. A few, however, do justify this move, notably Judith Butler. Butler's (1990a) deconstruction of 'the compulsory order of sex/gender/desire' that constitutes the 'heterosexual matrix' established her as one of the key theorists within both feminism and queer. In her earlier work Butler was critical of the ways in which psychoanalysis normalizes heterosexuality, whereby to be one sex is to necessarily desire the other (Butler 1990b). In discussing the feminist appropriation of Lacanian theory, she argues that it produces a 'false coherence in the form of a storyline about infantile development where it ought to investigate genealogically the exclusionary practices which condition that particular narrative of identity formation' (Butler 1990b: 332). Here Butler is clearly mobilizing Foucauldian methodology against psychoanalysis. Yet she was soon, in *Bodies that Matter* (1993), to argue for a 'Foucauldian redescription' of psychoanalysis, suggesting that it was possible to 'challenge the structural stasis of the heterosexualizing norm within the psychoanalytic account without dispensing with what is clearly valuable in psychoanalytic perspectives' (Butler 1993: 22). For Butler, the symbolic law that enforces sexual differentiation is not a universal fixed structure, rather it is a product of normative heterosexual reiteration. The reason why she sees psychoanalysis as 'valuable' is that she takes it to account for 'how certain regulatory norms form a "sexed" subject in terms that establish the indistinguishability of psychic and bodily formation' (Butler 1993: 22). She suggests that psychoanalysis is necessary to explain how subjectivity comes to be unthinkable without sexed subjectivity and to explain the 'identificatory processes [which] are crucial to the forming of sexed materiality' (Butler 1993: 17). For this reason she finds it necessary to recover the idea of the unconscious and to ameliorate Foucault's critique of repression to take account of the ways in which repression 'operates as a modality of productive power' (Butler 1993: 22).

Despite its apparent incompatibility with Foucauldian ideas, psychoanalysis is appealed to as if it were the only means of theorizing subjectivity – an assumption that we will contest more fully in Chapter 6. One of the curious effects of this queer coupling of psychoanalysis and Foucault is that it exacerbates the latent functionalism that has been noted in Foucault's work (Poulantzas 1978; Weeks 1981, 1989), in particular through his reintroduction of the concept of the normative. Where this is married up with the Lacanian idea of a symbolic law to which we are all subject, even if it is not a universal law, the result is close to the old functionalist sociology of social systems, where norms were assumed to be external to the individual and constraining, but were then internalized and so postulated 'as being constitutive, *rather than merely regulative*, of the self' (Dawe 1970: 210, emphasis in original). This is particularly clear in Butler's discussion of performativity as being more than mere performance since the former 'consists in a reiteration of norms which precede, constrain, and exceed the performer' (Butler 1993: 234).

This concern with the normative remains an ongoing theme in Butler's work, where it continues to echo some earlier conservative sociology: 'the norm appears to have a status and effect independent of the actions governed by the norm' (Butler 2004: 42). More generally the term heteronormativity has become common currency under the influence of queer theory (see Gamson and Moon 2004) and is used loosely and casually without regard to the limitations of its scope (Jackson 2006a). We can discern no critical awareness, within queer theory, of the chequered history of the norm in social theory or of the critiques to which the 'normative paradigm' has long been subjected (Dawe 1970; T. Wilson 1971). As in its sociological variant, the queer usage of the norm renders theorization of agency difficult. As in much poststructuralist theory, agency is explained either by the unpredictable eruptions of the unconscious or by recourse to an unexplained voluntarism (see McNay 2000, 2003).

Queer theory recycles other long-established sociological ideas, which are more in keeping with our own perspective. Among the unacknowledged antecedents of Butler's ideas about performance and performativity are Goffman (1969) and Garfinkel (1967), as well as earlier radically anti-essentialist theorizations of gender Kessler and McKenna (1978) and Delphy (1984). Moreover, the queer concern with the fluidity, contingency and multiplicity of subjectivity and identity resonates with interactionist ideas of the self as always in process. There are also, within queer, traces of interactionist theories of deviance. One of the central themes of queer theory is that heterosexuality and homosexuality are necessarily co-constituted. As Diana Fuss puts it:

> The language and law that regulate the establishment of heterosexuality ... is the language and law of defence and protection: heterosexuality secures its self identity and shores up its ontological boundaries by protecting itself from what it sees as the continual predatory encroachments of its contaminated other, homosexuality.
>
> (Fuss 1991: 2)

This personification reifies heterosexuality, but it also echoes earlier sociological accounts where one of the functions of deviance was said to be to maintain the boundaries of the normal. In her use of the inside/out trope, through which Fuss sees heterosexuality as being defined in and through its rejected outside, we are reminded of Becker's *Outsiders* (1963), in which deviance is a social construct that only makes sense in terms of an equally constructed normality.

We do not make these points merely to lament a lack of awareness of the sociological antecedents of current theorizations of sexuality, but in order to illustrate the problems consequent upon this forgetting. On the one hand this makes it impossible to ascertain what is innovatory and useful in queer and other purportedly new ideas (see Brickell 2006) while on the other it leaves us with attenuated critical skills through which to evaluate current theory. In particular, we want to emphasize the continued relevance of the interactionist tradition, which is more in keeping with our emphasis on the everydayness of sexuality and our scepticism of abstract theory that fails to illuminate ordinary lives. Thus, while we have noted some affinities between queer and interactionist perspectives, our preference is for the latter which, unlike queer, 'does not wish to lose its grip on the "obdurate empirical world"' (Plummer 2003: 520). This does not, however, signal a total rejection of poststructuralist or queer theories and we will draw on these where we find them fruitful.

The theoretical developments that we have discussed here owe a great deal to the existence of feminist, gay and queer political movements; of these, it is feminism, including lesbian feminism, which has most informed our own thinking. So far we have alluded to feminism but not yet fully engaged with it: we will go on to do so in Chapter 2.

Notes

1. Of course mid-twentieth-century thinking on sexuality was influenced by the sociology and sexology of earlier periods, but this work falls outwith the scope of this book. Morrow (2008) argues that sociologists are guilty of perpetuating their own 'repressive hypothesis' (Foucault [1978] 1981) by ignoring the work of early sociologists and dating the emergence of interest in sexuality to the late twentieth century, as a product of supposedly more 'liberal' times. We think Morrow rather overstates his case. We would not deny the existence of this early work, but maintain that what was innovative in the post-1960s work on sexuality was the sustained critique of essentialism. It is the origins of this development that we seek to explore here. Those interested in early sexology should consult the collections of historical documents edited by Jeffreys (1987) and Bland and Doan (1998). Morrow (2008) considers what early sociologists, including the 'founding fathers', had to say about sexuality. A more detailed study of mid-twentieth-century work can be found in Stanley (1995).
2. Kinsey et al. (1948) constructed a seven-point scale from 0, 'exclusively heterosexual', to 6, 'exclusively homosexual' (1948: 638ff.)
3. This is one of the sources of disagreement about how Freud's work should be interpreted.
4. She later pointed out, however, that she had used labelling theory only in a limited and 'mechanical' way in this article (see Weeks et al. 1981: 45).
5. It may have been Kenneth Burke's influence, as much as Goffman's, that inspired Gagnon and Simon's concept of sexual scripts; certainly the idea of scripts as governing self-reflection as well as interaction is closer to Burke and to Mead than it is to Goffman (see Burke 1945, 1950). Burke, as a public intellectual rather an academic, was not strictly part of symbolic interactionism but did, in 1982, win the G.H. Mead Prize (see Denzin 1992).
6. For further explanation see Chapter 2.

CHAPTER 2

FEMINIST ENGAGEMENTS: POLITICIZING THE PERSONAL AND ENGENDERING THEORY

Since the 1970s feminists have made major contributions to the critical analysis of sexuality. It is not difficult to see why this should be so, since the control of women's sexuality has historically been linked to their social location as men's dependants and subordinates, as virginal daughters and chaste wives or as mistresses and whores inhabiting the margins of respectable society. Even in the context of the greater sexual freedoms that have opened up in Western societies since the later twentieth century – the increasing separation of sexuality from reproduction and greater latitude for sexual diversity – gender asymmetries in sexual conduct persist and sexual violence towards women remains a major social problem.

With the revitalization of the Western women's movement in the late 1960s and early 1970s, the politicization of the personal moved sexuality from the realms of the intimate, private and individual into the political arena. Making the personal political, something that is part of a struggle for change, entails seeing it as social rather than as part of the natural order. As Christine Delphy put it: 'belief in the possibility of change implies belief in the social origins of the situation' (Delphy 1984: 211). There is thus an affinity between the feminist politics of the personal and the sociological imagination (Mills 1970), in that both transform personal troubles into public issues and both seek to locate individual biographies within social and historical contexts. While assuming the social origins of sexuality, feminists writing on sexuality in the 1970s did not necessarily engage with emerging social constructionist debates within sociology, but they brought new, politically informed insights to the critique of conventional, male-dominated heterosexual relations.

During the 1970s and the early 1980s feminists succeeded in bringing much that was previously taken for granted into question. Not only did they challenge the double standard of sexual morality, but also they questioned what counted as sex. Following Koedt's (1972) influential article 'The Myth of the Vaginal Orgasm', feminists challenged the definition of 'the sex act' and the conventional ordering of sexual conduct as foreplay leading to penetrative sex leading to (his) orgasm. Here the emphasis was on the ways in which a male-defined view of heterosexuality denied women sexual pleasure. Some began to go further, to challenge heterosexuality itself, to see it not as natural and normal, but as an institution central to the maintenance of male domination (Bunch 1975; Rich 1980). Here the concern was the way in which sexuality itself was implicated in the subordination of women. This was also the case in work on sexual violence and coercion, increasingly theorized not as an expression of men's natural urges, but as a form of social control designed to keep women in their place (Brownmiller 1975). The politics of sexuality was characterized both by the pursuit of sexual autonomy for women and by the struggle against sexual coercion and exploitation. There has, then, been an abiding tension within feminism between the analysis, on the one hand, of constraints on sexuality and the pursuit of sexual freedom, and on the other hand, of the oppression of women through sexual objectification, exploitation and coercion.

This tension was later to be encapsulated by the 'pleasure–danger' opposition (Vance 1984) and played out in the feminist 'sex wars' of the 1980s. The battle lines were drawn between libertarians – defining themselves as sex-positive and pro-pleasure – and radical feminists focusing on combating sexual violence and exploitation. Two issues arise from this. First, although this was an important political divide, the theoretical landscape of the 1980s cannot be reduced to the polarization between these two camps. There were many other debates ongoing at that time and it is important to understand their complexity in order to trace the genealogies of the ideas informing more recent theorizations of sexuality, to explain how some forms of debate were opened up while others were closed down. Second, the pleasure–danger dichotomy itself, the legacy of which is still with us, needs to be questioned. In this chapter we will chart the trajectories of some of the key tendencies within feminist thought from the 1980s onwards, explaining why certain routes were taken rather than others, before turning finally to a critical analysis of the opposition between pleasure and danger.

By the early 1980s there were a bewildering variety of competing feminist positions on offer. Feminist critique had begun from a shared assumption that the ordering of heterosexual relationships was detrimental to women, but from this starting point feminists followed a number of different paths. The differences that then emerged were in part political, deriving initially from the ways in which sexuality figured in varied and contested analyses of gender relations and wider social relations. The picture was further complicated by feminist engagements with the rapidly shifting terrain of social and cultural theory. Thus there was not even agreement on what sexuality might be – competing theories dealt with different objects at different levels of analysis and differing ideas about why sexuality should be a political issue. Often this period of feminism's history is imagined through a progress narrative, as part of the story of the 'cultural turn' (see e.g. Barrett 1992; Jackson 2001; Hemmings 2005), but actually a number of perspectives existed concurrently, jostling for attention.

What was at stake here was, in part, the relationship between gender and sexuality, whether they were seen as separable or not; they were variously regarded as part of the same phenomenon, as analytically distinct but empirically interconnected or as absolutely distinct from each other. Thus sexuality was, for some, to be approached primarily in terms of its relationship to gender division and hierarchy, while for others it was a specific area to be investigated in its own right. There were also divergences in how sexuality and gender were each conceptualized, in what dimension of the social they were located. So there were those who sought to analyse gender and sexuality in terms of social structure, how they worked in the maintenance of the existing gender or sexual order; those who were concerned primarily with culture or meaning, how gender and/or sexuality were constituted as meaningful cultural categories; those interested in the constitution and ordering of gender and sexuality in everyday interaction and practice; and, finally, those who focused on identity, subjectivity, the self or the psyche. Additionally, a further distinction arose between the analysis of sexuality (singular) as an area of social life or aspect of human experience and the use of the plural form, sexualities, in order to emphasize diversity in sexual identities, practices and lifestyles. Within all of the above there were theoretical disagreements, creating a complex, heterogeneous body of theory, not all of which, by any means, was sociological, but all of which had effects traceable within social theory.

Social structural analysis

Feminist theorizing in the 1970s, and arguably into the early 1980s, was dominated by forms of structural analysis addressing the systematic oppression of women, whether this was attributed to capitalism, patriarchy or some combination of the two. Where sexuality was included in such analyses, it was seen as in some way implicated in the maintenance of a particular social ordering of gender. Hence, implicitly at least, sexuality is conceived as analytically distinct from, but interrelated with gender. Those taking such a stance included not only the usual suspects, radical feminists, but also some Marxist feminists, as well as others not clearly aligned with either of these tendencies.

For some, sexuality was central to the maintenance of patriarchal domination mediated through the institutionalization of heterosexuality and/or enforced through sexual coercion and violence. One of the best known of such interventions is that of Adrienne Rich (1980), whose concept of 'compulsory heterosexuality' remains widely referenced today. In Rich's analysis, compulsory heterosexuality both kept women *in* (within its confines) and kept them *down* (subordinated by its institutionalization). She thus linked the social ordering of gender to the regulation of sexuality, but did not produce an entirely convincing account of the social construction of either. Although 'women' can be understood in her account as a socially constituted subordinate group, traces of essentialism remained in her assumption of a common womanliness uniting us all along a lesbian continuum. While she discussed forms of sexual practice that serve to control women, sexuality *per se* remained unexplored – and even lesbianism was largely divested of erotic import.

Others went further than Rich in pursuing the claim that men secure their dominance through the appropriation of women's sexuality. In Britain, France and the USA this view found its political expression among radical lesbians, who saw themselves as a vanguard of feminism and certainly not part of a continuum that could include heterosexual women who 'collaborated' with the enemy and colluded in their own subordination (see Duchen 1987; Jackson and Scott 1996; Jackson 1999). The British group, Leeds Revolutionary Feminists (1981), were among the more extreme exponents of this position. For them the act of heterosexual penetration itself was intrinsically oppressive to women, 'an extreme form of ritual humiliation' which, each time it is enacted, perpetuated men's power and women's subjection (Leeds Revolutionary Feminists 1981: 6–7). Not surprisingly, such feminists focused on the most coercive and violent aspects of sexuality, campaigning against pornography, rape and prostitution. This tradition of analysis is exemplified by, and was continued, in the work of Sheila Jeffreys, a member of the original Leeds group (see Jeffreys 1990, 1994a, 1994b, 1997).

A similarly critical account of intercourse, though one less damning of heterosexual women, was produced by Andrea Dworkin (1987). Dworkin, however, avoids the essentialism of the Leeds position, where the social significance of a particular sexual act is reduced to the act itself. Where the Leeds Revolutionary Feminists (1981: 7) asserted that 'no act of penetration can escape its function and symbolic power', and were scathing about heterosexual feminists' attempts to change the meaning of heterosex, Dworkin (1987: 152) saw such strategies as 'humane dreams that repudiate the rapist as the final arbiter of reality'.

A rather more sophisticated variant of the argument that women's subordination derives from men's appropriation of their sexuality came from Catherine MacKinnon who, in collaboration with Dworkin, is associated with campaigns against sexual violence and exploitation.

MacKinnon (1982: 515) argued that 'sexuality is to feminism what work is to Marxism: that which is most one's own, yet most taken away'. Just as the social organization of labour produces the class structure, 'the molding, direction and expression of sexuality organize society into two sexes – women and men' (MacKinnon 1982: 516). In taking sexuality to be analogous to work, MacKinnon avoids the essentialism of the revolutionary feminists, since she sees sexuality as 'a social process which creates, organizes, expresses and directs desire, creating the social beings we know as women and men, as their relations create society' (MacKinnon 1982: 515) and thereby locates gender in the social, rather than the natural, order. However, in our view she over-privileges sexuality as the ultimate origin of gender hierarchy and division. Other aspects of gender relations disappear from view or are rendered secondary, thus closing off the possibility of exploring their interconnections with sexuality.

Less reductive and more thoroughly anti-essentialist accounts of gender and sexuality were produced by French materialist feminists in the late 1970s and early 1980s. These feminists, intellectually organized around the journal *Questions féministes*, were associated with the pioneering French feminist, Simone de Beauvoir. In *The Second Sex* (first published in 1949), Beauvoir had identified sexual relations as integral to binding women into subordination. Of the consequences of romantic love for women, for example, she says: 'she chooses to desire her enslavement so ardently that it will seem to her the expression of her liberty ... she will humble herself to nothingness before him' (Beauvoir 1972: 653). The materialist feminists, following Beauvoir, sought to explore women's oppression in intimate relationships. Although using Marxist methodology, they saw patriarchal domination as requiring an explanation that did not reduce it to a side-effect of capitalism.

Like MacKinnon, these feminists saw the social division between women and men as analogous to a class relationship, but within a perspective that used a more explicitly Marxist method of analysis. Just as there can be no bourgeoisie without the proletariat, there could be no 'women' without men: 'there are no slaves without masters' (Wittig 1992: 15). Unlike MacKinnon, however, gender, in this formulation, does not derive from sexuality, but is the product of the appropriation of women's labour as well as their bodies (Delphy 1984; Wittig 1992; Guillaumin 1995; Leonard and Adkins 1996). Here gender division produces the homosexual/heterosexual division as well as the categories 'women' and 'men' (Questions féministes collective 1981), but neither women's subordination nor institutionalized heterosexuality were reduced to sexuality. Materialist feminists became divided, however, over the issue of political lesbianism. Monique Wittig became the standard bearer for those who saw lesbianism as the only truly radical strategy for combating male domination. Since, for Wittig, the category 'women' was founded on the heterosexual contract, lesbians could be seen as escaping its confines;

likening them to fugitive slaves, Wittig (1992: 32) famously declared that 'lesbians are not women'. Unlike the British revolutionary feminists, however, Wittig did not analyse heterosexuality solely in terms of sexual exploitation – for her, the heterosexual contract entailed the expropriation of women's sexual and domestic labour.

From the point of view of more conventional Marxism, the French materialists were heretical in applying Marx's analysis of the exploitation of labour to relations between women and men. Most Marxist feminists preferred to locate women's subordination elsewhere than in productive relations, but few had much to say about sexuality. There had been a tradition within Marxism of sexual libertarianism and 'free love', couched as resistance to reducing human sexual relations to property relations. Many feminists active within socialist and communist movements in the early twentieth century, such as the Russian revolutionary Alexandra Kollontai, had espoused such views (see Kollontai 1972). Later, libertarian Marxists such as Reich (1951) and Marcuse (1956, 1964), who saw the repression of sexuality as serving the capitalist social order, were influential among young sexual radicals in the 1960s and early 1970s. These theorists, however, had little to say about gender and most feminists were sceptical of the implications of their ideas – often seen as justifying the further sexual exploitation of women. There were a few who linked sexual liberation with women's liberation, such as the Red Collective ([1973] 1978) who, more in the tradition of early twentieth-century radicals than the gurus of the 1960s sexual revolution, saw the patriarchal family and monogamy as capitalist institutions that subordinated women. Unlike Reich and Marcuse, and in common with many feminists, they were highly critical of psychoanalysis.

In the 1970s and early 1980s it was more common for Marxists to focus on reproductive relations as a site of women's subordination. While it was not sexuality as such that featured in such accounts, the implication was that male sexual dominance derived from their control of women's reproductive capacities. There is a long and respectable tradition that facilitated this form of analysis, in that Marx's collaborator, Frederick Engels, had traced 'the world historic defeat of the female sex' back to the origins of private property and the consequent need for men to ensure paternity rights. Engels based his account on some decidedly dubious nineteenth-century anthropology which, by the 1970s, was discredited,[1] but this did not deter those seeking to make space within Marxism for an analysis of women's subordination that did not unduly disturb Marx's analysis of the history of modes of production. Women could be seen as ensuring the reproduction of class relations, with bourgeois women's sexuality harnessed to the transmission of capital to their husbands' legitimate heirs while proletarian women reproduced the proletariat through bearing and rearing the next generation of labourers as well as servicing the needs of existing workers (see e.g. McDonough and Harrison 1978).

Analyses such as these are vulnerable to charges of biological determinism, of reducing male domination to an effect of women's reproductive capacities. A more unusual variant of this approach, which attempts to evade this charge, is that of Mary O'Brien (1981), who argues that focusing on reproduction is no more biologistic than focusing on production: the latter is necessary to produce the means for our individual physical survival (food, shelter, etc.) and the former for our survival as a species. Thus both production and reproduction are socially ordered. She sees the historical conditions for the current organization of reproduction in the discovery, in our remote past, of men's role in reproduction. Rather than taking as given, as followers of Engels had, that men 'need' to ensure that they can identify their progeny, O'Brien (1981) asks why this is so. Her answer is that men are alienated from the products of their own contribution to reproduction. Since women carry children prior to birth, the sexual act resulting in conception is experientially linked to its product, the birth of a child; men, lacking this continuity, created it artificially through establishing relationships with women. She sees advances in reproductive technology as having the potential to alter current relations of reproduction, through severing the links first between sex and reproduction and subsequently between conception, gestation and birth (though avoiding the assumption made by Shulamith Firestone (1970) that this might free women from male domination). Whether O'Brien (1981) does avoid biological reductionism is questionable and, as with other analysts of reproduction, she tells us little about sexuality beyond its link to conception. Sexuality is not only about sexual acts, but also about the meanings they carry, the desires motivating them and the social interaction through which they are accomplished – and sexual acts themselves encompass a range of possibilities beyond those implicated in reproduction.

A further variant of structural analysis is that influenced by structuralism, exemplified by Gayle Rubin's (1975) classic and influential elaboration of the 'sex/gender system'. Writing from an anthropological perspective, Rubin was well aware of the many and varied forms of sexual practice documented throughout the world. But, in engaging with Lévi-Strauss's (1969) structural analysis of kinship, in which the exchange of women between kin is seen as foundational to human culture, she was also inclined to seek an underlying pattern to the diversity of human sexuality. It was this she encapsulated in the statement that every society 'has a sex-gender system – a set of arrangements by which the biological raw material of human sex and procreation is shaped by human social intervention' (Rubin 1975: 165). While noting the diversity of such arrangements, by relegating them to a footnote in order to concentrate on the structural 'traffic in women', Rubin (1975) missed an opportunity to explore in more depth the social construction of sexuality, as well as ceding ground to biological foundationalism.

One difficulty common to all these structural approaches is the way in which sexuality itself remains unexplored; it is more often taken as given, something to be contained, controlled or channelled, but not the object of analysis in its own right. This was later to lead Rubin (1984) to dissociate sexuality from gender. Part of the problem is that gender and sexuality are not phenomena of the same order and cannot be reduced to each other (Sedgwick 1990). While gender, as a fundamental social division, is amenable to some forms of structural analysis, sexuality is not. Sexuality is a sphere of life and, though it may be ordered by structural, institutional processes and may give rise to social divisions (such as those between heterosexuality and homosexuality), it is difficult to accommodate within a purely structural analysis (see Jackson 2006a, 2006b).

Dissatisfaction with structural analyses, especially their inability to explain subjective and experiential aspects of gender and sexuality, led feminists to look to alternatives. Rubin's appropriation of Lévi-Strauss, which was beginning to figure in some other feminist accounts of this period (e.g. Mitchell 1975), presaged a move from more materialist analyses to a concern with issues of culture, meaning and subjectivity. Those Marxist feminists interested in sexuality and subjective aspects of gender relations faced particular problems: sexuality was not easily accommodated within a Marxist framework while meaning and subjectivity could be addressed only through concepts of consciousness and ideology, which were found lacking for their inability to address women's attachment to, and investments in, aspects of feminine sexuality that feminists deemed oppressive. The notion of a dominant ideology resulting in 'false consciousness', denied women's active agency, failed to capture the complexity of women's subjective responses to their situation or the meanings of intimate relationships for them.

At this time many Marxist feminists turned to psychoanalysis, French structuralism and ultimately to poststructuralism and postmodernism in the search for more adequate analyses. They could, of course, have looked elsewhere to address Marxism's lacunae – to the interpretive sociologies we discussed in Chapter 1. These ideas were already in circulation and had been applied to the social construction of both gender and sexuality (Gagnon and Simon 1974; Plummer 1975; Jackson 1978a, 1978b; Stanley 1984) and to critique simplistic understanding of constructions of gendered selfhood current in mainstream sociology at the time (Stanley and Wise 1983). For reasons we will explain in detail later in the chapter, these sociological perspectives were sidelined by the main theoretical developments of the time, which followed a very different trajectory.

From structure to culture and subjectivity

These developments, associated with a shift of emphasis away from the material known as the 'cultural turn', were to lead in the 1980s and 1990s to the increasing influence of poststructuralism and postmodernism. The story, however, begins earlier and was to have a major impact on feminist approaches to sexuality. From the mid-1970s there was growing interest among Marxists and Marxist feminists in ideology, language and psychoanalysis, in Althusser's Shuehoal Marxism, Saussure's structural linguistics, Lacan's psychoanalysis and Lévi-Strauss's anthropology (Mitchell 1975; Coward and Ellis 1977). These bodies of theory were also central to the project of such radical theoretical journals as *Ideology and Consciousness* and *m/f*, launched in 1977 and 1978 respectively, which were instrumental in bringing 'French Theory' to an English-speaking audience.

Althusser's theory of ideology was pivotal to these developments. Althusser revised the older, economistic readings of Marx in which the economic base had determined all other (superstructural) aspects of the social formation. Instead Althusser suggested that the economic, the political and the ideological levels of the social were relatively autonomous, each having its own effectivity and materiality. Moreover, Althusser provided a means of connecting ideology with subjectivity in an ostensibly more sophisticated manner than had been possible with the old idea of false consciousness. In order to do so, he drew on Lacan's reinterpretation of psychoanalysis, conceiving of ideology as our imaginary relation to our real conditions of existence. Ideology was no longer conceived merely as concealing from us the 'truth' of our subordination to capital, rather ideology actively constituted us as subjects to the extent that it socially located us from the beginning of our lives – we are 'always already' subjects even before we are born (Althusser 1971).

For Marxist feminists, Althusser's view of ideology as relatively autonomous from economic relations was potentially attractive in that it created a space to theorize women's subordination without having to relate it to the capitalist mode of production. Further, in providing a way of annexing psychoanalysis to Marxism, there was now a ready means of explaining the ways in which femininity and masculinity were reproduced within our psyches. It was thus no longer necessary to view the social ordering of gender and sexuality as mere epiphenomena of capitalism. As Michèle Barrett (1980) noted, locating gender and sexuality at the level of ideology had some advantages over more traditional Marxist approaches:

> it avoids the unsatisfactory reductionism of attempts to explain very diverse sexual behaviour in terms of a rather forced notion of the 'needs' of capitalism ... and, perhaps most importantly, provides an explanation by which women come to 'collude' in their sexual oppression.
>
> (Barrett 1980: 60)

While Barrett had reservations, which we share, about severing all links between the material and the ideological,[2] others found this liberating.

One of the earliest signs of these developments among feminists was the rehabilitation of psychoanalysis. Previously most feminists had been sceptical of psychoanalysis, seeing Freud, with his deficiency model of femininity, as an apologist for patriarchy (Millet 1971; Jackson 1978a). The idea that all little girls suffer from 'penis envy', that they turn away from their attachment to their mothers as a result, that they later must give up 'active' clitoral sexuality in favour of passive vaginal sexuality in order to become functioning adult women, was hardly calculated to appeal to a generation of women seeking to assert their sexual and social autonomy. Juliet Mitchell, in *Psychoanalysis and Feminism* (1975), was the first to counter the prevailing view, but others were soon to follow, notably those involved in *m/f*, so that by the early 1980s there were a plethora of publications extolling the supposed virtues of appropriating psychoanalysis for feminism (Mitchell and Rose 1982; Henriques et al. 1984; Brennan 1989).

Mitchell's intent was not to advance the theory of sexuality as such, but rather to develop a new Marxist feminist explanation of women's subordination. She used Althusser's theory of ideology in conjunction with Lévi-Strauss's conceptualization of kinship to locate women's subordination at the level of culture. Lévi-Strauss's notion of the exchange of women had some resonance with earlier Marxist feminist theorizations of relations of reproduction, but related women's status as objects of exchange to the incest taboo which so preoccupied Freud and also to the symbolic realm of culture: thus women functioned both as objects of exchange and as 'signs'. Mitchell argued that patriarchal domination once had a material base, where kinship was integral to the socioeconomic order. With the development of capitalism, kin ties were no longer so fundamental to society and economy. As a result, women's subordination had become entirely cultural and ideological, reproduced in our psyches by the continual replaying of the Oedipal drama through which we are produced as sexed subjects. In arguing her case for the explanatory power of psychoanalysis, Mitchell introduced Anglophone feminists to the work of Jacques Lacan, albeit at this stage in a somewhat simplified form.

Lacan's rereading of Freud through structural linguistics was to prove crucial for the revival of psychoanalysis among Marxists and feminists (see Lacan 1977; Mitchell and Rose 1982). It enabled Mitchell and others to argue that feminists had misunderstood Freud. In Mitchell's original formulation, penis envy and the vaginal clitoral transference were not to be seen as literal indicators of women's innate inferiority and sexual passivity, but as symbolic, subordinating women to patriarchal culture. Soon, with the growing literature on psychoanalysis, feminists became acquainted with the idea that it was not the penis as a physical organ that guaranteed women's subordination, but the phallus as its symbolic representation that subjected us all to the law of the father (see e.g. J. Rose 1982, 1986). This supposedly purged psychoanalysis of the elements feminists found objectionable. We were urged to appreciate the importance of the unconscious and the structuring effect of language and the symbolic on both conscious and unconscious aspects of subjectivity.

The reasons why psychoanalysis found a ready audience among some feminists requires some explanation. Feminists were seeking a means of understanding how gender and sexuality were constituted at the level of individual subjectivity and, at the time, most conventional social scientific approaches to 'socialization' seemed both mechanistic and apolitical (see Henriques et al. 1984). Lacanian psychoanalysis provided a means of understanding how we became 'sexed subjects' that was both more complex and which addressed central feminist concerns. Psychoanalysis made sexuality (taken to incorporate gender) fundamental to our psyches and, moreover, in the less biologistic readings of the Lacanians, suggested that we are not born male or female but become 'sexed subjects' through our entry into language and culture. Moreover culture, conceived as phallocentric and governed by paternal law, was characterized as thoroughly male dominated, thus resonating with feminism. It was also suggested that, because of the unpredictability of the unconscious, masculinity and femininity were always precarious accomplishments, making them seem less inevitable. We have already suggested that part of its appeal lay in its potential 'fit' with Marxism – and this seems to have helped to secure its influence despite many critiques of its universalism, ahistoricism and residual essentialism.

Lacanian psychoanalysis is undoubtedly more sophisticated than cruder forms of Freudianism and is not so amenable to a biologistic reading – hence its perceived advantages for feminism. The drive, for Lacan, is not an instinct; it 'cannot be reduced to the order of need' (J. Rose 1986: 57). It has no predetermined aim or object but becomes ordered only through our entry into language and culture (though it still has a pre-social or supra-social existence). Similarly desire is not a need, but is constituted as 'lack' through the splits and losses consequent on our entry into the symbolic, and cannot, unlike a need, be satisfied. Moreover, the sex categories, male or female, to which we must be assigned in order to become speaking subjects are 'fictional' rather than given by nature, and women are not innately inferior, but subjected (see J. Rose 1982).

The emphasis on culture and the symbolic is suggestive of the social shaping of sexuality. Yet it is language and culture in general – not a specific language and culture – that produce desire and constitute us as 'sexed subjects', which makes it almost impossible to account for cultural variation and social change, to relate gender and sexuality to the local contexts in which our lives are lived, or to explain the everyday experience of sexuality. The ability of psychoanalysis to address everyday experience is further diminished by the insistence that what matters for our subjectivity is the unconscious, which 'undermines the subject from any position of certainty, from any relation of knowledge to his or her psychic processes and history' (J. Rose 1986: 52). There is little room for agency or reflexivity here; resistance to the gendered social order and the precariousness of our gendered identifications are products of the unpredictable eruptions of the unconscious (see McNay 2000). The idea of repression remains central, as that which cannot be allowed entry into language – the mysterious unconscious residue that lies outside the social. More fundamentally, for feminism, Lacanian psychoanalysis continues to conflate gender and sexuality. Not only are they analytically inseparable, preventing any exploration of their interrelationship, but also they are co-constructed: 'One either identifies with a sex or desires it, but only these two relations are possible' (Butler 1990b: 333). The problems this creates for theorizing lesbian desire or any form of gender/sexual identity outside the dualistic norm, might be thought to make psychoanalysis untenable for feminists – but this has not been its fate. Despite its shortcomings it has retained a tenacious hold on feminist studies of sexuality and subjectivity. Far more effort is put into trying to adapt psychoanalysis to feminist priorities, and into exploring diverse variants of psychoanalysis,[3] than into developing alternatives. Even when interest in structuralism gave way to poststructuralism and postmodernism, with their radical questioning of 'truth' claims, psychoanalysis was not dislodged.

The work of Foucault has been particularly significant in this context. Where Lacan's ideas can be situated at the juncture between structuralism and poststructuralism, Foucault is more often placed within poststructuralism or postmodernism (although he never associated himself with these intellectual movements). As we noted in Chapter 1, Foucault's writings provided a means of critiquing psychoanalysis, exposing it as another regime of truth as well as questioning the concept of repression on which it rests (though this has not prevented queer attempts to amalgamate his ideas with those of Freud). Foucault's approach has potential advantages for feminism in its radical anti-essentialism (sexuality has no existence outside the nexus of power/knowledge through which it is constituted) and in its anti-universalism (sexuality is the product of history). Such ideas resonate with feminists' concern with exploring how particular forms of femininity and female sexuality are constructed at particular historical moments and allow for historical and cultural variability. Foucault's perspective also has the potential to decentre sexuality, to bring into question the privileged place it occupies in late modern society and culture although, as we will see, this is a potential often missed by some of his acolytes.

Foucault himself was not very interested in women or in gender relations. Although, in the first volume of *The History of Sexuality*, the 'hysterical woman' is one of the four figures he identifies as emerging from the nineteenth-century deployment of sexuality (Foucault 1981: 105), women are barely mentioned elsewhere in his work. Nonetheless the insights he offers have been taken up, with varying degrees of enthusiasm, by many feminists and it is rare to find a feminist text on sexuality written after the 1980s that does not reference him. Feminists have drawn on both Foucault's ideas and his analytical methods, but have applied them in new ways, highlighting the discursive construction of gender and the gendered constitution of sexuality (see e.g. Diamond and Quinby 1988; Bartky 1990; Ramazanoğlu 1993). His work also, of course, had a major impact upon queer theory and thus on the critique of heterosexuality (see Chapters 1 and 4).

There are, however, aspects of his work that we, in common with some other feminists, find more problematic. First, although his notion of power as productive rather than repressive is valuable, the idea of power as dispersed, as everywhere and nowhere, leaves us without the means of effectively analysing power *over* others and the production of systematic inequalities – including those of gender. Foucauldian libertarians are thus able to focus on power as regulating sexuality, defining the 'charmed circle' of the normative and outlawing the transgressive (Rubin 1984), while giving insufficient attention to the power relations *within* some forms of sexual transgression, such as prostitution and pornography (see Jackson 1996a, 1996b). Second, the emphasis on discourse, even where it includes discursive practices, does not adequately address everyday, interpersonal interaction and the meanings negotiated within it – which are, for us, crucial to understanding sexual relations. Foucault has also been taken to task for his lack of theorization of agency, for ignoring it in his earlier work and simply assuming it in his later work on technologies of power (Foucault 1988; McNay 2000). Finally, as we indicated in Chapter 1, Foucault's sex/sexuality formulation conflates gender and sexuality – though with fewer fatal consequences than in their psychoanalytic entanglement. Somewhat ironically, in Foucault's suggestion that sex 'is *produced* by the apparatus of sexuality' (Foucault 1980: 210, emphasis in original), and in the inclusion of the male–female distinction in 'sex', there is an echo, albeit a theoretically distant one, of MacKinnon's argument that the social shaping of sexuality 'organizes society into two sexes' (MacKinnon 1982: 516).

The missing dimension: interaction

Significant dimensions of sexual life are missing from both psychoanalytic and Foucauldian approaches: everyday interpersonal interaction, the meanings deployed within it and the agency and reflexivity it entails.[4] Moreover both make it difficult to disentangle gender from sexuality. The interactionist perspective that we outlined in Chapter 1 does, however, address these aspects of sociality and sexuality. It provides the analytical tools to link culture and subjectivity to everyday interaction and practice, to place sexuality in the context of wider social relations and to explore the relationship between gender and sexuality. Interactionism as a whole, however, has remained a minority perspective, even within sociology, and is little known outside it. The intellectual climate could now be more favourable, given the ease with which interactionism can be integrated with some aspects of poststructuralism (Denzin 1992), and its resonance with 'conceptualizations of the social in terms of process, flux and movement' (Atkinson and Housley 2003). The interactionist perspective on sexuality has, we believe, considerable potential for feminist analysis but has, along with other interpretive sociologies, been neglected or derided by most feminists.

The reasons why feminists have ignored or dismissed interactionist accounts, as we indicated earlier in the chapter, can be traced back to the theoretical debates of the 1970s and 1980s. Interactionism's exclusion from mainstream feminist thought at this time might be partly attributable to its own shortcomings, particularly its inattention to the systematic structural inequalities characteristic of late capitalist societies. This deficiency, however, is arguably shared by psychoanalytic and Foucauldian perspectives,[5] but the former had, courtesy of Althusser's theory of ideology, a ready means of articulation with Marxism, while Foucault's *History of Sexuality* became appropriated as part of the move towards a poststructuralism post-Marxism (see Barrett 1991). While sexuality is not, by our definition, a structural phenomenon, it is subject to institutional ordering and regulation and is closely bound up with gender, a fundamental social division. We accept, therefore, that to explain these aspects of sexuality, a more materialist, structural analysis is required. But since interactionism is a 'modest' theory that makes no totalizing claims (Plummer 2003), there are no barriers to using it in conjunction with other perspectives that might illuminate different aspects of the social. Moreover, interactionism's focus on the everyday practical actualities of life makes it more consonant with materialist analysis than is often recognized (see Jackson 2001, 2006a). However, it was initially condemned for its perceived lack of an easy fit with Marxism and subsequently forgotten in the enthusiasm for Foucault.

Feminists using interpretive sociologies in the 1970s and early 1980s were an embattled minority and, if lucky enough to have interactionist or phenomenological work published,[6] often found themselves misunderstood and pilloried. Liz Stanley and Sue Wise's *Breaking Out* (1983), which drew on interactionism and ethnomethodology, is a prime example. It was grossly misrepresented by its critics and damned as essentialist, individualist, and as both overly abstract and anti-intellectual (see Stanley and Wise 1993: 9–13). We have memories of giving papers on the social construction of sexuality at this time and of being met with incredulity, primarily from Marxist feminists, that we could even think of abandoning the concept of repression – although many of them, within a very few years, happily embraced Foucault's more fashionable critique of the repressive hypothesis. Until the English translation of Foucault's *The History of Sexuality* became widely available, Gagnon and Simon (1974) offered the only available theory of the social construction of sexuality. Yet most feminists ignored their work completely and most of those who did engage with it were sceptical or hostile. It is worth considering in some detail the objections that were raised since they help to explain why so promising a theory was rejected.

Given the pervasiveness of the concept of repression, and its currency within Marxist circles, it is perhaps understandable that Gagnon and Simon's anti-essentialism may have been a little too radical for some. Mary McIntosh (1978), for example, carefully framed her exposition of Gagnon and Simon (1974) to distance herself from their rejection of the biological bases of sexuality. In her terms 'they go so far ... as to claim that sexuality is socially scripted rather than a product of innate drives'. She suggested that 'we need not go all the way with Simon and Gagnon' to recognize the cultural variations in human sexuality. These are, she says, 'based, no doubt, on biological structures, and on generic drives ... but they are not determined by them' (McIntosh 1978: 56). Thus, while she sought to establish the social basis of sexual relations she stepped back from embracing a fully sociological explanatory framework. She concluded that psychoanalysis was preferable because 'it enables the theorization of the specific differences between men and women, whereas the scripting approach leaves the content of the scripts a contingent matter' (McIntosh 1978: 64). What McIntosh saw as a disadvantage has to us always seemed an advantage in that scripts can and do change, not only historically but contextually, allowing for human agency and interaction. McIntosh's critique is very much of its time: not only have radically anti-essentialist perspectives since become commonplace, but also the psychoanalytic 'fixing' of gender difference as inescapable is now less acceptable.

Many of McIntosh's reservations were, not surprisingly, echoed by Michèle Barrett, with whom she frequently collaborated. Barrett's *Women's Oppression Today* (1980) was a highly influential overview of feminist theory written when Althusser's influence was at its height and psychoanalytic theory was becoming more popular among Marxist feminists, but before Foucault had made an impact. It is therefore illustrative of the dominant theoretical trajectory of feminism at the time and the ways in which interpretive sociologies were brushed aside. In discussing Althusser, Barrett briefly notes that his was not the only challenge to Marxist economism at the time:

> Indeed this has gone beyond the confines of Marxism itself, as can be seen in the rise and popularity of subjectivist sociologies (phenomenology and ethnomethodology, for example) seeking to explain 'reality' in terms of the negotiation of intersubjective social situations. Some of these last developments have claimed to be particularly helpful in

describing male-female transactions, and to be relevant to an understanding of gender identity and gendered interaction.

(Barrett 1980: 30)

This, however, is mentioned only in passing, referenced via a footnote to Garfinkel and to Gagnon and Simon, before she returns to the significance of Althusser's theory of ideology, the space it gives to theorize 'the oppression of women as a relatively autonomous element of the social formation' (Barratt 1980: 31) and the contribution of psychoanalysis. Although she is gently critical of the latter, noting the need to historicize it, it is clearly what she considers to be the mainstream of feminism's challenge to Marxism, from which 'subjectivist sociologies' are an insignificant distraction. The choice of the word 'subjectivist' is itself significant since it carries connotations of being insufficiently social.

Interactionism later figures briefly in her chapter on femininity, masculinity and sexual practice. First, she notes, interestingly, a parallel with Simone de Beauvoir whose 'stress on the shaping of consciousness and gender identity through interaction is echoed in the school of sociological work on sexuality using the interactionist perspective' (Barratt 1980: 52).

This is followed by a very brief, oversimplified account of the idea of sexual scripts, but Barrett does observe that the implication is 'that the very definition of sexual behaviour is open to question, and that behaviour can legitimately be regarded as "sexual" only in so far as the actor defines it as such' (Barrett 1980: 52). This, however, is not followed up. While she admits that this perspective has produced interesting 'studies on the subjective negotiation of sexuality', citing Plummer's *Sexual Stigma* (1975), she then produces the standard criticisms:

> In common with all work derived from an interactionist perspective, however, it tends to suffer from the weaknesses of this approach in specifying why particular forms of behaviour are learnt and not others; it does not adequately address the question of whether social and historical conditions may prescribe the appropriateness of one script rather than another, or make some scripts but not others available.

(Barrett 1980: 53)

While there is some justice in these criticisms, a lack of attention to 'social and historical conditions' is truer of psychoanalysis, to which Barrett then directs her attention. This she clearly regards as a far more significant attempt 'to break away from reductionism, and to locate sexuality and gender identity in the specificity of historical ideological processes' (Barrett 1980: 53). In contrast to the one paragraph (two-thirds of a page) in which she outlines and then dismisses interactionism, she devotes nine pages to psychoanalysis (Barrett 1980: 53–62), mostly to Mitchell (1975). She is not entirely uncritical, and in the course of her assessment interactionism is accorded another passing mention, as sharing with psychoanalytic feminism 'the tendency to locate sexuality entirely in the realm of ideology' (Barrett 1980: 60). Such accounts, she says, cannot explain differential responses to the processes described, 'the conditions under which a given subject may or may not respond to them and how necessarily determining they are'. In this context she says of interactionism that 'deviant sexual socialization is so well accounted for that one can barely see the overall pressures towards conformity' (Barrett 1980: 60–61). Presumably here she is thinking of Plummer's (1975) work on homosexual identity – as it is hardly applicable to Gagnon and Simon (1974) themselves, who devote most of *Sexual Conduct* to more normative forms of sexuality.

It is a little later that she makes her most startling – and inaccurate – claim about interactionism. In discussing the need to avoid tying gender and eroticism too closely together, she suggests that interactionism 'tends to conflate gender and sexuality in its accounts of learned behaviour and identity' (Barrett 1980: 63). This interpretation is both erroneous and inexplicable since Gagnon and Simon (1974) make an explicit analytical distinction between the two, a distinction followed up in feminist work of the time (Jackson 1978a, 1978b, 1978c). Notably, this is a criticism far more applicable to psychoanalysis, and it was in critiquing psychoanalysis that Gagnon and Simon underlined the importance of distinguishing between sexuality and gender, but Barrett fails to notice this. She continues to promote psychoanalysis and disparage interactionism. In discussing the controversy over the vaginal orgasm, she asserts that the rediscovery of the clitoral orgasm 'did not tally with women's lived experience of intercourse' and suggests that psychoanalysis might be useful here in 'demarcating the psychic processes that underlie the pleasure of this experience'. In the very next sentence Barrett (1980: 66) says that what is needed is 'an understanding of pleasure in terms of meanings, definitions, the discourse of pleasure' – precisely what interactionism supplies and psychoanalysis does not.

This cavalier misrepresentation and dismissal of interactionism in order to clear the path for psychoanalysis, coming from one of the most authoritative feminist theorists of the time, helped to confirm the view that interactionism was irrelevant for feminism. It almost disappeared from view as most erstwhile Marxist feminists, including Barrett (1991) herself, turned to Foucault, Lacan, Derrida and other French theorists for explanations of subjectivity and sexuality. It was interactionism's lack of materialism that first condemned it, but the move from materialist to cultural analysis ironically served only to marginalize it further. Its next mention in a major text on feminist theory came from a materialist who had resisted the 'turn to culture', Sylvia Walby (1990).

Walby's materialism was not grounded in Marxist orthodoxy in the way that Barrett's was, and she had sympathies with the French materialist radical feminism of Christine Delphy (Delphy 1984; Walby 1986). She was also far less appreciative of psychoanalysis, seeing Freud as irredeemably patriarchal and attempts to rescue him as essentialist and ahistorical (Walby 1990: 110–113). She is, however, also critical of interactionism, although she has been fairer than Barrett in giving a fuller, more sustained, account of interactionist approaches to sexuality and acknowledging its feminist exponents (Walby 1990: 113–15). She also recognizes that it has its strengths 'in its critique of the biologism of orthodox Freudian thought and the concepts it introduces for a sensitive sociological analysis' (Walby 1990: 115). In Walby's eyes, however, it is fatally flawed by the taint of liberalism – something which, by definitional fiat, places it outside the realms of respectable feminist theory. In dubbing interactionism 'liberal', Walby identifies the same basic shortcomings raised by Barrett: that interactionism lacks any concept of 'an overarching social structure', cannot explain 'systematic gender inequality in sexual relations' and offers 'no account of where sexual scripts themselves come from'. She applies this to a specific example – an article on rape written by one of us (Jackson 1978b). She argues that this analysis was rendered more adequate by the concept of patriarchal power, but that this 'is inadmissible within the symbolic interactionist perspective' (Walby 1990: 115). This may be a fair point, but what she then goes on to say is not: that this 'account succeeds in its analysis of rape precisely as it moves outside a symbolic interactionist framework' (Walby 1990: 115).

It is the case that this article sought to relate rape to the patriarchal relations of contemporary society – it would be hard to imagine rape existing without male domination. But we thought then, and we continue to think now, that this does not *make* men rape, it provides the structural conditions that enable men to exercise power (sexual or otherwise) over women, but does not directly determine their conduct. To explain how men come to rape, we need to explore the construction of both male and female sexuality, the ways in which men are able to make sense of their own actions in relation to their potential victims in particular settings in such a way that rape becomes possible. This is what the article sought to achieve. It was never intended to provide a complete explanation for rape, but rather to apply C. Wright Mills' precept that: 'A sociological conception of motives ... translates the question of "why" into a "how" that is answerable in terms of a situation and its typical vocabularies of motive' (Mills 1940: 440). It was suggested that vocabularies of motive for rape were embedded in everyday heterosexual scripts. If the argument was successful it was precisely because, and not as Walby would have it, in spite of, its interactionist analytical method.

Walby and Barrett were engaged in evaluating the state of feminist theory in the course of advancing their own explanations of women's subordination as a whole and it is therefore not surprising that they both rejected perspectives that did not fit within their theoretical preferences. It might be expected that those more modestly concerned with sexuality would be more receptive to Gagnon and Simon's interactionism, but this was not always the case. Annabel Faraday (1981), for example, does not contest the theoretical framework offered by interactionism, but focuses on exposing the sexism she sees as inherent in Gagnon and Simon's depiction of female sexuality in general and lesbianism in particular. The effect of her acerbic criticism, however, was to hammer another nail in the coffin of interactionism. For her, Gagnon and Simon's emphasis 'on the social construction of sexuality suggests a revolutionary alternative to essentialist and drive reduction models' but 'by neglecting any analysis of the ways in which men and women negotiate or fail to negotiate sexual meaning, they substitute one reductionist explanation – that of "gender" for that of drive' (Faraday 1981: 122).

Faraday demonizes Gagnon and Simon as patriarchal purveyors of a model of female sexuality as inherently passive, adaptive to male needs and simply reflecting their 'femininity'. What particularly arouses her ire is their depiction of lesbianism as 'a conformity greater than deviance' – by which they mean that lesbians, according to the evidence available at the time, acted sexually more like heterosexual women than gay men – that they were more interested in loving sexual relationships than casual cruising. This is not something many feminists would object to – and indeed some radical feminists have taken this to confirm lesbians' moral superiority to both gay and straight men (see e.g. Jeffreys 1990). Faraday, however, takes issue with this as one more indication of Gagnon and Simon's failure to accord women agency or autonomy.

Some of Faraday's misgivings derive from the language Gagnon and Simon used. Not simply the sexist language (corrected in the second (2004) edition), but also other terminology current at the time, such as talking of 'the male', 'the female', 'the lesbian' – which now reads as essentializing – and their reificatory use of 'society'. When this is compounded by other concepts, such as sexual object choice, this can give the impression of a very negative attitude to women and to lesbians in particular. Faraday (1981) extracts from this as much damning evidence she can:

> In their brief discussion of 'the lesbian', Gagnon and Simon define 'her' as a woman who 'differs from other women only in the gender of the object that engages her sexual attention'. That is, lesbian women are not seen as choosers or definers but rather as women whose 'sexuality' happens to latch on to other women, described here as 'objects'.
>
> (Faraday 1981: 120, quoting Gagnon and Simon 1974: 176)

This is both unjust and disingenuous. In the first place the idea of an 'object' in this sense is not meant as objectifying; this is common terminology in studies of sexuality, used to refer to the gender of sexual preference and remains current in psychoanalytic parlance (where it rarely raises an eyebrow). The idea of something 'engaging' someone's sexuality need not be read as passive as 'just happening to latch on to'; to be engaged implies active *engagement*. The sexism of the language of *Sexual Conduct* might now cause problems of interpretation, but it was written in an era when gender-neutral language had yet to become standard and the use of 'man' and 'he' to mean everyone, while 'women' meant only women, was commonplace. Feminists frequently challenged this, so Faraday was right to point out that Gagnon and Simon could be read as suggesting that only men are involved in the interpretive processes they describe – hence her sarcastic commentary on their representation of 'the problems of "our hero" in deciding whether or not a situation is sexual or not' (Faraday 1981: 121).

It is certainly the case that *Sexual Conduct* is riddled with all manner of sexist assumptions – it was, after all, a product of its time – and we would not contest this. Moreover, as Mary McIntosh noted, they also failed to problematize 'the specificity of men and masculinity' in relation to homosexuality (see Weeks et al. 1981). But this, she admits, was a shortcoming of which she was equally culpable in her discussion of the homosexual role (McIntosh 1968). However, Faraday's reading of Gagnon and Simon is decidedly uncharitable. In lifting some of the more problematic passages out of context, she presents Gagnon and Simon as men who regard women as intrinsically lacking in autonomous sexuality and as simply existing to service men's pre-given needs. Our interpretation of Gagnon and Simon is more sympathetic. In foregrounding gender in the shaping of sexuality (both male and female) they are not seeing this as determining sexuality but as providing the parameters within which we become sexual and make sense of ourselves as sexual subjects. They were also working with the existing research of pre-1970s USA – a time when the majority of women were constrained by traditional expectations of sexual propriety and chastity, by their assumed destiny as wives and mothers, when, as many feminists pointed out, women were expected to respond to men's desires rather than express their own, when few were able to develop, much less express, an autonomous sexuality. In other words, they were describing the forms of sociosexual scripts available to men and women then, not prescribing how women should be or how they intrinsically are. Indeed a great deal of research since, after feminism had made its impact, suggests that autonomous desire remains problematic for women (see e.g. Holland et al. 1998; Tolman 2002). This much more recent – and feminist – work on heterosexuality resonates with one of the passages that Faraday finds so objectionable, and which she takes to represent 'the crux of their perspective: only men can and do define situations; women only "act like women"':

> sexuality for the female has less autonomy than it has for the male, and the body (either of the self or of others) is not seen by women as an instrument of self-pleasure. This vision of sexuality as a form of service is continuous with the rest of female socialization.

(Gagnon and Simon 1974: 182, quoted by Faraday 1981: 122)

Interactionism, then, was represented by its critics as at best beset by the limitations of liberalism, at worst an exemplar of patriarchal posturing. What self-respecting feminist would even consider utilizing it? We were among the few who did think it worth pursuing and, while it has been bypassed by the mainstream of Marxist and later poststructuralist theory, we continue to think it is fruitful for feminist analysis. We will demonstrate its utility throughout this book, but at this point it is worth summarizing what we, as feminists, see as the advantages of the ideas first developed by Gagnon and Simon (1974). First, it is radically anti-essentialist, allowing us to think of the differences between men's and women's sexuality as the consequence of social processes rather than differential repression, thus avoiding the pitfalls of either taking male sexuality as the norm or valorizing an essential feminine sexuality as morally superior. Second, by distinguishing analytically between gender and sexuality, it allows us to theorize the relationship between them without deciding in advance (as in psychoanalysis) how that interrelationship is manifested. Third, because it is not deterministic and is predicated upon a reflexive social self, it also allows for variation *within* gender categories, for social and cultural change and for human agency. For the same reasons, it provides a viable alternative to psychoanalysis in accounting for the processes by which we become sexual and for the exploration of the sexual self. In so doing it locates sexuality in the context of the everyday social fabric of our past and present lives. Finally, in treating sexuality as fully social it brings into question the 'special' status of sexuality. This, for us, is highly significant since we have always been wary of forms of feminism that over-privilege sexuality either as the root cause of women's subordination or, as in the case of psychoanalysis, the basis of human psychic functioning.

Challenging the 'specialness' of sexuality enables us to get it back into proportion as simply one aspect of social life among many. The heat generated by the so-called sex wars, which we identified at the beginning of this chapter as a key moment in feminist engagements with sexuality, might have been lessened by an appreciation of the 'ordinariness' of sexuality. By the time the opening salvos in the battles between libertarians and anti-libertarians were fired, however, interactionism was fading from view. Those opposed to the radical feminist emphasis on sexual violence and exploitation framed their theory primarily in Foucauldian terms. In the remainder of this chapter we want to consider some of the consequences of the importance accorded to sexuality within the sex wars debates.

Rethinking 'the fallacy of misplaced scale'

'The fallacy of misplaced scale' is a phrase coined by Gayle Rubin (1984) in her contribution to *Pleasure and Danger* (Vance 1984), the collection of papers published from the 1982 Barnard conference, often taken to mark the beginning of the sex wars. In Rubin's paper, now a feminist classic, 'the fallacy of misplaced scale' encapsulates the idea that 'sexual acts are burdened with an excess of significance' (Rubin 1984: 279), so that sexual transgression attracts disproportionate opprobrium, condemnation and policing, with oppressive consequences for sexual minorities. While we concur with Rubin's view that sexual issues tend to be inflated out of all proportion in late modern societies, we see this as double-sided. It may be, as Rubin argues, that this has historically been associated with 'sex-negativity', but it is no longer only the puritanical or 'sex-negative' members of the population who lack a sense of proportion – so too do those who see themselves as 'sex-positive'.

Just as there is a long tradition of condemning forms of sex deemed 'immoral' as undermining the very fabric of our civilization, there is also a tradition of seeing in sex the key to human freedom and personal fulfilment. Sex itself is seen as something special and apart from everyday life – either as a uniquely exciting, ecstatic experience enabling us to transcend mundane everyday life or as uniquely dangerous, threatening to return us to barbarism. This is, as we have argued elsewhere (Jackson and Scott 2004), the source of a number of contradictions in our current sexual climate – the more so as it is possible for individuals to hold these opposing views simultaneously – thus the Moral Right can claim that sexual excess threatens social decline while at the same time claiming that sex is so special, so central to cementing the social bond of matrimony, that it must be protected and reserved as a sacrament unique to this relationship. On the other hand, those who condemn the moralists most forcefully produce their own contradictions, reifying the pleasures to be gained from transgression *per se*.

It is this 'fallacy of misplaced scale' that we wish to unpick here, for it is this which has, in part, produced the tension between pleasure and danger within feminist thinking and activism around sexuality. It is not that we wish to deny the lived reality of this tension, the ways in which it maps onto everyday experience. Feminists have both sought to create spaces for women's pleasure and fought against sexual coercion and violence. As women and as feminists we cannot help but be aware of both pleasure and danger as potentials to be negotiated in our daily sexual (and wider social) lives. What concerns us here is that the ways in which debates on sexuality subsequently became polarized led to the assumption that sex in itself is either good, positive and pleasurable or inherently bad, oppressive and dangerous. For example, it became possible for one camp to define themselves as 'sex-positive' and their opponents as 'sex-negative', as if being positive about sex were an unimpeachable virtue and being negative about sex an unforgivable vice. Actually their opponents – those who campaigned on sexual violence and exploitation – did not claim that sex itself was a bad thing, rather that the current ordering of sexuality led to the objectification, humiliation and exploitation of women. Some have, however, seen heterosexuality as so inextricably bound up with male domination that any woman who claims to enjoy sex with men must be irredeemably masochistic. The problem here is identifying sexuality as *the* source of women's subordination, thus once again singling out sex as somehow more important than any other aspect of the social (paradoxically a view that both sides share: sex is either a route to liberation or the root of oppression). Our argument is that sex in itself is neither good nor bad, neither uniquely pleasurable nor uniquely dangerous, neither intrinsically oppressive nor liberating; it becomes so through the particular social conditions under which our sexual lives are lived.

This dichotomous thinking about sex is itself the product of social and historical contexts and meanings, of the way in which Western societies have 'invented' an importance for sexuality (Gagnon and Simon 1974). As Foucault asks: 'how have we come to be a civilization so peculiar as to tell itself, through an abuse of power which has not ended, it has long "sinned" against sex?' (Foucault 1981: 9). The fallacy of misplaced scale relies on sex being seen as different from any other social or physical activity, even those activities that might also carry risks. For example, in relation to current debates about obesity it would be seen as ridiculous to argue that eating in and of itself was either good or bad, either pleasurable or dangerous.

The decades since the publication of *Pleasure and Danger* (Vance 1984) coincide with the period of Foucaults influence. Yet Foucault's work has often been read only selectively by those on the libertarian side of the divide, the so-called 'pro-sex' lobby, who often frame their case in terms of Foucault's call for a return to bodies and pleasures while sidestepping the central insights of his critique of the repressive hypothesis. They are quite happy to speak from within the repressive hypothesis to make use of one of the planks Foucault identifies as sustaining it, what he calls 'the speaker's benefit':

> If sex is repressed, that is, condemned to prohibition, non-existence and silence, then the mere fact that one is speaking about it has the appearance of a deliberate transgression. A person who holds forth in

such language places himself [*sic*] to a certain extent outside the reach of power; he [*sic*] upsets established law; he somehow anticipates the coming freedom.

(Foucault 1981: 6)

Such transgression can be flaunted all the more if one is acting rather than merely speaking, engaging in performances that flout sexual convention (e.g. S&M) or acting in defence of 'sexual outlaws' (*pace* Rubin 1984). But 'transgression' is not necessarily transgressive: it does not inevitably change the social order through which we live our lives (Wilson 1993).[7] Part of the problem arises from lacunae in Foucault's own analysis, as Nancy Fraser (1989) pointed out; it is difficult to see how resistance in the name of bodies and pleasures might work, given that our bodies and pleasures are so marked by the disciplinary deployment of sexuality. While Foucault argued for the constitutive effects of power in producing sexuality, he had little interest in exploring how desires are constituted at the level of our subjectivities. Those interested in theorizing pleasure often, therefore, turned to psychoanalysis to fill this gap, bypassing the much more useful interactionist perspective (see Chapter 6).

One effect of this is that many of those interested in theorizing pleasure have worked in the realms of high theory, drawing on poststructuralist and psychoanalytic traditions. Meanwhile, those working on the risks and dangers of sex have more often busied themselves with empirical investigations of, for example, violence against women and are therefore exposed to the charge that they are atheoretical, even anti-intellectual, as well as 'sex-negative'! The latter is by no means necessarily the case, of course, but it does produce incommensurability between the two sides: we are not comparing like with like. We would argue for a need for theory, but are interested in ways of theorizing the sexual that have some purchase on the empirical world, which can enable us to make sense of sexual lives as they are lived, the mundane, the ordinary and the routine as well as the exotic, ecstatic, risky or coercive. This means we must consistently treat sex as part of the social: our desires and pleasures as well as the constraints upon them, the risks, dangers and pleasures associated with the sexual as part of the wider social context and shaping of sexual life rather than intrinsic to sex itself. If we imbue sex itself with either pleasure or danger, then we are treating it as outside the social. We need to stop thinking about sex as special and start treating its pleasures and dangers in the same way as we would pleasures and dangers associated with any other aspect of social life.

Feminist depictions of the pleasures of sex often represent sex only in its most ecstatic and exciting forms (see e.g. Hollibaugh 1984; Grosz 1995b; Segal 1997). There is little room in much academic, or indeed popular, thought on sexuality for sex that is routinely comfortable, cosy or cuddly – such 'vanilla' pleasures are treated with contempt (see Califia 1981). But why? We do not expect, and would not want, every meal to be a banquet: we are sometimes satisfied with the simple pleasures of comfort food while at other times we seek out more exotic taste experiences. Why should we regard sex any differently? In setting sex up as something that always has to be ecstatic and considering ourselves failures if it is not, in following injunctions to pursue better and better sex we are as much in the grip of power as we would be facing prohibitions against sex (see Heath 1982; Jackson and Scott 1997). Another tendency that appears in writings on sexual pleasure, especially from the pro-sex, pro-pleasure lobby – and in much commonsense thinking – is that risk, danger and transgression themselves make sex 'sexy'. This is yet another instance of forgetting that sex is socially constructed: it is not that risk and danger, in themselves, are sexy or exciting, but rather that certain sorts of risk and danger have come to be defined as erotic.

Some forms of risk are a turn-off rather than a turn-on: there is nothing erotic about chlamydia. Few women would regard the risk of pregnancy as adding to their sexual pleasure but may nevertheless experience heterosex as pleasurable despite this possible risk. Historically heterosexual penetrative sex has carried the greatest risks for women and now carries increasing risks for men, but this form of sex, while it may provide excitement through being risky, is unlikely to be marked out by sexual radicals and outlaws as transgressive but rather as boring, safe and mainstream. Indeed, it is the quintessence of 'normal' sex. The pleasures of risk taking have most often been foregrounded in relation to 'transgressive' sexual desires (Hollibaugh 1984) or practices such as 'S&M' (Califia 1981) and here there is a gulf between those 'playing' with power and those concerned with the actualities of violence against women. While lesbian S&M can hardly be regarded as the greatest threat to feminism, we would argue that no pleasures should be beyond critique and that understanding the social sources and meanings of power is equally relevant to both sides of the debate.

In all such debates, however, it is difficult to find a place beyond the battle lines from which to speak. To take another example, most feminist work on prostitution has become polarized between those seeing it as a form of woman abuse and those arguing that it is either a form of work or an example of transgressive sexual practice to be celebrated. Yet there is good feminist work being done that illustrates the complexity and variability of women's work within the sex industry and its irreducibility to either abuse, work or sexual expression (see e.g. O'Connell Davidson 1998, 2002, 2006; Chen 2008). Those involved in explicating these complexities, however, often find themselves caught in the cross-fire or accused of being unwilling to take a stand.

The difficulties we currently have in thinking about sex derive from an inability to see it as simply part of everyday social life, and therefore to analyse it as we would any other aspect of sociality. Only when we stop seeing sex as 'special' and somehow outside the social will we get it into proportion and view its attendant pleasures and dangers not as attributes of sex itself but simply part of a wider social landscape in which pleasures and dangers attend almost everything we do as social beings. In Chapter 3 we will apply this analysis to the conditions under which sexual lives are lived within late modernity.

Notes

1. The misapprehensions of this early anthropology included the assumption that women did no productive labour in simple societies and the idea that matriliny was the earliest form of kinship and descent.
2. Ironically Barrett was later to surmount her reservations, with the help of Foucault, abandoning not only the material-ideological link, but also the concept of ideology itself, explicitly aligning herself with post-Marxism (Barrett 1991).
3. Other psychoanalytic theorists who have been popular among feminists include Luce Irigary, who famously challenged Lacan and suggested that women's specificity and radical alterity were denied by our phallogocentric culture, the object relations theory of Melanie Klein, and its more sociological variant developed by Nancy Chodorow.
4. This difficulty is resolved in some theoretical and empirical accounts by suggesting that we 'position ourselves' within discourses (see e.g. Weedon 1987; Renold 2005). But this strategy, as McNay (2000) notes, simply introduces an unexplained voluntarism.
5. Of course apologists for psychoanalysis claim that it does address the conditions of women's subordination (Mitchell 1975, 1982; J. Rose 1982, 1986), but it locates these within interpersonal familial relationships and psychic processes, at best in civilization *per se* rather than in historically specific social formations.
6. Publishing this kind of work was not easy at a time when mainstream journals and publishers were still wary of feminism and most of the alternative outlets were controlled by Marxists. The launch, in 1978, of *Women's Studies International Quarterly* (later *Women's Studies International Forum*) at last enabled work that did not conform to current orthodoxies to gain a foothold in the public domain.
7. Nor should we assume that what is pleasurable is unambiguously good, that pursuing individual desires and pleasures is emblematic of freedom as the pro-sex lobby tends to. We cannot insulate desire and pleasure from critique but should always ask where those desires and pleasures come from.

CHAPTER 3

MODERNITY AND ITS DISCONTENTS

Any adequate theorization of sexuality must place it in historical and cultural context. Since sexual relations and practices are embedded in the social, it follows that they are subject to change, rather than being fixed by 'nature', and cannot be expected to remain constant over time and place. More fundamentally, our modern Western understanding of what sexuality *is* derives from specific historical circumstances: 'Sexuality, human experience of the sexual, is as old as language, as old as human being; "sexuality" [a] particular construction of that experience, goes back little more than a hundred years' (Heath 1982: 11).

Heath (1982), like many other historians and theorists, dates the emergence of 'sexuality' as a concept, and the basis of modern understandings of sexual life, to the late nineteenth century. While this is a key moment in the modernization of sex, it is not the beginning of the story. Foucault, on whom Heath bases much of his argument, dates the incitement to discourse that led to the construction of 'sexuality' to the earlier, post-Reformation development of a confessional culture. Other processes also contributed to the modernization of sexuality, in particular the ways in which sex was brought into the 'civilizing process' (Elias [1939] 1994) and how it was implicated in the reordering and reconceptualizing of differences and relations between women and men (Poovey 1988; Laqueur 1990). Where commonsense thinking about the history of sexuality tends to emphasize recent changes – the supposed consequences of the 'sexual revolution' or the demise of Victorian morality – academic research and theory direct our attention to significant earlier changes. Following this lead, we would suggest that to understand the characteristics of late modern sexuality we need to take account of a longer history and be alert to continuities as well as discontinuities. We will therefore begin with a brief discussion of change from the late medieval period in Europe onwards, explaining how the preconditions for the modern idea of sexuality emerged. We will then go on to consider how sexuality changed as modernity advanced before exploring the tensions and contradictions characteristic of sexual life in late modernity.

From lust to sexuality

All witchcraft comes from carnal lust, which is in women insatiable.

(*Malleus Maleficarum*, Sprenger and Kramer 1486, in O'Faolain and Martines 1974: 221)

Most women, happily for them, are not much troubled by sexual feelings of any kind.

(*The Functions and Disorders of the Reproductive Organs*, Acton 1857, in Laqueur 1990: 196)

These quotations call attention to both continuities and discontinuities. The latter are, perhaps, more immediately striking, the most obvious disjunction being the reversal of representations of women's sexuality: where, between the fifteenth and nineteenth centuries, did all that lust go? What brought about such a radical shift in opinion about women's 'nature'? From the standpoint of the present we might also want to know how Acton's (1857) view of 'normal' women as asexual came to be replaced by a state of affairs where lack of desire in women is seen as pathological, as symptomatic of 'female sexual dysfunction' (FSD). There is also a more subtle change evident here: while women are defined in relation to men in both cases, the earlier statement assumes a difference of degree, a quantitative difference between women men – both are prey to carnal sins, but women are more so. In the later instance, we have a qualitative difference, where women are radically other than men, virtually opposite in their characteristics: men are naturally sexual, women are naturally asexual.

There are, however, some constants within these transformations. First, the voices we hear in these historical pronouncements are those of men with the power to define women. These are authoritative voices, invested with the right to speak and be heard, though the locus of authority has shifted from the Church to the medical profession – Sprenger and Kramer were Dominican friars, Acton was a gynaecologist. The views of these men may have been extreme even for their own time, but they nonetheless had material effects on women. The *Malleus Maleficarum* became the witch-hunters' handbook during the European 'witch craze' of the sixteenth century, in which the majority of those tortured and burned at the stake were women. While not all nineteenth-century physicians agreed with Acton's view that women were totally without sexual feeling, most considered that respectable women were incapable of autonomous desire. Evidence of such desire was thought to be associated with gynaecological problems, justifying the ovariectomies and clitoridectomies performed on Victorian women.

A further continuity apparent in these quotations is their sex-negativity. For the Dominicans, lust was a sin; for Acton and his contemporaries, sexual feeling was 'troubling'. The suspicion of the flesh deriving from the Christian tradition persisted, although the frame of reference had shifted from morality to medicine. This development was indicative of wider social change in which the regulative power of the Church had given way to secular controls and, by the nineteenth century, to the scientific authority of medical and other experts. It was these experts who began to define sexuality, in a more modern sense, as an object of scientific investigation and as an aspect of the inner self.

The emergence of the modern Western idea of the sexual, then, depends on a particular history. Western society has changed, but this change is located within a specific cultural heritage so that the modernization of sexuality depends upon a complex configuration of continuity and discontinuity. While we will be focusing in what follows primarily on the transformation of medieval lust into modern sexuality, we remain cognizant of significant constants. Among these are the androcentrism of knowledge, the definition of women in terms of masculine norms and a heritage of anxiety about carnal appetites, strongly associated with suspicion of women.

Most commentators agree that in medieval Europe what we now think of as sexuality was not thought of as integral to the self, but as a bodily appetite. Carnal desires were potentially sinful, and subject to regulation by church and secular authorities, but were taken for granted as part of the human condition. Elias's (1939) study of etiquette manuals reveals a lack of shame attached to bodily functions and an openness of speech about them, which would have been shocking to later generations. There is other historical evidence that supports this. First, the records of the Church or 'Bawdy' Courts, which routinely dealt with cases of fornication and adultery, reveal much about the morals and manners in the late medieval and early modern period (Hair 1972; Quaife 1979). These records are marked by a frankness of speech that would be considered inappropriate in polite circles even today. Those confessing to such sins, for example, often gave more detail than a simple confession required. A young man confessed that he had first committed the sin of fornication with a young woman against a stile and 'at first he could not come at her ... until he made her hold up her leg and then he came at her closely' (Quaife 1979: 173). Respectable witnesses did not shrink from depicting in detail others' sexual misdemeanours or repeating their coarse language, as in the case of a vicar's wife whose deposition against a man accused of adultery repeated his boast that he had 'fucked ten old women of this parish' and 'fucked Kent's wife, the miller, to flitters' (Quaife 1979: 54).

Another feature of evidence given in the courts is that it is indicative of the lack of privacy available for illicit encounters, so that many found themselves before the courts because they had been, quite literally, caught in the act. The majority of the population lived in small dwellings in which there was a lack of specialized space for different functions, such as eating or sleeping – most would not even have had a bed to call their own. Wealthy people also lacked basic privacy. They may have had private bedchambers, but frequently expected their servants to sleep in the same room so that they were on call when needed. Large houses and palaces were usually built without corridors until the seventeenth century so that one person's bedroom might be a through route to others' rooms. It was not just illicit but all sexual conduct that was open to public gaze, to the sight of children as well as adults. It was considered perfectly acceptable to discuss sexual matters in the presence of children, for the barriers that have since been erected between children and adults did not exist in their modern form (Jackson 1982; Elias [1939] 1994).

From the seventeenth century onwards greater propriety was observed in relation to bodily functions and greater modesty became the norm. Elias discusses this in terms of the advance of the 'frontier of shame' surrounding the human body: 'the wall between people, the reserve, the emotional barrier erected ... Between one body and another, grows continuously' (Elias 1994: 138). Not only did sexual acts now require greater privacy, but also the sexual realm could no longer be discussed so openly in polite society. This trend became particularly pronounced in the later years of the nineteenth century:

> In the civilizing process, sexuality ... is increasingly removed behind the scenes of social life and enclosed in a particular enclave, the nuclear family. Likewise, the relations between the sexes are isolated, placed behind walls in consciousness. An aura of embarrassment ... surrounds this sphere of life. Even among adults it is referred to officially only with caution and circumlocutions. And with children, particularly girls, such things are, as far as possible, not referred to at all.
>
> (Elias 1994: 148)

Foucault (1981) offers a somewhat different interpretation of these historical trends since he is less concerned with changes in standards of conduct or mental attitude than with the construction of sexuality as an object of discourse. He detects an early manifestation of incitement to discourse in the church confession manuals of the Reformation. Prior to the Reformation, confessors were instructed to extract a detailed account of sinful sexual conduct, which parallels the full confessions historians have noted in the records of the Bawdy Courts. In the post-Reformation period, however, much greater circumspection was observed in eliciting details of acts: questions were less direct, the language used more decorous. Thus far Foucault appears to be observing the same trend as Elias. For Foucault, however, this is secondary to a much more important shift from the mere regulation of conduct to the injunction to speak of every inner desire:

> According to the new pastoral, sex must not be named imprudently, but its aspects, its correlations, and its effects must be pursued down to their slenderest ramifications: a shadow in a daydream, an image too slowly dispelled, a badly exorcised complicity between the body's mechanics and the mind's complacency: everything had to be told ... shifting the most important moment of transgression from the act itself to the stirrings ... of desire. ... Under the authority of a language that had been carefully expurgated so that it was no longer directly named, sex was taken charge of, tracked down as it were, by a discourse that aimed to allow it no obscurity, no respite.
>
> (Foucault 1981: 19–20)

This incitement to discourse, which began in the seventeenth century, was the starting point for the putting of sex into discourse that culminated in the nineteenth-century science of sex. Foucault famously saw the Victorian era not as a period in which sex was denied or repressed, but one in which there was a discursive explosion around sexuality (see Chapter 1). What Foucault plays down, however, is the importance of redefinitions of gender in this process. He identifies the 'hysterization of women's bodies' as one of four key strategic deployments of sexuality, initially discernible in the eighteenth century, which anchored the nineteenth-century construction of the sexual, along with the 'pedagogization of children's sex', the 'socialization of procreative behaviour' and the 'psychiatrization of perverse pleasure'. Women's bodies, he tells us, were pathologized; they were seen as beings 'saturated with sexuality' (Foucault 1981: 104). And in a sense they were, in that women were considered to be governed by their unruly reproductive capacities, but Foucault misses the converse of this, that women were also considered to be lacking in autonomous desire.

The period from the late eighteenth to early nineteenth centuries saw a reordering of gender relations, particularly among the increasingly influential bourgeois classes. This entailed a redrawing of the boundaries between public and private life, in particular a separation of work from home, which effected the exclusion of bourgeois women from the world of work and commerce. This was accompanied by what has been called 'the domestic ideology', an ideology of separate spheres in which women were deemed 'by nature' to be unsuited to a life beyond domesticity (Davidoff and Hall 1987; Hall 1992). When set alongside the civilization of sex described by Elias and the increasingly restrictive standards of propriety operating in bourgeois circles, the redefinition of women as creatures devoid of sexual desire becomes more understandable. Women were expected to be pure in thought and deed as guardians of the domestic haven, a space protected from the threat of physical and moral pollution posed by the outside world.

A key aspect of this restructuring of gender relations was that women were no longer regarded merely as inferior to men, but as radically other. This extended to the understanding of their bodies as well as their minds. According to Thomas Laqueur (1990), during this period the 'one sex' model of human reproductive organs and functions, which had prevailed since antiquity, gave way to the 'two sex' model with which we are familiar today. Female reproductive organs had previously been seen as homologues of male organs – the vagina as an inverted penis, the ovaries as testes and so on, as evinced by the medical illustrations of the time. Such ideas persisted in everyday discourse into the nineteenth century, after they had disappeared from medical literature, as in the following little rhyme:

> … though they of different sexes be,
>
> Yet on the whole they are the same as we,
>
> For those that have the strictest searchers been,
>
> Find women are but men turned outside in.

(Anon., quoted in Laqueur 1990: 2)

Laqueur also suggests that the transition from the eighteenth to nineteenth centuries was marked by the disappearance of the female orgasm. Where it had once been seen as essential to conception, within a few decades all mention of it had vanished from medical texts. These shifts were not, Laqueur (1990) argues, a result of new scientific evidence but of new ways of seeing. Indeed, modern medical knowledge could as easily be interpreted within a one sex model – a difference of degree between women and men – as within the two sex view of men and women as opposite sexes (see e.g. Oudshoorn 1994). In other fields of medicine, too, the nineteenth century saw an increasing preoccupation with establishing fundamental differences between women and men (Schiebinger 1989). The effect was to underline and justify women's fundamental difference from men.

The degree of scientific scrutiny to which sex became subject can be seen as an aspect of an ongoing project of rationalization with its roots in Enlightenment thought. Rationalization can also be understood as a broader process with a longer history underpinning the civilizing process

(Elias 1994). For Elias, what is central to the development of civilized manners and conduct is the control of affect and bodily desires. The advance of the 'shame frontier' is a key component of this. Sex, as an embodied and emotional practice, is thus increasingly hedged around with controls and restrictions and 'relegated to the realm of secrecy' (Elias 1994: 154). Even today, when secrecy has diminished, the idea of sexuality as unruly, intractable and resistant to rational management persists. In what follows we will discuss the ways in which the rationalization of sex since the nineteenth century has left its mark on late modern understandings of gendered sexuality. We will begin by addressing some familiar ideas about the modern self, which are often seen as central to this rationalizing process.

Rationalizing sex

Since the rise of postmodern theorizing, it has become conventional to depict the modernist conception of self, deriving from the Enlightenment, as a rational unitary self. In one of the founding statements of this position, Jane Flax tells us that postmodernists 'seek to throw into radical doubt beliefs still prevalent ... but derived from the Enlightenment' (Flax 1990a: 41). In so doing postmodernists construct a story about the Enlightenment, 'a master narrative' against which they deploy their own rhetoric. Central characters or themes in this story are the 'stable coherent self' and 'a form of reason capable of privileged insight into its own processes and into "the laws of nature"' (Flax 1990b: 30). The self of this narrative is the core of our individuality, and carries with it the notion of an essential inner self, which somehow exists outside the social order we inhabit and is the basis of human rationality, freedom and autonomy.

The story, of course, is one told of Enlightenment Man – for this unitary, rational and free individual is posited as male, is a representation of a masculine ideal of self. This is recognized by Flax, who also implies that Enlightenment Man is a straw man, set up by postmodern theorists in order to be knocked down again, rather than a universally held view. We would argue that a version of a modernist – and masculine – conception of self does exist within Western culture, but that its internal contradictions have long been apparent. It has always been somewhat precariously constructed, with its supposed rationality, stability and autonomy threatened from within by the very cultural dualisms to which postmodernists are always drawing our attention – between nature and culture, mind and body, reason and unreason, thought and emotion, order and chaos – all of which are implicated in the opposition between male and female.

Each term within these binaries, of course, requires its obverse; each is constructed in relation to its 'other'. As Zygmunt Bauman points out, 'the negativity of chaos is a product of order's self-definition ... Without the negativity of chaos, there is no positivity of order; without chaos, no order' (Bauman 1990: 165). The existence of these socially constructed dualities suggests not a confidently unified rational self, but a self in struggle, the forces of culture, mind and reason fighting to control nature, the body and the irrational. Mastery over unruly nature has been identified as central to the project of modernity by Bauman and also by a number of feminists (see e.g. Jordanova 1989). The nature which man (*sic*) struggled to know and master was not merely outside himself – associated with women and with the alien (and often colonized) other – but also nature within himself. Man struggled to exert self-control, mind *over* matter. This idea of self-control in many respects represents older ideas of mind–body dualism (the long Christian tradition of the struggle to resist temptations of the flesh) translated into the idiom of modern rationality. It is also a feature of the longer process of civilization and increasing 'affect control' depicted by Elias (1994).

Although the origins of the modern self are usually located in the eighteenth century, a product of Enlightenment, the nineteenth century is characteristically represented as a high point of these binaries, especially in so far as they provided a template for the reconstruction of gender boundaries that underpinned Victorian morality. In this era, with woman defined as radically other than man, masculine science strove to dominate feminine nature, to make the mysterious feminine visible and subject to masculine mastery (Jordanova 1989). Yet important as the nineteenth-century reordering of gender was, the binary divides so created were not always secure. Not only were constructions of 'woman' internally contradictory, as feminists have long noted (Poovey 1989; Smart 1992), but also the model of man was not as unassailable as it might appear. On the contrary, 'manliness', a major preoccupation of the Victorians, had to be striven for (Mangan and Walvin 1987). What differentiated men from women was not that one possessed a 'natural' side which the other lacked: both were deemed to have a 'natural' being but were not equally governed by it.

Sexuality has occupied a pivotal and also problematic place in the construction of the binary divide of gender and of all the other dichotomies associated with it. At first sight it would seem that sexuality 'obviously' belongs on the side of nature, the body and unreason – the feminine side (hence the idea of women as saturated with sex, governed by their sexual organs). Yet there is also a tradition, dating from the nineteenth century, of active sexuality as masculine and as rationally ordered – a drive that women lacked. The idea of sexuality as a natural yet rational 'drive' has, we will argue, become more prominent as modernity has progressed. Its irrational aspects, on the other hand, have increasingly become associated with emotion rather than sex. The emotional meanings of sex have become a locus of resistance to rationalization, a desire to hang on to the 'specialness' of sexuality, whether in the name of romance, morality or both. This, too, is gendered with women's desire for love often finding itself in opposition to masculine notions of rational sex. Sexuality as a drive is masculine, autonomous, goal-driven, rational as opposed to the feminine, emotional side which threatens autonomy; hence the masculine conception of sex and the feminine conception of love which still haunt us today (Cancian 1990).

Controlling male passions

The split between the rational and irrational self is a recurrent motif in nineteenth-century accounts of sexuality, accounts produced largely by white middle-class men. Sexuality was understood as an intrinsically masculine 'drive', yet for men sexual desire and activity were far from being unproblematic expressions of their individual masculinity. Manliness, a bourgeois virtue, was in many respects something to be achieved through mastery over those 'natural' urges that threatened to subvert it. In this respect, sexuality came to exemplify a broader characteristic of modern existence, the desire to transcend nature which, according to Bauman, had become associated with disorder and chaos:

> raw existence ... becomes now nature: something singularly unfit for human habitat – something not to be trusted and not to be left to its own devices, something to be mastered, subordinated, remade so as to be readjusted to human needs. Something to be held in check, retrained and contained, transferred from the state of shapelessness into form – by effort and by application of force.
>
> (Bauman 1990: 165)

In keeping with this mistrust of nature, the manly man strove to control himself, and the self in need of control was the bodily, sensual, animal self, the site of both baser instincts and unruly emotions – although the latter could be tamed, cultivated as 'finer feeling' (Battersby 1989). Sexuality was central to this struggle for self-rule, and was often represented as a spirited horse reined in by a strong rider (Heath 1982). The truly virile man bridled his passion and restricted the occasions and frequency with which he could give it its head. In addition to equestrian metaphors, sexual activity was also represented in the economic idiom of nineteenth-century capitalism. A man's goal was to conserve his bodily resources, to invest them wisely and with discretion lest he end up 'spent'. If this physical and fiscal bodily management failed, it was believed, a man became weakened, dissolute, potentially diseased and emasculated (Heath 1982). Bourgeois manliness thus represented the triumph of reason over passion, of saving over spending; the man who could so govern himself was made fit to govern others: women, the working class and the outposts of Empire.

Women, assumed to be mentally weaker, were less capable of the strength of will necessary to raise them above their animal natures: 'a man possesses sexual organs, a woman is possessed by hers' (Otto Weinenger 1906, quoted in Kent 1990: 24). Thus men were endowed with autonomous sexual drives, actively controlled, whereas women were governed by sexual functions passively endured. The model of femininity this produced was contradictory and contested (Poovey 1989). Women were constructed as saturated with sexuality, in that they were ruled by their sexual and reproductive functions, but as morally pure because they lacked the autonomous sexual drives of men. Yet women were seen as having a potential for desire that could be activated by the sexual advances of a man. For example, writing in the 1860s, W.R. Gregg, a commentator on prostitution and the 'problem' of single women, characterized women's desire as 'dormant' until 'excited' by 'undue familiarities' and 'almost always till excited by actual intercourse' (quoted in Poovey 1989: 5). Where science was posited as a means by which men could know and control others, especially women, religion was thought of as the best means by which women could control themselves – in other words through an appeal to their faith rather than their reason.

Religion was an adjunct to male self-control, as in the ideal of muscular Christianity (Mangan 1987), but it was science that promised men both self-knowledge and knowledge of the other – hence the relentless search for scientific explanations of the way we are, which persists to this day. The nineteenth century was the high point of so-called 'scientific racism' as well as a period in which the foundations were laid for biological explanations of gender and sexuality. In the same period there was a development of the human sciences, in particular, psychology (N. Rose 1989), which tapped into ideas about the inner self in constructing a developmental model premised on the unfolding of innate proclivities which could be observed and measured. The inner self, though posited as the source of the capacity for reason and moral judgement, was also the locus of sensuality and emotion. The nineteenth-century construction of sexuality as an intrinsically male drive positioned it as the core of masculinity and of man's essential self (Heath 1982). Individuality and manhood, the supposed products of reason, were thus seen to be crucially determined by unreason, by bodily being. While science itself stemmed from human (or male) reason, the model of human beings it constructed was one that was biologically driven.

Sexuality, seemingly located on the side of nature and the body – over which man exerts control but to which woman succumbs – has slipped over to the side of rationality and autonomy largely through scientific discourse. The very 'naturalness' of sex has been used to rationalize it: what should place it on the side of irrationality actually serves to define it as rational. The 'natural' has become associated with the biological, and science has increasingly constructed biology as governed by its own rational laws. Nature is no longer understood as the brutish obverse of culture but as a rule-governed realm in its own right. This entailed a shift in conceptualizations of nature from a religiously based nativism to scientific nativism (Connell and Dowsett 1992). Within a religious world view human nature was deemed to be inherently sinful, a result of our fall from grace, but this coexisted with a more positive view of the 'natural order' as god given (and of nature more broadly as God's gift to humanity). To indulge in carnal acts outside morally approved contexts on the one hand confirmed humanity's fallen nature, but on the other hand was 'against nature' and hence against God's ordained social and moral order. While this older religious notion of nature persists in some circles, it has largely been supplanted by a more scientific understanding of the natural world.

Modern scientific discourse has constituted human nature, and nature in general, as orderly in a new sense – as amenable to rational classification and explanation. Hence it has become possible for sexuality, and in particular male sexuality, to be posited as a rational force. The discovery of the physiology of conception, for example, was cast in terms of this model. The sperm was understood anthropomorphically and androcentrically as pursuing its mission with single-minded determination: the intrepid adventurer fighting his way to the ultimate prize – or the prince capturing the elusive princess (Martin 1991).

Taylorized sex

During the twentieth century the rationalization of sexuality became increasingly scientific. Currently evolutionary psychology represents the apotheosis of rational choice as the foundation of human sexual desires; differences between male and female desire are understood as products of our genes' drive to perpetuate themselves (Dawkins [1976] 2006; for a critical view of this argument, see Jackson and Rees 2007); the human capacity for sexual pleasure dissociated from reproduction turns out, after all, to guarantee our reproductive success through cementing heterosexual bonds (Diamond 1997). When lust was a sin, it was something to be 'wrestled with and defeated' (Connell and Dowsett 1992: 50); now indulging it can be understood as fulfilling a rationally ordered genetic purpose.

Sex has also been claimed by medicine, making possible a discourse of health and illness. Where once this opposed unhealthy, pathological sex to wholesome, normal sex, increasingly sexuality is talked of in the idiom of health promotion and lifestyle choices. Initially sexual health was indicated by fulfilling physical and psychological needs. It has also meant avoiding the risk of infection, but recent concern about HIV and other sexually transmitted infections (STIs) exists side by side with injunctions to enjoy sex – albeit safer sex – to the full. Alex Comfort tells us that 'there is no occasion for panic, or for losing out on the joy of sex – simply for informed caution' (Comfort 1996: 19). Currently, 'healthy sex' ranks along with high fibre, low fat diets as part of the personal management of bodily vitality. Lack of interest in sex or inability to perform is now medically defined as 'dysfunction' (Marshall 2002).

These trends towards rational constructions of the sexual, coupled with a pedagogic approach to the management of everyday life, have contributed to what might be called the 'Taylorization of sex' (Scott and Freeman 1995; Hawkes 1996). This metaphor is borrowed from analyses of the history of the labour process. F.W. Taylor's philosophy of 'scientific management', developed in the 1890s, was based on the assumption that work could be broken down into its constituent parts, into physical motions, which could be timed and ordered to maximize efficiency (Taylor 1911). It paved the way for forms of mass production based on Fordist principles (pioneered by Henry Ford in the assembly line production of automobiles). Taylorization and Fordism are associated with deskilling the labour force, or with limiting their skills to those needed for specific, repetitive tasks. In extending this idea to the analysis of sexuality, we are not suggesting that sexual activity is seen as totally unskilled. Rather, we argue that sexual skills are defined and delimited in specific ways. The social construction of sexual aptitude assumes that these are not craft skills passed down through generations, but require specialist training founded on expert knowledge. In this respect, sexuality has become caught up in the rationalizing motor of modernity.

This process was fostered by the 'sexualization of love' and 'eroticization of sex' during the twentieth century (Seidman 1991). Where conjugal love was, in the nineteenth century, defined as primarily spiritual, it has come to be seen as increasingly carnal. Gradually, over the course of the twentieth century, sexual desire and activity became highly valued as means of cementing heterosexual relationships, with this view being well established by the 1950s and 1960s (Finch and Summerfield 1991; Richards and Elliott 1991). Good sex thus came to be seen as fundamental to a successful relationship, hence the perceived need to educate couples in the ars erotica. Sex became incorporated into the lexicon of romance, raised above its association with the bestial and primitive. Sex itself became civilized. Old anxieties about the debilitating consequences of sexual excess gradually gave way to a new emphasis on the need for sexual experience in the quest for improved sexual performance. As the tie between heterosexuality and reproductive goals was loosened, sex acquired new purposes: individual fulfilment in the service of maintaining heterosexual coupledom. This led to an emphasis on sexual skills and an increased Taylorization of sex, the production of rationalized means of producing pleasure.

Nineteenth-century sexology had been concerned with codifying and classifying sexual practices, with who should do what, with distinguishing the perverse from the normal (Foucault 1979; Heath 1982; M. Jackson 1994). During the twentieth century the emphasis shifted to how heterosexual acts should be performed. It is as if once the parameters of normality had been set in terms of normative monogamous heterosexuality, attention could then be given to what the 'normal' couple did (Kinsey et al. 1948, 1953) and how they could do it better (Masters and Johnson 1966). The tardis of modern heterosexual practice was being opened up: what looked on the outside to be a closely confined space was revealed to be a much larger arena for sexual exploration. This space, however, was far from infinite and remained bounded by the dictates of compulsory heterosexuality (Rich 1980) and very specific and gendered assumptions about the ways in which sexual activity should proceed, a strictly linear trajectory which it should follow. The Taylorization of sex assumed a series of stages to be gone through before the final output: foreplay leading to coitus culminating in orgasm.

As the twentieth century progressed, the sexualization of love and the eroticization of sex required that women's sexual pleasure was given greater attention than it had been in the nineteenth century, but only in the service of male sexual needs. This is why some feminists have seen this development as an eroticization of women's subordination (see e.g. Jeffreys 1990; M. Jackson 1994). Similarly men were expected to exercise self-control not, as previously, in restricting the frequency of intercourse and ejaculation, but in the interests of producing a competent sexual performance. The assumption of an innate spontaneous male sexuality and a quiescent female sexuality, which could be awakened only by a man, persisted. Early in the twentieth century sexual advice books were predicated on the assumption of an active, skilled male sexuality and a passive responsive female sexuality. The husband became both seducer and mentor, who must learn the techniques of arousing a woman's desires in order to teach her how to express them: 'Woman is a harp who only yields her secrets of melody to the master who knows how to handle her' (Van de Velde 1928, quoted in M. Jackson 1994: 164).

These early sex manuals assumed that men needed to be taught what to do and women needed to be taught what to feel, where to feel it and how to adopt the proper attitude in order to be appropriately appreciative of a husband's performance. Paradoxically, although women were now assumed to have a sexual instinct, they needed instruction in order to recognize it. The assumption of feminine passivity persisted throughout the twentieth century, although it gradually was eroded with more emphasis on women as active rather than merely responsive partners. Sexual reciprocity came to be seen as a central ingredient of successful marital and other heterosexual relationships (Finch and Summerfield 1991; Richards and Elliott 1991). Women as well as men are now expected to acquire skills, so they too can share in the performance anxiety once reserved for men.

Seidman (1991) has argued that uncoupling sex from reproduction ultimately created the potential for undermining heterosexual monogamy: once erotic pleasure became a goal in its own right, it was no longer necessarily tied to the marital bed. Nevertheless, the most usual way in which this new freedom is played out is through heterosexual recoupling. The balance between proscription and prescription in the regulation of sexuality has shifted in the direction of the latter. Sex is now seen as positive, playful and life-enhancing. Where once it was thought to bring out the beast in us, it is now more often seen as having the potential to bring out the best in us (although the idea that sex has a dark and dangerous side has not disappeared). We are now faced with injunctions to 'do it' in ever more exciting and exotic ways. Good sex has become a key life goal and a source of personal fulfilment: sex as secular salvation. Rather than being seen as a problem in itself, sex is more often presented as an individualized solution for life's problems. If we get our personal sexual lives right, contentment will follow – a reversal of the relationship between private troubles and public issues which Heath (1982) has termed the 'sexual fix'.

By the 1980s, good sex had become a mark of distinction. Now in advertising, magazines, coffee table books, media advice and a proliferation of 'how to do it' DVDs, we constantly receive a series of messages about sex. Sex – if it is 'safe' and heterosexual – is natural and therefore 'healthy'. There is a differentiation between 'good' and 'bad' sex, just as there is between 'good' and 'bad' taste. Through good, technically proficient, sex we both ensure the experience of pleasure while expressing our 'individuality'. Being 'good at sex' is increasingly equated with other indices of 'having style', like wearing the right clothes or having the right mobile technology – a qualification for and an indicator of our worldly success and social integration. Indeed, the evocation of sexuality in advertising relies on these associations.

What 'good sex' entails, however, is not always clear. Sometimes, as in advertisements, it is left to our imaginations. In many advice books we are told that imagination is essential for good sex, but are nonetheless offered detailed instructions. Alongside these explicit sex manuals are self-help books which hark back to earlier understandings of sexuality. John Gray (1996) describes male and female sexuality in terms reminiscent of Van de Velde. 'Great sex for women' is dependent on 'her partner's skilful and knowing touch', whereas 'great sex for men' is experienced through 'the results of his efforts' in which his partner's fulfilment is 'his ultimate quest and victory' (Gray 1996: 12).

Sex, then, is 'natural' and yet we must endlessly be guided in how to do it. Being told how to do what supposedly comes naturally is a feature of much advice for women and has often been commented on by feminists, particularly in relation to child care manuals (Hardyment 1983; Richardson 1993; Everingham 1994). The irony of this has also occasioned feminist humour: 'If I get my feminine instincts naturally, I'm not having you telling me how to be a woman!' (Anonymous cartoon, mid-1970s). In part this contradiction arises from the emphasis on education and training, which is a key feature of the modern world. We now have to be taught how to eat, how to exercise, and so on – activities once deemed natural. These activities have also become highly individualized and to a great extent Taylorized in the form of diet and exercise plans produced by a host of 'experts'. For the privileged, this involves personal relationships with their trainer, beautician, dietician or therapist. To cater for the less privileged there is a huge market for 'how to do it' advice on everything from practical skills – such as gardening and cooking – to self-improvement, developing your confidence, your speaking skills and the quality of your orgasms. Indeed, the tone of modern sex manuals is in some respects not too different from cookery books, offering step-by-step recipes for better sex. Commenting on women's letters to the magazine *Forum* in the 1970s, Sheila Jeffreys says: 'They advised each other on how to swallow semen in the same way in which they would advise each other on how to remove red wine stains from the carpet in another kind of women's magazine' (Jeffreys 1990: 114). Or, we might add, advice on a new way of reducing the stains on the sheets!

A further set of contradictions is revealed here. Sex is pleasurable, but it must also be worked at. We now have access to ever more detailed instructions on how to perform more sexual tasks more skilfully. The implication is that we only have to work harder and practice in order to achieve the best possible outcome – often defined as simultaneous, or at least separately electrifying, orgasm. We are also encouraged to work on other aspects of our bodies for the sake of our sexual satisfaction. Alex Comfort (1996: 241) warns that obesity reduces our options for novel positions and energetic sex. Jane Hertford informs us that being fit and healthy enhances pleasure and that regular exercise will give us the 'strength, balance and flexibility for more interesting positions' (Hertford 1997: 10).

'Good sex' is also supposed to be spontaneous, not merely mechanical (see Gray 1996: 145). The performance should seem effortless so that the work and practice behind it remain hidden. Few of us would be impressed with a new lover who had the instruction manual open on the bed (although this might be acceptable for established couples and pornography often is used in this context). There are, however, a number of 'pocket guides' available to aid last-minute revision (see e.g. Hertford 1997). To be perceived as 'good' at sex, it must seem a natural talent. Good sex is also assumed to indicate sexual and therefore emotional compatibility – a sign of true love. Bad sex, however, does not negate the possibility of love; it is often taken as simply a lack of proficiency which can be overcome by diligence and practice in an atmosphere of 'trust'. For those who are truly dysfunctional, remedial classes have been offered by organizations such as

Relate,[1] tightly structured courses to be followed in order to achieve competence (Lewis et al. 1992; Clark 1993). More recently therapeutic interventions are more likely to be pharmacological.

Ideas about competence, however, remain highly gendered. Until recently, if women were seen as candidates for therapeutic intervention, this was largely seen as a problem 'in their heads', a mental 'block' to be overcome. The model was one of repression causing 'impaired desire' or 'orgasmic dysfunction' from which women need to be 'liberated' (Clark 1993: 29). Male 'dysfunctionality' was, and continues to be, more likely to be located in the body, localized in the penis – now increasingly equated with 'erectile dysfunction'. What has changed in the age of Viagra is that the male model of sexual dysfunction is increasingly applied to women, with a search for a physical cause and a pharmacological remedy for 'female sexual dysfunction' (Moynihan 2003).

Despite the elaborate and varied sexual practices recommended in modern sex manuals, the syntax of heterosexual sex has largely remained unaltered: intricate foreplay still leads ultimately to coitus. However skilled a man might be with hands or tongue, if his penis is not up to it, he has failed in his performance. This is the focus of most male sexual anxiety and most of the therapy on offer to men has taken the form of elongating the sexual sentence (Bardeleben et al. 1989; Scott and Freeman 1995), deferring coitus while the man learns control – but successful coitus is still the aim (see e.g. the detailed instructions offered by Comfort 1996: 237). Late twentieth-century male sexuality was as much about self-control as its nineteenth-century counterpart, but the object of control had changed. Nineteenth-century medics worried about the debilitating consequences of too frequent ejaculation, and advised men to restrain their impulses (Heath 1982) modern sexologists concerned themselves with; impotence and especially 'premature' ejaculation and offered advice on self-control in the interests of better performance. Performance took precedence over pleasure, with such folk remedies as doing multiplication tables to stave off premature ejaculation. Where male performance anxieties were concerned, women were meant to be supportive – massaging egos and even the penis itself, sometimes very precisely, as in the 'squeeze technique' (see Masters et al. 1986). By the turn of the millennium, however, male self-control was increasingly being replaced by chemical control with Viagra being prescribed to enable men to achieve and maintain erections.

Pharmaceutical solutions to mechanical sexual problems, however, do not necessarily reduce concerns and anxieties about sexual technique and expertise. Where shame once attached to sexual activity *per se* (Elias 1994), now it attaches to doing it badly. Sexuality is still singled out as a special area of life; to be bad at sex is worse than being bad at anything else. It strikes fundamentally at our identities in a way which having no aptitude for sport or gardening would not. It is acceptable to admit lack of skill in most social arenas, or to seek to acquire a new skill – but this is not true of sexuality. Whereas sex manuals for married couples early in the twentieth century assumed that both partners were relative beginners, now beginner status is something to be got through as fast as possible, preferably without revealing the incompetence of the novice.

Sex, while increasingly Taylorized, is not entirely amenable to this process. An important aspect of sexuality, bound up with its 'specialness', is our emotional investment in sexuality and sexual relationships, the persistent irrationality of our desires, wanting relationships which are not good for us, the agony of sexual jealousy and the leap of faith required to trust a partner – indeed, the felt need for trust itself. These emotional tangles are catered for by yet another genre of self-help books – all the twelve-step programmes offering us rational guides for variously overcoming or indulging our irrational emotions, including sexual addiction.

Flexible sex?

In recent years tensions in the Taylorized model have become more apparent and the public discussion of sexuality has, in many respects, taken on a post-Fordist flavour (Scott and Freeman 1995), with the emphasis on adaptability, versatility and reskilling. These goals, however, are difficult to attain given the anxiety that still surrounds sex, the emotional weight it carries and the continued proliferation of expert knowledges, which suggest that we should be the authors of our own sexual scripts while simultaneously telling us what those scripts should be. This post-Fordist turn, moreover, does not fundamentally challenge the gendered context within which heterosexual relations occur.

One such tension was exposed in the mid-1980s when, in response to HIV/AIDS, instructions were issued by public health agencies about safer sex. The Taylorized model was applied and the common assumption appeared to be that condoms could simply be inserted as a punctuation point, a comma in the sexual sentence (Bardeleben et al. 1989). There was at this time some optimism in relation to a development of a less penetrative focus to heterosex, chiming with existing feminist concerns (Coward 1984), but where feminists sought radical disruption of sexual syntax, challenging the coital imperative, public discussion continued to assume that condoms were the solution. Penetration was thus preserved by preservatives. Getting men to use them, however, was not so simple. Public discourse around safer sex in this period can be understood within a post-Fordist frame, with a focus on reskilling and increased flexibility. Heavy male sex work, with the emphasis on performance, seemed to be of less value and female negotiating skills came to the fore. Meaningful negotiation, however, requires an equal starting point and most health advice disregarded the inequalities within the gendered dynamics of heterosexuality (Holland et al. 1990). The emotional meanings of sexuality were largely ignored, especially for women, for whom being 'carried away' is constructed as central to the romance of the sexual encounter. In the end, this public discussion offered minimal challenge to male sexuality and women were still left to do the 'care work' around sex.

This was true of other arenas where post-Fordist discourse seemed to be the order of the day. Since the 1980s much discussion in women's magazines has stressed adaptability and the development of new skills. In 1992, in an article on how to make good heterosexual sex sensational, *Cosmopolitan* magazine (quoted in Hay et al. 1994) suggests that the woman who can do this 'knows how to turn any setting, even the kitchen counter, into the backdrop for sensational sex, and has the surfaces cleared, clean and ready for any spontaneous action'. Spontaneity, it seemed, required both planning and hidden domestic labour. Old feminine skills were being put to new uses: not just those of housewifery, but also the traditional feminine ideal of being adaptable and responsive to male demands (sexual or otherwise).

Reskilling is a prevalent theme in manuals for established couples, who are instructed on spicing up their sex lives and maintaining monogamy when routinization has set in. For example, John Gray (1996) has chapters entitled 'How to Rekindle the Passion', 'Mechanical Sex versus Spontaneous Sex' and 'Passionate Monogamy'. The paradox here is that routinization is combated with increased rationalization; the goal is to restore spontaneity, variety and specificity (what is best for you and your partner) but by choosing from a set menu. Where individuality is expressed through choice, and sexual freedom could once mean multiple partners, in the face of sexual risk choice is seen as something best exercised within the monogamous couple.

The opening up of varied options for sexual activities is still, for the most part, taking place within relatively constrained parameters, in which monogamous heterosexuality may have been modified, but retains its hegemony and remains structured around gender hierarchy. Since the 1990s, however, a discourse of sexual flexibility has been in vogue, challenging the fixity of heterosexuality and homosexuality, destabilizing the boundary between them, and representing queer and bisexuality as readily available off-the-peg lifestyle choices. This 'postmodern' sexuality has been much discussed in academic writing (Butler 1990a; McRobbie 1996) and sometimes in the media. While ambiguous sexuality may be a style accessory for the few, for the majority of the population, anything outside heterosexuality is regarded at best with ambivalence rather than embraced as a fashionable and positive ambiguity. Moreover, the ability to participate in such circles is often the prerogative of a privileged few with access to the necessary economic, social and cultural capital (Hennessy 2000; Taylor 2004). In many respects the normalization of homosexuality has occurred without undermining institutionalized heterosexuality (Richardson 2000, 2004, 2005a, 2005b; Seidman 2002, 2005, 2009).

For all its emphasis on flexibility, post-Fordist sexuality is still constructed in terms of a rational choice model and is more an extension of some of the underlying principles of Taylorization than a challenge to it. Just as 'disorganized capitalism' (Lash and Urry 1987) is not a departure from capitalism's goal of maximizing profit, but merely a new means of attaining that goal under changing conditions of the world market, so post-Fordist sex is still geared to the maximization of male pleasure within the context of the commodification of sex and global risk (Scott and Freeman 1995). Indeed, the redefinition of sexual problems as 'dysfunction' and the availability of Viagra have reinforced phallocentric definitions of what sex is.

The language of function and dysfunction has, in much medical discourse, replaced older ideas of 'normality'. Whereas what was 'normal' could be defined in relation to either social or statistical norms, functionality and dysfunctionality are exceedingly elastic concepts (Marshall 2006). While this elasticity may seem consonant with the idea of flexibility, it has served to reinforce and rigidify the same old sexual sentence in which penetration of a vagina by a penis is what sex is all about. Thus while expectations of functionality can constantly be raised and definitions of dysfunctionality broadened to encompass a host of very varied problems, what is functional remains tied to heterosexual coitus (Marshall 2002).

Take the widely cited assertion that 43 per cent of women suffer from female sexual dysfunction (Moynihan 2003). This figure has been extrapolated from Laumann et al.'s (1994) US National Health and Social Life Survey, from those who answered 'yes' to having had one of seven experiences in the previous year, including: not enjoying sex, not wanting it, not achieving orgasm, pain or lubrication difficulties. Having experienced any one instance of any of these things could thus place a woman in the 'dysfunctional' category. By this definition a figure of 100 per cent would not be surprising. It seems that if women do not want sex – penetrative sex – all the time, and if they do not enjoy it, all the time, they are dysfunctional. It is rather like saying that someone who does not approach every meal with appetite or does not find every meal enjoyable or satisfying suffers from an eating disorder. If sexual desire and pleasure have become compulsory, essential to being defined as 'healthy', the 'sexual fix' described by Heath (1982) has become tyrannical. It may also be that the availability of Viagra for men has further entrenched the notion of coitus as men's right within a relationship and shortened, rather than lengthened, the sexual sentence. The research of Annie Potts and her colleagues suggests that this may be the case, exemplified by the following statement from a heterosexual woman whose partner uses Viagra:

> [Viagra use began] during a time when I was trying to impress upon him that foreplay would be a nice thing ... that this was, you know, quite an important part of making love so when Viagra came along the whole foreplay thing just *vanished*, I mean, it wasn't even a

suggestion it was: 'OK, I've taken the pill, we've got about an hour, I expect you in that time to be acquiescent'. (48 year old woman).

(Potts et al. 2003: 704)

Emotional entanglement and the rationalization of intimacy

Sexual encounters are not merely physical. Both Taylorized and post-Fordist constructions of sexuality ignore the emotionality, the ideas of naturalness and spontaneity that complicate the choices we make around sexuality. These choices also continue to be limited by, and negotiated within, gendered power relations (Holland et al. 1990; Phillips 2000; Tolman 2002). Moreover, in many respects these constructions are descendants of models of sexuality as rational and goal-oriented. Resistance to the rationalization of sex is still seen as irrational – whether 'trusting to love' rather than condoms or seeking romance and emotional reassurance rather than playful experimentation – especially when these forms of resistance come from women.

There are those who argue that we are undergoing a convergence between men's and women's sexual and romantic aspirations, that we are moving towards androgynous love (Cancian 1990) or the 'pure relationship' (Giddens 1992). There may be a trend in this direction, but what evidence we have from sociological studies, from the 1980s onwards, indicates that women have continued to invest more in love than men, that many men are still inclined to see sexual contact as a panacea for problems in a relationship while women rarely view sex as an unproblematic signifier of intimacy, but instead desire emotional intimacy as a precondition for sex (L. Rubin 1983; Cancian 1990; Duncombe and Marsden 1993; Langford 1995; Potts et al. 2003).

Masculinity continues to be associated with tight emotional control, and lack of male expressiveness has, over the last few decades, continued to be reported by sociologists as an issue in many heterosexual relationships (Mansfield and Collard 1988; Duncombe and Marsden 1993; Langford 1995). Men are no longer seen as endangered by sexual excess, as they were in Victorian era, but emotional excess may still, it seems, 'unman' them. The potential dangers of sex for men have been defused by an increasingly rationalized approach to the pursuit of pleasure and its anxiety reduced by pharmaceutical remedies. Emotions, however, are still deemed mysterious and unknowable. Sociologists have colluded with this, hence their greater (recent) willingness to deal with sexuality rather than the emotions bound up with it. Sexuality is treated as rational, knowable, even quantifiable – as in the British national sex surveys which neatly classify complex practices into active or passive, penetrative or non-penetrative sex (Wellings et al. 1994; Johnson et al. 2001). Much research and theorizing on the sociology of the emotions has not been concerned with the sphere of the intimate, but with work relationships (Hochschild 1983; James 1989) and where intimacy does become the focus, it is often conceptualized in the language of 'emotional labour' and caring work (Duncombe and Marsden 1993). While we regard this as an important feature of heterosexual relations, it still provides a means of avoiding talking about sexuality as a highly emotionally charged area of social life.

Emotion is the last refuge of the irrational, especially those emotions most closely associated with sexual desire. Yet emotions themselves are coming to be seen as susceptible to rational intervention. Emotions are viewed positively when properly expressed and properly managed and men's emotional 'inadequacy' is seen as an inability to manage and express their emotions properly – they need to be 'put in touch with them'. The repressive model we are so familiar with in discourses around sexuality is now also deployed in relation to the emotions. Advice manuals in this area suggest that we should uncover the 'truth' of our emotions, whether it be women confronting their emotional 'neediness' (see e.g. Norwood 1985) or men recovering or coming to terms with their primeval masculinity (Bly 1990; Hood 1999). While some versions of this discourse seem to privilege women as emotionally knowledgeable, we should be as sceptical of the repressive hypothesis in this context as we are in relation to sexuality. Women's emotional competence may well derive from their social location as carers and dependants but we should be wary of valorizing what is symptomatic of subordination, however tempting it might be to deride men's emotional incompetence (Jackson 1995). Emotions are as much socially constructed as sexuality; both are constructed *and* managed.

This idea of emotional management parallels the widely held assumption that the rational management of sexuality is a good thing, and that sex itself, properly managed, is a good thing. Yet the ways in which the concept of rationality is deployed in relation to sexuality and emotionality differ, and are also always in tension with ideas of emotionality as spontaneity. This gives rise to two competing discourses of rationality and sexuality, or perhaps competing versions of the same discourse, since they share ideas of sexuality and emotionality as innate essential human attributes. The version of rationalization we have been concentrating on is the rational pursuit of pleasure through sex. There is, however, another version: moral conservatism. Whereas rationality in the former is understood in terms of an opposition between sexual efficiency and inefficiency, the moral conservative version opposes order to chaos. Where the former is predicated on scientific constructions of rationality, the latter rests on an older, originally Christian, idea of a 'natural order', governed by divine ordinance.

These discourses intersect where they identify a series of sexual 'problems' variously classified as sickness, maladjustment or addiction. Here both address assumed differences between men and women as a site of much sexual malaise, but whereas one offers a patriarchal solution, the other offers personal remedies that take little account of the social bases of gender divisions. Moreover, moral conservatives emphasize social chaos and seek social order, while those advocating therapeutic solutions are concerned only with quelling the turmoil within the individual. Moral conservatives see untrammelled lust as leading to social chaos: promiscuity, homosexuality, unmarried mothers – all linked to the decline of the family – are seen as destabilizing the natural order. Rationality here is understood as reimposing moral order upon sexuality, locating it once again within the sanctity of patriarchal marriage. Sexuality is seen as too 'special' to be debased through promiscuity or perversion. Within the discourse of rational management, there is less concern with a social, moral order and more emphasis on the individual. The pursuit of pleasure itself – for both men and women – is the object of rational governance, but even here there are notions of troubling excess: the sex addicts or the women who love too much (Giddens 1992; Schrager 1993). A phalanx of self-appointed experts now informs us about optimum levels of sexual activity and emotional investment in sex and tells us that deviations from the ideal are amenable to rational therapeutic management. We are encouraged to engage in self-surveillance, identifying problems within ourselves and working on them to effect a cure. Whether modern sexual ills are understood as indicative of a lack of 'moral fibre', or as symptomatic of 'dysfunction' or ignorance, they are seen as susceptible to rational remedial action. Moral re-education and self-restraint on the one hand, or therapy and self-knowledge on the other, are attempts to impose order on chaotic desires.

What these discourses of moral and therapeutic management suggest is that there are always elements of human sexuality that elude rational control. Despite all the discursive strategies through which sex has been constructed as rational, the idea that it is irrational persists and appears to be integral to the ways in which sexuality is understood in everyday life. Psychoanalysis is one means of dealing rationally (and, purportedly, scientifically) with the irrational. By locating irrationality in the unconscious, the rationality of the conscious mind is preserved – except when disturbed by 'eruptions' of the unconscious. Since the unconscious is also a repository of repressed sexual desires, sexuality is the effective source of the irrational within the unconscious. Thus despite the rationalizing processes that we have described, psychoanalysis has provided a way of understanding sexuality as intrinsically irrational, albeit amenable to 'scientific' explanation and therapeutic intervention.

Change, continuity and contradiction

It is widely assumed that late modern societies are becoming more sexually open, regardless of whether this is seen as positive or negative. A number of commentators have drawn attention to the liberalization of both sexual regulation and wider sexual attitudes since the 1960s, which, superficially at least, have enabled a freeing up of sexuality. There is empirical evidence from survey data, such as British Social Attitudes surveys, of the acceptance of premarital heterosexual sexual relations being widespread since the 1980s, and, more equivocally, greater tolerance of gay sexuality among younger generations (Harding 1988; Heath and McMahon 1991; Barnett and Thomson 1996). Younger people have also been reporting earlier first sex and increased numbers of sexual partners since the late 1980s (Wellings et al. 1994; Johnson et al. 2001). There is also evidence from numerous smaller qualitative studies of a diversity of sexual communities, values and practices within late modern societies. The impression of a sexually variegated and freer society is reflected in representations of sexuality and intimate relations in popular culture and reinforced by the everyday knowledge gained from living in a social environment increasingly saturated with sexual imagery.

What are we to make of such trends? The answer is far from clear. There are those who urge caution over too eager a celebration of new sexual freedoms. Feminists, for example, point to the continued existence of gender hierarchy in heterosexual relations and the persistence of sexual violence. They have also long been aware that sexual liberation could impose new forms of constraint (Jackson and Scott 1996). Early Foucauldian accounts concurred, in that the incitement to have more and better sex is as much a function of power as are injunctions against sexual activity (see e.g. Heath 1982). More recently, however, sociologists have been more inclined to celebrate diversity and fluidity in sexual relations in keeping with these late or postmodern times as, for example, in Giddens' (1992) account of 'plastic sexuality' and the 'pure relationship' and Roseneil's (2000) identification of 'queer' tendencies in contemporary sexual mores. Yet a queer lifestyle is not equally accessible to all, not even to all lesbians and gay men, but only to those with the economic and cultural capital necessary to access the increasingly commodified cultural spaces that queer inhabits (Hennessy 1995, 2000).

'Progress' towards liberalization is, in actuality, very uneven and gives rise to a number of antinomies and associated anxieties. These anxieties centre on the specialness of sex, its status as extra-ordinary, as somehow separable from everyday social practices and routines – a source of ecstasy that lifts us beyond the mundane but which is also uniquely problematic and troublesome. Making sense of these tensions entails more than an awareness of both continuity and change. It is not simply that some things change while others stay the same, it is that these changes and continuities throw up tensions and contradictions around sexuality which, we feel, are indicative of a persistent unease about the sexual that sits side by side with an acceptance of greater sexual freedom and diversity. In the remainder of the book we will explore some of these contradictions.

Note

1 'Relate' is the major marriage guidance organization in the UK. For an analysis of their work, see Lewis et al. (1992).

CHAPTER 4

IS HETEROSEXUALITY STILL COMPULSORY?

The critique of heterosexuality is now central to much theorizing about sexuality, but the institution and the practices associated with it are undergoing change. Some of the major theorists of our time have, in recent decades, made optimistic predictions about the changes we are witnessing. Are we, as Giddens (1992) argues, undergoing a 'transformation of intimacy' towards more democratic and flexible relationships? Might the increasing economic independence of women and the rise of movements for women's and gay liberation even herald the 'end of patriarchalism', as Castells (2004) would have it? A few feminists, too, have suggested that the ideal-typical heterosexual family no longer occupies centre stage in Western societies as families and domestic arrangements become more diverse or even 'queer' (Stacey 1996; Roseneil 2000; Roseneil and Budgeon 2004). So are we seeing a queering of intimate life? We are not so sure.

We would not, of course, deny that major changes have occurred since the 1950s. We have, after all, come a long way from the days when gay male sex was a criminal offence, when lesbians risked losing custody of their children and unwed mothers were coerced into giving up their babies for adoption. Domestic, intimate and sexual life has become more variegated and there have been major advances in the rights of sexual minorities. But the 'world we have won', as Weeks (2007) points out, throws up new dilemmas and anxieties. Many of the antinomies and tensions associated with sexuality, to which we alluded in Chapter 3, accrete around the institution of heterosexuality. The queer impetus towards transgressing and destabilizing heterosexual norms coexists with the naturalizing of homosexuality as an innate proclivity. Greater public openness to sexual diversity and the granting of citizenship to sexual minorities exist alongside continued homophobic harassment, bullying and violence in schools, workplaces and on the streets (Hennessy 2000).

Within heterosexual relationships, egalitarian ideals are embraced but inequitable distributions of labour and resources persist; women are becoming more independent and aspire to more democratic relationships, yet levels of domestic and sexual abuse of women show no sign of declining. Tolerance of premarital, even casual, heterosex and of marital breakdown and serial relationships coexists with the continuing reification of monogamy.

It might be suggested that these tensions are likely to abate over time, that they are merely symptomatic of the uneven advance towards a more open, democratic sexual culture. Yet the antimonies inherent in the changes through which we are living seem, at least in part, to be produced by those very transformations; they are not merely leftover debris of bygone prejudices blocking the road to sexual progress. We argue that although the boundaries of normative heterosexuality have shifted, along with the ways in which those boundaries are regulated, heterosexuality retains its hold as the 'normal' and normative form of human sexuality (Seidman 2002, 2009; Richardson 2004, 2005a, 2005b) and is taken for granted as such in much of everyday life. This being the case, we maintain, the sociological critique of heterosexuality has by no means outlived its usefulness.

In order to explore the current status of heterosexuality and the competing academic claims being made about it, it is important to keep both heteronormativity and gender division in mind. Institutionalized heterosexuality is a key site of intersection between gender and sexuality, implicated both in the perpetuation of gender hierarchy and in the marginalization of alternative sexualities. To explain this further, we need to say more about the history of debates in this area, drawing together some of the material on queer and feminist theory that we have discussed in previous chapters, before outlining our own approach.

Why question heterosexuality?

Despite the loosening of normative constraints on sexuality and the increased visibility of forms of sexuality that transgress, subvert or unsettle the heterosexual norm, heterosexuality itself still goes largely unchallenged in everyday life. Until the 1990s this was largely the case in mainstream sociology, too, though the roots of a critique of heterosexuality go back to the feminist and gay liberation movements of the 1960s and 1970s. Until fairly recently, for example, sociologists studied marriage and family life without apparently noticing that these were heterosexual institutions – and it would not have occurred to most of them to think about how heterosexuality might, for example have been implicated in shaping wider social relations such as the labour market or workplace cultures. This is now changing as the critical insights of feminist, lesbian, gay and (more recently) queer scholars have gained more credence within the discipline.

There are very good reasons why, as sociologists, we should question heterosexuality – and why questioning heterosexuality is in keeping with the foundations of the sociological enterprise. First, sociology is and should be concerned with questioning the taken-for-granted, both at the level of commonsense understandings of the social world and in terms of the wider social order. Sociology is thus concerned with denaturalizing what might otherwise be taken as given 'facts of life'. Second, sociologists have long been aware that understanding a given set of social relations requires interrogating the normative as well as the transgressive, questioning social privilege as well as exposing disadvantage. There is also a well-established critical tradition of sociology that has always been concerned with injustice and inequality, which should extend to the injustices and inequalities associated with heterosexuality. It is very much in keeping with the exercise of a sociological imagination that the gender inequalities within heterosexual relationships and the marginalization and oppression of lesbians and gay men – what were once seen as 'personal troubles' – should now be thought of as public issues, and that the biographical details of individual sexual and intimate life should be understood in historical and social context (cf. Mills 1970). If we are serious about analysing sexuality as socially constructed, or prevailing patterns of intimate relationships as products of a particular society and culture, then heterosexuality, so central to both, must become an object of scrutiny.

Unsurprisingly, given the political interests at stake, it was from gay, lesbian and feminist movements for liberation that the impetus for the critique of heterosexuality came. In the early 1970s both gay and feminist movements concurred in critiques of patriarchal, heterosexual institutions, such as the family, and there was a sense of a common cause. As Seidman (2009) points out, though, there were always differences of emphasis: while gay liberationists focused primarily on sexual liberation, feminists focused on gender oppression. It should be noted, however, that much of the feminist work at the time, like mainstream sociology, did not name heterosexuality as the object of analysis and critique (Jackson 1999). Nonetheless in addressing the patriarchal structures that shaped family life, revealing women's discontents with heterosexual relationships, bringing to light the problems of sexual violence and challenging the androcentric definition of 'the sex act' (the coital imperative), feminists laid the foundations for a thoroughgoing critique of heterosexuality – though the elaboration of that critique was left to lesbian feminists such as Adrienne Rich and Monique Wittig (see Chapter 2).

The concept of 'compulsory heterosexuality' proved to be one of the lasting legacies of this early stage of theorization. While associated particularly with Rich (1980), this idea of heterosexuality as an imposed order was very much 'in the air' at the time and underpinned many lesbian feminist and gay liberation arguments, evident in Wittig's (1980) dissection of the heterosexual contract and in many other analyses of the 1970s and 1980s (see e.g. Radicalesbians 1972; Bunch 1975; Gay Left Collective 1980; Gough and Macnair 1985). The importance of the concept of compulsory heterosexuality was that it identified a socially formed structural order of patterned sexual-gender divisions and hierarchies (Seidman 2009) This, as Seidman notes, marked a fundamental break with the individualist reformist tendencies of both earlier homophile movements and liberal feminism (Seidman 2009). Heterosexuality was therefore seen neither as a matter of choice nor as ordained by nature, but as a social institution. The concept of compulsory heterosexuality brought something new to the sociological understanding of sexuality since the early social constructionist approaches, with their roots in interactionism and phenomenology,[1] did not attend to structural constraints.

It is notable that many feminist variants of the critique of heterosexuality were not only addressing sexuality. While some identified the appropriation of women's sexuality as a primary 'cause' of women's subordination (MacKinnon 1982; Jeffreys 1990), most linked it to other aspects of subordination. Charlotte Bunch viewed heterosexuality as fundamental to women's marginalization as secondary workers in the labour market and as upholding 'the home, housework, the family as both a social and economic unit' (Bunch [1975] 1997: 55–56). Adrienne Rich (1980), too, saw it as an economic relation encompassing sexual divisions of labour and Monique Wittig conceptualised the category of sex as itself as 'the product of a heterosexual society in which men appropriate for themselves the reproduction and production of women and also their persons by means of ... the marriage contract' (Wittig [1982] 1992: 7). An understanding of heterosexuality that includes more than just sexuality was to remain central to many later feminist analyses, and is fundamental our own perspective. Sexual relationships and practices, as we have repeatedly emphasized, occur in wider social contexts and this is particularly important in the case of heterosexuality precisely because it *is* normative and institutionalized. It is not only the boundaries of heterosexuality that have been policed, but also heterosexual conduct itself so that, as Steven Seidman (2002, 2005) points out, there are hierarchies of respectability and legitimacy among heterosexuals. Moreover, since heterosexuality is founded on relations between men and women, it is inextricably bound up with gender relations.

The development of feminist and queer critiques

Early feminist debates became mired in the furore around political lesbianism and subsequently the heated debates of the 'sex wars' between the libertarian 'pro-sex' lobby and anti-violence feminists (see Chapter 2). There was, therefore, something of a hiatus in feminist debates around heterosexuality until the 1990s, when its resurgence coincided with the emergence and growing influence of queer theory. Feminists continued to emphasize male dominance in hetero-relations, as well as the privileging and institutionalization of heterosexuality, but in the context of the 1990s the debate was less acrimonious and more productive – though this was by no means guaranteed by the way in which it was reopened.

In 1992, the journal *Feminism and Psychology* published a special issue on heterosexuality which was, in many respects, framed from within the old debates. Sue Wilkinson and Celia Kitzinger,[2] the editors of the special issue and the subsequent book (1993), were committed to political lesbianism and this is very evident in their introduction; for example, they reassert the idea that no act of heterosexual penetration can, under current social conditions, escape its meaning as an enactment of male domination. The special issue could be seen as an exercise in 'outing' heterosexual feminists who were invited to answer the question: 'How does your heterosexuality contribute to your feminism?' (Wilkinson and Kitzinger 1993: 33). Not surprisingly most found this a difficult question to answer: whereas lesbianism can be seen as a political identity and in itself a form of political opposition, heterosexuality – because it is normative – cannot readily be seen that way. Quite apart from the difficulty of answering this question, it also had the effect of focusing too narrowly on the issue of identity rather than encouraging a wider analysis of heterosexuality. Whatever its failings, this initiative did revive the debate and while some took offence (as many heterosexual feminists had in the first round of debates on political lesbianism), many more engaged with the question or found ways of creatively sidestepping it and exploring other aspects of heterosexuality. The debate ran on for some three years in the pages of the journal and longer elsewhere and, as it did so, broadened out to include many aspects of heterosexual practice and experience.

One of the most critical reactions to Wilkinson and Kitzinger's project came in Lynne Segal's *Straight Sex* (1994). If the former reprised the radical lesbian role of the late 1970s and early 1980s, the latter took up the mantle of the affronted heterosexual feminist. Segal is critical of the condescension with which Wilkinson and Kitzinger treat their heterosexual contributors, yet, with at least equal condescension, describes those who participated in the project as 'foolhardy' and as a 'selected sample of victims' (Segal 1994: 215). She reads the responses of feminists genuinely seeking to confront and analyse their own heterosexuality as a wrongheaded defensiveness – but her own project in *Straight Sex* could equally be read as defensive, albeit with a more heterosex-affirmative bent; she concludes that straight feminists 'have everything to gain from asserting our non-coercive desire to fuck if, when, how and as we choose' (Segal 1994: 318). Throughout she emphasizes heterosexual women's agency and the potential pleasures of heterosex – neither of which we would dispute in themselves – but in so doing frequently abstracts sexuality from its social context and accords it far too much transformative potential. In a later article this is even more evident; here she suggests that 'sex easily *threatens* rather than confirms gender polarity' and that in consensual sex 'all the great dichotomies (activity/passivity, subject/object, heterosexual/ homosexual slide away' (Segal 1997: 86, emphasis in original). In this account it is as if bodies meet without any social context and as if sex is somehow capable of dissolving gender divisions and inequalities. Such overblown claims say little about the actual conditions under which everyday heterosexual relations are practised and offer even less to a sociological critique of heterosexuality.

Fortunately, many feminists refused both the agenda set by Kitzinger and Wilkinson and that of Segal and rose to the challenge of developing analyses of heterosexuality in which critiques of its institutionalization were kept distinct from the condemnation of heterosexual feminists. Greater attention was given to disentangling the relationship between heterosexuality as an institution, practice and identity. By the mid-1990s it was clear that the renewed attention to heterosexuality was producing far more nuanced accounts of it than had previously been possible from the more polarized stances of the early 1980s. One illustration is the collection edited by Diane Richardson (1996), which included, for example, contributions on heterosexuality in relation to social policy (Carabine 1996), domestic life (VanEvery 1996), masculinity (Robinson 1996), sexual desire (Hollway 1996), first heterosex (Holland et al. 1996), the impact of normative heterosexuality on lesbian sexuality (Wilton 1996) as well as more general articles on the current state of play within these debates. Although these contributions came from very varied political and theoretical perspectives, and from self-identified lesbian, queer and heterosexual feminists, the new mood of the debates was summed up by the closing contribution from Carol Smart, in which she argues for the need to move on from seeing heterosexuality *only* as a form of oppression and to 'appreciate differences of experience and meaning' among women (Smart 1996: 177).

Many feminists were also engaging with queer theory, including its critical stance on sexual and gendered identities and its emphasis on destabilizing the binary divisions between women and men and hetero and homosexualities. Both feminism and queer theory contributed, sometimes separately and sometimes in dialogue, to the revitalization of analyses of heterosexuality. As in the feminist and gay liberation writings of the 1970s, there are shared assumptions – most notably a continuing commitment to questioning the inevitability and naturalness of heterosexuality – but there are differences of emphasis within and between feminism and queer. These centre on the two rather different grounds for critiquing heterosexuality: first, its privileged, normative status, and second, its relationship to gender division and hierarchy. For feminists, the former is related to the latter; for queer theorists, the former is the main issue.

As Seidman (2005) has pointed out, queer analysts of institutionalized heterosexuality have 'focused exclusively on its role in regulating homosexuality' and, while they theorize how 'homosexuality gains its coherence in relation to heterosexuality, the impact of regimes of normative heterosexuality on heterosexuality has largely been ignored' (Seidman 2005: 40). A further problem here, from our perspective, is that although queer theorists seek to trouble heteronormativity, they are relatively unconcerned with what goes on *within* heterosexual relations. This has a rather paradoxical consequence given the queer insistence on the fluidity and instability of sexual and gender categories: heterosexuality comes to be seen as a monolithic entity, positioned simply as a 'unitary concept' (Smart 1996: 170), a norm to be destabilized. For most queer theorists, heteronormativity is understood in cultural terms, as discursively constituted and hence, as Seidman (2009) points out, compulsory heterosexuality is no longer understood as a social structural phenomenon. In the process, gender is frequently displaced from the central place it occupied in earlier critiques. Feminists, because they continue to be concerned with gender hierarchy, are more likely to retain an interest in analysing institutionalized heterosexuality as a structural phenomenon, but they are also more concerned with exploring the micro-politics of everyday heterosexual relations and practices. While the former can lead back, once more, to treating heterosexuality as a 'unitary concept', the latter alerts us to the complexities of heterosexual lives.

The competing priorities within and between feminist and queer accounts can be illustrated with reference to two of the key texts that reoriented debate in the 1990s. One of these was, of course, Judith Butler's *Gender Trouble* (1990a), which can be seen as both feminist and queer (see Chapter 1). Butler, unlike many other queer theorists, does accord gender a central place and, indeed, puts the interrelationship between gender and heterosexuality firmly back on the theoretical map. Her interest, however, was primarily in gender difference and in unsettling the category of women by asking whether it achieves 'stability and coherence only in relation to the heterosexual matrix' (Butler 1990a: 5). She defines the heterosexual matrix in a footnote as 'that grid of cultural intelligibility through which bodies, genders and desires are naturalized' and acknowledges that she is drawing on both Wittig and, to a lesser extent, Rich:

> to characterize a hegemonic, discursive/epistemic model of gender intelligibility that assumes that for bodies to cohere and make sense there must be a stable sex expressed as a stable gender ... that is oppositionally and hierarchically defined through the practice of compulsory heterosexuality.
>
> (Butler 1990a: 151n.)

While there is reference to hierarchy here and to 'the practice of compulsory heterosexuality', the emphasis on the 'discursive/epistemic' foundations of the heterosexual matrix shifts it away from the social structural and into the realm of the cultural. Hence it is heterosexuality's normativity and the possibilities for destabilizing it that preoccupy her. While recognizing that gender is both regulatory and coercive in its imposition, gender is conceived as hierarchical only in relation to its cultural intelligibility rather than in terms of wider social relations – despite her debt to Wittig. Butler reads Wittig in relation to poststructuralist and postmodern theory, rather than as a materialist feminist text, and thus divests it of much of its import as a social-structural critique of institutionalized heterosexuality, in particular its emphasis on the appropriation of women's bodies *and* labour.

By contrast, another landmark publication of the 1990s, which also draws on Wittig, is firmly located within social-structural critique: Chrys Ingraham's analysis of 'the heterosexual imaginary' (1996)[3] as an ideological device that masks the ways in which gender has consistently been defined from a heteronormative perspective. Drawing attention to the construction of 'women' and 'men' as mutually attracted 'opposite sexes', she argues that sociologists (including feminists) have failed to see the heterosexual ends to which this gender divide is directed. As she points out, the definitions of gender employed by feminist sociologists indicate that it is a binary 'organizing relations *between* the sexes' (Ingraham 1996: 186; emphasis in original).

Like the original French materialist feminists, Ingraham defines heterosexuality as an institution that regulates far more than our erotic lives. She suggests that it 'serves as the organizing institution and ideology ... for gender' (Ingraham 1996: 187) and is implicated in the operation of all social institutions at all levels of society, from family to workplace to the state. We are not convinced that heterosexuality should be accorded such causal primacy, though we would accept that heterosexuality is *an* organizing principle of many aspects of social structure and social life, and an important one. For example, it is possible to relate all gendered aspects of work and employment to heterosexuality. But does this give heterosexuality primacy? Are gendered labour markets and wage differentials heterosexual in themselves or are they simply related to the social organization of heterosexual family life? Is it heterosexuality that orders, even constructs, gender rather than the other way around? The problem here is that it is possible to argue links from either direction, so that causal or logical priority is difficult to determine. Defining heterosexuality so broadly that it encompasses all aspects of gendered relations, and then collapsing heterosexuality and gender into one term – heterogender – does not, for us, represent an adequate solution to the problem of conceptualizing their interrelationship. While gender and heterosexuality are so closely entwined that it is not easy to unravel their intersections, we need to retain the capacity to do so.

Ingraham's (1996) argument certainly provokes us to think about the ways in which heterosexuality may order gender relations – as well as vice versa. However, something has slipped out of our grasp in this analysis: sexuality in the wider sense of erotically significant desires, practices, relationships and identities. Although Ingraham starts from the issue of erotic attraction, the erotic then disappears from the gender-heterosexuality relation although clearly in some way implicated in it. A further issue in both Butler's and Ingraham's analyses is that both tend towards the unitary model of heterosexuality – in Butler's case because of the emphasis on heteronormativity and in Ingraham's case as a result of an almost exclusively structural analysis.

The problems we have identified suggest that a more adequate analysis of heterosexuality has three prerequisites: first, to tease out the relationships between gender, sexuality and heterosexuality, second, to think more broadly about the sociality of heterosexuality in terms of structures, practices, meanings and subjectivity, and third, to keep in mind both the normativity of heterosexuality and its relationship to gender division and hierarchy. It is to this analysis that we now turn our attention. In so doing we will be drawing heavily on previous work on this theme (especially Jackson 2006a, 2006b), but also a wealth of theorizing and research on heterosexuality that has accumulated since the 1990s.

Definitional difficulties and conceptual slippages

Part of the problem in analysing heterosexuality's interconnections with sexuality in general and with gender is that there is no consensus on the definition of these terms: they are applied to different objects at different levels of analysis. Their meaning is imprecise, slippery and shifts with context. For example, the term 'heterosexuality' can denote a mode of erotic attraction, and/or a cultural norm, and/or an institution involving wider social relations between women and men, and/or a set of practices. 'Sexuality' can be understood primarily in terms of the hetero/homo binary, or the straight, gay, lesbian or bisexual identities deriving from it, or as encompassing a fuller range of desires, practices and identities. 'Gender' can mean a social division between women and men, and/or a cultural distinction, and/or the content of gender categories, conventionally defined as femininity or masculinity. Our preference is to opt for the broader definitions of these terms. While this risks collapsing a great deal of sociocultural complexity into a small number of concepts, this is preferable to narrowing them down with the greater risk of losing sight of significant portions of social life. Our own definitions, while broad, are particular and it is worth restating and elaborating the brief outline of them that we gave in the Introduction.

Gender, for us, denotes the division or distinction *between* women and men, female and male, these binary categories themselves (the products of the distinction/division) and the characteristics and identities embodied through membership of those categories. Gender is thus a social division and a cultural distinction, given meaning and substance in the everyday actions, interactions and subjective interpretations through which it is lived. If gender is to be understood as fully social, 'then principle of partition itself' (Delphy 1993: 3) is crucial; if gender categories have no natural existence they cannot pre-exist the division and distinction through which they are constituted. While, as Judith Butler maintains 'permutations of gender which do not fit the binary are as much a part of gender as its most normative instance' (Butler 2004: 42), in our view, such variations could not be understood as gender without the division that constitutes and defines gender in the first place. Departures from the binary norm are located as such in relation to that norm, as variations on or combinations of masculinity and femininity or as interstitial or transitory between them.

While the binary division of gender is a persistent and resilient feature of social and cultural life, it has historically coexisted with very different understandings of the division itself (see e.g. Laqueur 1990) and with historical shifts and contemporary variation in how gender is lived. Within individual, socially located biographies, gender is enmeshed with other social inequalities (such as class and racial divisions), with other identities deriving, for example, from class, ethnic or regional affiliations as well as from the local exigencies of individual biographies. Yet despite considerable potential for variation *within* gender categories, and even increasing visibility of departures from the normative binary, the divide itself remains entrenched. As Delphy (1993) suggests, one of the defining features of gender is the coexistence of variability in its content with the intractability of gender division.

In using 'gender' to denote all aspects of the distinction and division between male and female, along with those variations that seem to depart from the normative binary, we reserve the terms 'sex' and 'sexual' for all that pertains to the erotic. While 'sex' denotes carnal acts, 'sexuality' is a broader term referring to all erotically significant aspects of social life and social being – desires, practices, relationships and identities. It refers, then, to a whole sphere of life. Sexuality is not, therefore, reducible to the heterosexual/homosexual binary – although this is an important aspect of its social organization. As a sphere of life it encompasses a multitude of desires and practices that exist across this divide and within homosexuality and heterosexuality respectively.

We are, then, making an analytical distinction between sex and sexuality on the one hand and gender on the other. While some make the case for the irreducibility of the former to the latter in order to create a space for the theorization of sexuality *per se* (Rubin 1984; Sedgwick 1991), we do so in order more effectively to theorize their interrelationship. Without an analytical distinction between them, we cannot effectively explore the ways in which they intersect; if we conflate them, we are in danger of deciding the form of their interrelationship in advance. Yet, while analytically separable, gender and sexuality are empirically interconnected (Gagnon and Simon 1974). If we ignore the empirical linkage between them, there is a danger of abstracting sexuality from the social. Sexual practices, desires and identities are embedded within complex webs of non-sexual social relations (Gagnon 2004), most, if not all, of which are gendered. Sexuality is gendered, for example, through its conventional or normative feminine and masculine expression as well as being the foundation of the hetero/homo binary. Yet it is ordered not *only* by gender, but also by other social divisions, relations and identities (Whittier and Simon 2001).

One good reason for maintaining the analytical divide between gender and sexuality is that once the latter is understood as social and far exceeding the boundaries of reproduction, it cannot be mapped directly onto the former (cf. Sedgwick 1991: 29). Herein lies a difficulty: sexuality and gender may be interrelated but they are rather different and not directly comparable social phenomena. Sedgwick (1991: 29) argues that 'the whole realm of what modern culture refers to as "sexuality"… is virtually impossible to situate on a map delimited by the feminist defined sex/gender distinction'. While we would endorse Sedgwick's queer project in so far as sexuality, as she says, exceeds male–female difference and 'the choreography of procreation' (Sedgwick 1991: 29), our understanding of gender leads us to posit an alternative view: that sexuality and gender differ because the former is a sphere or realm of social life while the latter, while encompassing a range of subjective meanings and everyday practices, is a fundamental social division.

For those of us interested in the social construction of sexuality, it is necessary to take seriously the idea that what makes an act, a desire or a relationship sexual is a matter of social definition: the meanings invested in it (see Gagnon and Simon 1974). These meanings are contextual and variable and hence sexuality has no clear definitional boundaries; what is sexual to one person in one context may not be to someone else or somewhere else. It might be said that gender is a matter of social definition too – and in a sense it is. As a social division, however, it is also a ubiquitous feature of social life. Gender is often taken by queer theorists, as it is by Sedgwick (1990) to define 'the space of differences between men and women', with these categories understood as co-constructed and relational. And so they are. Understood more sociologically as categories produced by social division, however, they are more: they are hierarchical categories associated with inequalities of labour and resources; they pervade all aspects of sociality, locating men and women differently in virtually all spheres of life. Social divisions are not always binary, and not always sharply defined, but these are a particular feature of gender, dividing members of society into two discrete categories. Many aspects of gender may be more fluid and variable, less definable, but the division itself remains remarkably fixed and stable.

Gender pervades all aspects of social life and sexuality is no exception. So although we cannot map sexuality directly onto gender, we can and should explore the variety of ways in which sexual desires, activities and relationships are gendered. In so doing, however, the distinction between sexuality as a sphere of social life and gender as a social division should be kept in mind. If we compare sexuality and gender with work and social class, perhaps this will be clearer. Work is a sphere of life and not in itself a social division, yet its social organization gives rise to class, which is a social division, and is also implicated in gender division. Sexuality is a sphere of life, which need not necessarily be associated with social division but is, as currently socially ordered, associated with both gender and the social division between homosexuality and heterosexuality.

What is more comparable with gender in this sense, then, is the binary divide and social division between heterosexuality and homosexuality. Thus we produce greater conceptual congruence with gender by pluralizing sexuality – speaking of 'sexualities' rather than 'sexuality'. This move, however, is not usually made with that intent, but rather with the aim of recognizing diversity in sexual identities and practices within as well as between heterosexuality and homosexuality (see e.g. Plummer 1985). Moreover, while it might offer us a set of categories relatable to gender, it produces other problems. First, it directs attention away from the broader scope of sexuality (singular) as a field of study and sphere of life and limits explorations of the gender–sexuality linkage to the ways in which gender is related to sexual 'identities'. Second, and importantly, if heterosexuality becomes conceived as simply one of a number of sexualities, albeit a hegemonic one, this might prevent us from seeing the broader social contours of institutionalized heterosexuality and the effect that this has on homosexuality.

Heterosexuality should not be thought of as simply a form of sexual expression. It is not only a key site of intersection between gender and sexuality, but also one that reveals the interconnections between sexual and non-sexual aspects of social life. As an institution, heterosexuality is, by definition, a gender relationship, governing relations between women and men, ordering not only sexual life but also domestic and extra-domestic divisions of labour and resources (Ingraham 1996; VanEvery 1996). Thus heterosexuality, while depending on the exclusion or marginalization of other sexualities for its legitimacy, is not precisely coterminous with heterosexual sexuality. Heteronormativity is effective because it defines not only normative sexual practice but also a normal way of life. Heterosexually is both sexual and asexual, publicly institutionalized yet a personal relationship, maintained through everyday practices yet so routinely that it appears unremarkable. Thus while heterosexuality is thoroughly gendered, precisely how it is gendered as institution, practice and experience is variable.

So what can we conclude from all this? If sexuality as a field of inquiry and a sphere of social life entails more than the homo/hetero binary, then it is crucial to retain a means of analysing the ways in which all facets of sexuality and all sexualities may be gendered. Since all aspects of social life, sexual and non-sexual, are also gendered, then we need to be able to think about how this gendering process is related to heterosexuality without deciding the issue in advance. If heterosexuality as an institution entails more than specifically sexual relations, we should consider both the actualities of social relations between heterosexual couples (in and out of marital and monogamous relations) and how heterosexuality is implicated in the ordering of wider aspects of social life (cf. Ingraham 1996). This suggests that the intersections between gender, sexuality and heterosexuality are exceedingly complex and by no means unidirectional.

The lack of consensus on definitions derives, in large part, from differing conceptualizations of the social. The analysis of gender, sexuality and heterosexuality has been approached with different aspects of social relations in mind – from the subjective to the discursive to the institutional – and from a variety of perspectives. While there is broad agreement that gender, sexuality and heterosexuality are social (rather than natural) phenomena, the social is perceived from a variety of rather different angles. It is not a case of some having a clearer view than others, but rather that the social is multifaceted and what is seen from one angle may be obscured from another. Following earlier analyses (Jackson 2006a, 2006b), we suggest that sexuality, gender and heterosexuality intersect in variable ways within and between different dimensions of the social; the way gender, sexuality and heterosexuality intersect may not be the same in each dimension. We cannot, for example, deduce the everyday sexual desires and practices of a heterosexual couple from the way heterosexuality is institutionalized. In order to understand the complexity of heterosexuality, then, we need to appreciate the complexity of sociality.

Dimensions and intersection

Gender, sexuality and heterosexuality are constituted within and across a number of different dimensions of the social. If we are to understand the complexity of their interconnections a certain degree of theoretical eclecticism is necessary, drawing on the diverse insights that competing perspectives have to offer. We have in recent work (Jackson 2006a) suggested that the social can be thought of in terms of four intersecting dimensions. First, there is what might be called the structural dimension of the social, the patterned social relations that shape the social order at a macro level where gender figures as a hierarchical social division and heterosexuality is institutionalized, most obviously through such mechanisms as legal systems. Second, all social relations and practices are imbued with meaning,[4] which encompasses the language and discourses constituting our broad cultural understandings of gender and sexuality and the more context-bound meanings negotiated in the everyday social interaction. Third, there is the 'everyday', the routine social practices through which gender and sexuality are constantly constituted and reconstituted within localized contexts and relationships. Fourth, in and of the social, there are social agents or subjects, sexual and gendered selves who through their embodied activities construct and make sense of everyday gendered and sexual interaction.

Conceptualizing these facets of the social is not without difficulties: the choice of metaphor carries certain implications. The term 'levels' used in some earlier work (Jackson 2001) makes sense in that it conveys a distinction between larger patterns of social relations – such as the workings of global capitalism – and those day-to-day social relations that more immediately impinge upon our lives. Yet precisely because the concept of 'levels' maps so easily onto the distinction between the macro-social and the micro-social, it implies a hierarchy in which the higher levels determine the lower. This is not our intention. Rather we are suggesting that we consider the social from both the top down *and* the bottom up, because this enables us to see different aspects of sociality. Moreover, one of the dimensions we have identified, that of meaning, cuts across the conventional macro–micro divide. The term 'facets' then begins to seem preferable, since it captures the idea that what might be seen from one angle is obscured from another. Facets, however, have edges implying a sharp delineation between them, whereas we envisage less rigid boundaries. The idea of dimensions, though not a perfect metaphor, better captures the idea of interconnections that are not hierarchically ordered.

These analytical distinctions between structure, meaning, practice and the self are intended as devices enabling us to begin to explore the varied ways in which gender, sexuality and heterosexuality intersect. It should be clear that this endeavour does not entail a total theorization of the social or some kind of theoretical synthesis allowing these dimensions of the social to be seen as a unified whole. On the contrary, what we seek to demonstrate is that although these dimensions of the social are interrelated, they cut across each other as well as intersecting, producing disjunctions between and within them. The connections between gender, sexuality and heterosexuality operate differently at different points within a complex webs of interconnections strung across, between and within dimensions. Moreover, it is difficult, if not impossible, to focus on all of these at once, thus we generally have only a partial view of multidimensional processes. In focusing on one aspect of the social, others slip out of sight and analytical tools that illuminate one point may cast little light on another.

We can now begin to sketch an outline of the complex picture that begins to emerge when different dimensions of the social are taken into account, a picture of connections between gender, sexuality and heterosexuality which are manifested variously within and between dimensions, are not always unidirectional and where the linkages are stronger at some points than at others.

The structural dimension

While gender has been considered a structural phenomenon, implicitly at least, in past feminist debates on patriarchy and explicitly so in materialist feminist analyses (see e.g. Delphy 1993; Ingraham 1996), sexuality and heterosexuality are less often approached from this angle. As we have seen, though, there are exceptions in the continuing tradition of materialist feminism exemplified by Ingraham. Elsewhere the concept of compulsory heterosexuality, once seen in structural terms, has now been recast, through its queer incarnations, as cultural (Seidman 2009). This emphasis on culture reflects the displacement of the concept of social structure by postmodern scepticism and the recent sociological emphasis on the fluidity of the social (Adkins 2002). We would argue that there is still a need for a 'view from above', a means of appreciating patterned inequalities in distributions of resources, divisions of labour and hierarchies of advantage and disadvantage, which situate men and women in a hierarchical relationship and which privilege heterosexuality.

In appealing to the structural we are envisaging neither fixed nor foundational underpinnings to social and cultural relations of the kind found in some forms of *structuralism*, nor some overarching social structure that determines all aspects of social life. Social structures are subject to historical change and cross-national variability; for example, capitalism, while a global phenomenon, does not take identical forms even within the wealthy countries from which transnational capital is controlled. Social structures, or what Ingraham terms 'social totalities', 'are not monolithic, but consist of unstable patterns of interrelations and reciprocal determinations' (Ingraham 1996: 171).

By our definition, sexuality is itself not a structural phenomenon; gender and heterosexuality, however, can be thought of as structural. Despite changes and variability in the ways that gender is lived, the division of gender remains entrenched and continues to be associated with material inequalities. Moves towards gay citizenship rights may have made it easier to live outside heterosexuality, but have not seriously undermined heterosexual dominance (Seidman 2002). As Seidman points out, normative heterosexuality 'not only establishes a heterosexual/homosexual hierarchy but also creates hierarchies among heterosexualities', between 'hegemonic and subordinate forms of heterosexuality' (Seidman 2005: 40). The current hegemonic form no longer necessarily requires marriage, but nonetheless enshrines monogamous coupledom as the ideal and this in turn is reflected in much state policy and institutional practices defining which interpersonal relationships are socially validated (Carabine 1996; Richardson 2005a).

Within the structural dimension of the social the connections between gender and heterosexuality are particularly strong – hence Ingraham's notion of heterogender as the 'asymmetrical stratification of the sexes in relation to the historically varying institutions of patriarchal heterosexuality' (Ingraham 1996: 169). Institutionalized heterosexuality is by definition gendered and the heterosexual contract is a powerful mechanism whereby gender hierarchy is guaranteed (cf. Wittig 1992). This is manifested not only in heterosexual couple relationships (still the nexus of familial relationships despite their increased variability and instability) but also, for example, in gendered labour markets. Gender-segregated occupational structures, and their associated wage differentials, historically associated with particular economic and labour relations within heterosexual families, have persisted despite the decline in the male breadwinner wage and continue to impact on both employment opportunities and the organization of domestic life (see e.g. Irwin 2005).

While attention to the structural dimension of the social enables us 'to link the local to the macro level of analysis' (Ingraham 1996: 171), specific structural linkages between gender and heterosexuality cannot be assumed to *determine* other points of connection within other dimensions of the social. For example, we cannot deduce from the structural relationship between gendered labour markets and gendered divisions of domestic labour how each heterosexual couple organizes household chores. How structural constraints impinge on everyday life, differentially enabling and/or constraining our patterns of existence, is a matter for investigation.

Where does sexuality as such figure here? While it is not in itself a structural phenomenon, it is of course ordered in crucial respects by the intersection of heterosexuality and gender. Moreover, if structural phenomena have enabling and constraining effects on other dimensions of the social, sexuality will not be immune to those effects, particularly since it is always embedded within wider, non-sexual relations. As such, it is also affected by social divisions other than those of gender and heterosexuality–homosexuality. One illustrative example is class. Consumer capitalism has accommodated queer practices as lifestyle choices (Evans 1993; Hennessy 2000), but these are not equally available to all; for example, working-class lesbians may not feel comfortable in fashionable queer spaces and may lack both the material accoutrements and cultural capital facilitating entry to such spaces (Taylor 2004). The celebration of queer lifestyles by the materially privileged rests upon the exploited labour of the underprivileged who produce the commodities on which that lifestyle depends – and here it may be not only localized class differences that are implicated, but also global inequalities (Hennessy 2000). Among heterosexuals, too, there are class differences in the extent to which women, in particular, can escape the normative regulation of sexual conduct. Those who are financially independent can exercise more choice in their sexual relationships as well as in other aspects of their life. Here we can also see how structural inequalities have effects within other dimensions of the social, on meanings, practices and subjectivity. For example, working-class women who are too obviously sexual are more likely to provoke public distaste, even disgust, than middle-class women with independent lifestyles (Skeggs 2003). The forms of cultural capital available to us by virtue of our class location also impinge on the resources we can draw on in making sense of our sexual lives and fashioning sexual selves (Skeggs 2004). Thus opportunities to escape the most conventional forms of heterosexuality are not equally distributed.

Meanings: discursive and interactional

Structural and institutional patterns give rise to and are sustained by forms of understanding whereby they appear natural or inevitable, and it is here that the normalizing effects of institutionalized heterosexuality are evident. As well as shading into the structural/institutional, however, the dimension of meaning shades into everyday practice as part of the world-taken-for-granted and is implicated in the constitution of subjectivity. Meaning thus cuts across macro and micro aspects of social relations. At the level of society and culture as a whole, gender, sexuality and heterosexuality are constituted as objects of discourse and are subject to normative regulation through specific discourses in circulation at any historical moment. At the most fundamental level, these discourses serve to distinguish male from female, to define what is sexual, to differentiate the 'normal' from the deviant.

Here there is room for, and evidence of, fluidity and change, particularly within popular culture (Roseneil 2000). Yet the admission of greater sexual diversity has limits. Seidman (2002: 160) suggests that the 'normalization' of gay characters in US cinema requires that they be 'gender conventional, committed to romantic-companionate and family values, uncritically patriotic and detached from a subculture'. Thus being gay becomes 'normal' without overly unsettling heteronormative ideals. It may be that less conventionalized representations of lesbian, gay or queer individuals exist within the British media, but still, we would suggest, with little import for the hegemonic status of heterosexuality. It has been suggested that the boundaries of the normative are being redrawn, separating the 'good homosexual' or 'normal gay' from the 'dangerous queer' or the bad citizen (Smith 1997; Seidman 2002, 2005). The advancement of gay citizenship rights has, moreover, been paralleled by the increasing acceptance of the idea that homosexuality and heterosexuality are innate proclivities, thus enshrining gays and lesbians as permanent minorities (Rahman and Jackson 1997; Seidman 2002; Richardson 2005a, 2005b).

Yet it is undeniable that considerable shifts have occurred in the meanings of both normative and non-normative sexualities. Such change is inexplicable if norms are conceived simply as properties of a cultural order external to us. Any norm, as Butler says, 'renders the social field intelligible and normalizes that field for us' (Butler 2004: 42). If heteronormativity and gender norms have this effect, it is because they circulate not only through the wider culture but also within everyday interpretive practices. However, while they may govern intelligibility at that level, meaning is not simply dictated by cultural norms, but is also negotiated in, and emergent from, the mundane social interaction through which each of us makes sense of our own and others' gendered and sexual lives. Here the normative is mobilized as a condition for the intelligibility of the social, informing the 'natural attitude' (Schutz 1972; Kessler and McKenna 1978), but the intelligibility so produced is, nonetheless, a 'practical accomplishment' (Garfinkel 1967). So, for example, most of the heterosexual population, most of the time, takes for granted the existence of 'men' and 'women' as given categories of people who 'naturally' form sexual liaisons with members of the 'opposite' gender. Yet the everyday 'doing' of gender and heterosexuality in the ethnomethodological sense, producing a sense of an intelligibly gendered and heterosexually ordered world, entails a variety of cultural competences and complex interpretational processes, evident even in the simple act of attributing gender to another person (Kessler and McKenna 1978; West and Zimmerman 1987). The interpretive work this involves goes unnoticed because it is so habitual that it is assumed that we are simply recognizing a natural fact. Thus in so far as heteronormativity persists in everyday meaning-making, it is contingent upon being constantly reaffirmed. Hence it can potentially be unsettled or renegotiated, although we need to be aware of how any such challenges can be accommodated back into the 'natural attitude'.

Within the dimension of meaning we can see how gender and sexuality constantly intersect, where the construction of gender difference is bound up with the assumption of gender complementarity, the idea that women and men are 'made for each other' (Katz 1995; Ingraham 1999). Hence the boundaries of gender division and normative heterosexuality are mutually reinforced. However, as Kessler and McKenna (1978) suggest, within everyday interaction the attribution of gender appears to have primacy in that we 'do' gender first. We recognize someone as male or female before we make any assumptions about heterosexuality or homosexuality: we cannot logically do otherwise. The homosexual/heterosexual distinction depends upon socially meaningful gender categories, on being able to 'see' two men or two women as 'the same' and a man and a woman as 'different' (and thus select and interpret many potential differences and similarities between individuals in order to 'recognize' those that signify gender difference).

The homo/hetero binary, however, by no means exhausts the gendered meanings of sexuality. Where heterosex is concerned, the heteronormative assumption that women and men are 'made for each other' is sustained through the commonsense definition of vaginal penetration by the penis as '*the* sex act'. As we pointed out in Chapter 3, feminists, along with some HIV/AIDS activists, have tried to dislodge this assumption, but, in the Viagra age, it is more entrenched than ever (Marshall 2002). The idea of gender complementarity further presupposes that men and women are naturally different in their sexual desires and proclivities. While some of the old familiar stereotypes may have been eroded, it is the degree of difference and the forms of difference that are changing – not the idea that there *is* a difference. Popular self-help manuals for heterosexual couples continue to promote the idea that male and female sexuality are naturally different and we must learn to live with it (see e.g. Gray 1996); popular science continues to represent evolutionary psychology, based on the reproductive imperative, as 'fact' (Potts 2002; Jackson and Rees 2007; McCaughey 2008).

Everyday interaction and practice

In discussing everyday meanings, it is virtually impossible to separate them from the practices they reciprocally order and are ordered by. Gender, sexuality and heterosexuality are thus continually produced and reproduced within the third dimension of the social, where they are lived out by embodied individuals. In everyday life we 'do' gender, sexuality and heterosexuality in two senses. In the first, ethnomethodological, sense this 'doing' produces a socially intelligible 'reality' as a 'practical accomplishment' through everyday interpretive interaction (Kessler and McKenna 1978; West and Zimmerman 1987). In the second sense 'doing' refers to actual practical activities – whether having sex, dressing for work or organizing a night out – constructing a gendered, sexual or heterosexual performance. In both senses, however, social interaction with others is essential to practice, to our ability to negotiate and fit ourselves into ongoing social activities.

The doing of social life (in both senses) can be seen as heteronormatively ordered. Butler comments that when norms 'operate as the normalizing principle in social practice, they usually remain implicit, difficult to read, discernible most clearly and dramatically in the effects they produce' (Butler 2004: 41). This is where close attention to what actually goes on in the everyday dimension of social practice can help, since then norms are visible not only in their effects, but in the process of their reproduction. An example of this is Celia Kitzinger's discussion of displays of heterosexual identity through talk (Kitzinger 2005). Using the techniques of conversation analysis, she demonstrates how heterosexuals continually produce themselves and others as heterosexual. This is most evident in sexual banter or talk about marriage and relationships, but it also occurs within very ordinary conversations, which are not ostensibly about sexuality or relationships, where 'nothing special' is going on but where heterosexuals routinely and repeatedly display their heterosexuality. For example, heterosexual kinship terms (husband, wife, mother-in-law, etc.) are dropped into talk in passing, others are referred to in relation to their spouses and individuals identify themselves as part of a couple through the use of 'we'. All this passes without comment because of the shared background assumption of heterosexual normalcy – but when lesbians and gay men use such conversational devices, for example, referring to a same-sex partner, this can disrupt taken-for-granted assumptions and therefore the flow of interaction. Kitzinger's analysis allows us to see the process of normalization in action, in the everyday process of its production, where normative heterosexuality is available as a resource, but is also an ongoing accomplishment.

Heterosexuality is reproduced and renegotiated in everyday life not only through talk, but also through routine activities in which gender, sexuality and heterosexuality interconnect. Gender asymmetry is a key feature here, but takes variable forms. In their daily lives women are frequently identified and evaluated in terms of their sexual availability or attractiveness to men and their presumed 'place' within heterosexual relationships as wives and mothers. At work, for example, the increased sexualization and aestheticization of labour can result in particular standards of (hetero)sexual attractiveness impinging on women's self-presentation and job opportunities (Adkins 1995; Black 2004; Liu 2008) while assumptions about domestic responsibilities affect both the implementation of and resistance to equal opportunities policies (Cockburn 1991). Here gendered assumptions seem to be informed by heterosexual ones. But this does not apply in the same way to heterosexual men. While womanliness is almost always equated with (hetero)sexual attractiveness and (heterosexual) domesticity, manliness can be validated not only through (hetero)sex, but also through physical or mental prowess, courage or leadership abilities (Connell 1995, 2000). Where a man's heterosexuality goes unquestioned, his gender is less bound to and defined by (hetero)sexuality than that of a woman; but if his heterosexuality is in doubt, he might well be perceived as less than a man, since the boundaries of acceptable masculinity are still policed through homophobia (Kimmel 2005). When either men or women breach heteronormative conventions, moreover, they are equally susceptible to being defined by, reduced to, their sexuality.

Thinking specifically about how heterosexual sex confirms femininity and masculinity, gender asymmetry works in a different direction. Among young people, first heterosex may make a boy a man, but it does not make a girl a woman (Holland et al. 1996). Impotence, now called 'erectile dysfunction', is said to emasculate a man: the promise of Viagra is to keep men 'forever functional' as men (Marshall and Katz 2002). There is little evidence that the women partners of such men feel that their femininity is undermined by a lack of penetrative sex (Potts et al. 2003). However, far more than sex goes on within heterosexual couples, who 'do' heterosexuality (and simultaneously do gender) as much through divisions of labour and distributions of household resources as through specifically sexual practices, as they negotiate and potentially struggle over their mundane gendered and heterosexual routines.

The sociality of the self

How do we come to be the embodied gendered and sexual individuals who enact these practices, but who nonetheless have the capacity to renegotiate gender divisions and resist dominant constructions of sexuality? How is heteronormativity reproduced at the level of subjectivity while clearly not keeping everyone within its bounds? Answering these questions adequately, in our view, requires a conceptualization of a social self rather than a psychoanalytic notion of the psyche. As we will argue in more detail in Chapter 6, the idea of the social self, originating from the work of G.H. Mead, provides a view of the self as social while allowing for agency through the emphasis on interpretive practices. Here the self is not a fixed structure but is always 'in process' by virtue of its constant reflexivity, the dialogue between self as subject and as object. It is a product of socially located biographies and of ongoing interaction between self and others and is temporally located through the interpretive interplay between past and present. The self is not separate from the social but a dimension of it since it is the possession of reflexive selves, our ability to locate ourselves in relation to others, which makes sociality possible.

The interactionist tradition allows for the analytical separation of gendered and sexual aspects of the self, seeing them as empirically and contingently, rather than necessarily, interrelated (Gagnon and Simon 1974, 2004; Jackson 2007). This means that particular forms of gendered and sexual selfhood are culturally and historically specific; particular modes of self-construction become available at different historical moments in specific social locations (Plummer 1995; Whisman 1996). Moreover, gendered and sexual selves are never fixed, but continue to be reflexively renegotiated or reconfirmed throughout our lives allowing for considerable variation. This does not mean that we are free to make and remake our sexual selves as we choose – we are constrained by the cultural resources available to us and by the prevailing taken-for-granted view of the natural in the social milieu we inhabit but, because these are resources rather than determinants, variability is possible and agency is a factor even in conformity (see Chapter 6).

In modern Western societies, gender attribution seems to be foundational to the self in that the moment we are born, through a crucial act of social categorization, we are ascribed a gender (Kessler and McKenna 1978; Kessler 1998). From this perspective, a gendered sense of self precedes awareness of ourselves as sexual (see Gagnon and Simon 1974, 2004; see also Chapter 5). As soon as we turn to heterosexuality, however, the picture changes, because children come to understand non-sexual aspects of heterosexuality – families, mothers and fathers, for example – long before they gain access to specifically sexual scripts or discourses. This heteronormative ordering of the social becomes taken-for-granted, a resource available for reconceptualization, as sexually significant once children become sexually aware.

The heteronormative order, however, is by no means absolute, heterosexuality is not guaranteed and there is no single form of heterosexuality (or of homosexuality, lesbianism or bisexuality); self-formation is a variable process. What is significant, however, is how central gender continues to be, whatever the outcome, although there are multiple ways of being male or female. For young heterosexuals, becoming sexual is profoundly gendered (Wight 1996; Holland et al. 1998; Tolman 2002) and so are sexual relations in later life (Duncombe and Marsden 1996; Potts et al. 2003). Becoming lesbian and gay does not entail a loss of gender since homosexuality, as much as heterosexuality, is defined by gender. Yet it does require negotiation of the different ways of investing gender with erotic significance and different forms of gendered self-understanding. In particular, lesbians and gay men are called to account for themselves in a way that heterosexuals are not – accounts being generally expected or offered when conduct departs from normative expectation (M. Scott and Lyman 1968). That heterosexuals are not called upon to tell stories about 'how they got that way' is indicative of heteronormativity's effects, but we should not neglect the significance of gender within the heteronormative contexts in which our selves are forged.

Sexuality and social change

The account we have given of these intersections is far from exhaustive; there are, no doubt, many other connecting threads that could be pulled out and examined. One advantage of attending to the complexity of these intersections within the multidimensional social, however, is that it may enable us to make more sense of changing sexual times, to understand why some things change while others stay the same, why there are tensions and antinomies within our current sexual world. It may help guard against overgeneralized views of social change and to develop a more satisfactory account of the place of heterosexuality in contemporary societies. This brings us to the question posed by the title of this chapter: is heterosexuality still compulsory?

The case for undermining compulsory heterosexuality rests first on changes in sexual mores, second, on the apparent decline of the traditional patriarchal heterosexual family, and, third, on the increasing visibility and acceptability of non-normative sexualities and the rights gained by sexual minorities. To take the case of sexual mores first, there has undoubtedly been considerable change here. Over the past hundred years heterosexual sex has become increasingly separated first from reproduction and then from marriage. The historical 'eroticization of sex' and 'sexualization of love' (Seidman 1991) initially established sexual pleasure as essential to a happy marriage. But once sexual activity could be seen as pleasurable in itself and once contraception became more widely available, the moral injunctions that tied sex to the marital bed lost much of their force: sex could be envisaged as a recreational activity with no necessary relation to reproduction, marriage or even commitment. Moreover, if sex could be indulged in purely for pleasure, or for love unencumbered by the bonds of marriage, there was less reason why heterosexual sex should be seen as the only legitimate form of sexuality. It is these conditions that Giddens (1992) encapsulates in the term 'plastic sexuality'.

The change in heterosexual relations is most marked with regard to women's sexuality. There has been an apparent erosion of the sexual double standard and an increasing emphasis on women's right to sexual pleasure and to freedom of sexual expression. Detailed discussion of women's sexual pleasure has become widespread throughout popular culture and there is now far more openness about and information on the intimate details of female sexuality than there was even in the 1960s and 1970s. It also seems to be the case that women themselves are more sexually active and have far more partners than in the past (Johnson et al. 2001). Some women, especially young women, are now out there pursuing sexual pleasure in a way once reserved for men.

This, however, is only part of the picture, for some asymmetries persist while others are being reinforced. Among the old ones is, of course, the double standard. It may have been eroded but by no means entirely. Young women remain concerned with maintaining appropriately feminine sexual respectability while representing themselves as sexually desirable (Skeggs 1997) and continue to struggle to assert their own desires within heterosexual relationships while continuing to be troubled by sexual violence and coercion (Holland et al. 1998; Phillips 2000; Tolman 2002). At the same time there has been a renewed emphasis on the 'naturalness' of sexual difference in popular culture. Evolutionary psychology has had a major impact on popular understandings of science and underpins, for example, virtually every television documentary purporting to inform us about the 'science' of sexuality (Jackson and Rees 2007). The predatory male is thus reconstructed as an inevitable part of our evolutionary heritage (McGaughey 2008). This pseudo-scientific discourse of sexual difference also permeates self-help guides to 'better' relationships in which women and men are represented as being intrinsically different, indeed even from different planets; John Gray's Mars and Venus series (Gray 1992, 1996) continues to be widely read. Such differences are held to be irreducible and the way to make relationships work is to understand the 'other' or, rather, to persuade women to make allowances for men since these books are marketed primarily for women. The appeal of these accounts might lie in an underlying philosophy of a 'different but equal' relation between the sexes. This idea is seductive in that it promises equality without challenging what people think is central to their sense of gendered and sexual self; yet it also naturalizes gender, leaving no space for a critique of femininity and masculinity as social constructs, still less of men's conduct in relationships as a product of their historical dominance (McGaughey 2008). 'Scientific' theories have replaced morality as arbiters of normal and normative heterosexuality.

The pursuit of greater freedoms within heterosexuality also brings new pressures, particularly in the urge to sexual perfection. Sex can no longer be taken for granted; rather it must be constantly improved upon in the pursuit of perfection (see Chapter 3). And where performance anxiety was once reserved for men, women now share in it. Sexual fulfilment has come to be seen as a life-goal in itself – the key to personal happiness (Heath 1982). More than physical sexual satisfaction is sought as both sex and the relationship itself become projects to be worked at and worked upon with the assistance of self-help book and expert advice. This is accompanied by an increased medicalization of sex and a broadening of the definition of what constitutes sexual dysfunction. Indeed, the idea of 'functionality' can intensify performance pressures; it is no longer enough to be normal, the goal is optimal functionality.

While social theorists speak of desire as constructed, 'plastic' and fluid, the medical profession is determined to fix it. This medical 'fix' has two dimensions. First, sexuality is 'fixed' in the sense of being innate, objective, measurable and physiological, something to be diagnosed as functional or dysfunctional. Second, it is 'fixable'; it is something to be 'corrected' or 'cured' when found to be dysfunctional through a surgical or chemical fix. The latter, in particular, has come to the fore recently with the search for a female equivalent of Viagra and through attempts to establish 'female sexual dysfunction' as an accepted diagnostic category. Here the new essentialism is often mobilized in combination with a pseudo-feminist discourse. Once women's sexual problems were seen as being 'all in their heads'; now they are redefined as physiological and therefore 'real', which is taken to indicate that they are now treated more seriously.[5] Women's sexuality is being 'fixed' in terms of readiness for vaginal penetration (Marshall 2002) and thus an andocentric, heteronormative view of what sex *is*.

The drive to sexual perfection and the medicalization of sex do not so much reinforce compulsory heterosexuality as render heterosexuality *compulsive*. A successful heterosexual must seek out sex and perform it well. The potential anxieties this creates are lived out in a world where sexual relationships are no longer as predictable as they once were. This instability is central to Anthony Giddens' (1991) thesis that we are witnessing a 'transformation of intimacy', accompanying the separation of sexuality from reproduction, increasing female autonomy and greater gender equality. The result is the democratized 'pure relationship', where trust is maintained through mutual disclosure and which 'is continued only in so far as it is thought by both parties to deliver enough satisfactions for each individual to stay within it' (Giddens 1991: 58). Giddens maintains that we are moving from romantic love, based on lasting commitment, to a 'special person' to a more contingent 'confluent love' in which we seek a 'special relationship' (Giddens 1991: 61–62). In this context the quality of the sexual relationship can be seen as part of what keeps it going.

If Giddens were correct, the transformations he identifies could be seen as signalling the demise of compulsory heterosexuality – the heterosexual contract becomes voluntary and fragile. However, as his many feminist critics have noted, Giddens' argument is more conjectural than empirically grounded and ignores evidence of continuing inequality in heterosexual relationships (see e.g. Duncombe and Marsden 1993, 1996; Jamieson 1999; Langford 1999; Evans 2003). There have certainly been changes in patterns of heterosexual relationships as a result of the increased participation of women in paid labour, falling rates of marriage, rising average age at marriage, more people remaining single and falling fertility rates – trends evident throughout the wealthier countries of the world (see Castells 2004). But such trends conceal a great deal of diversity and complexity. We cannot deduce from them a widespread disintegration of heterosexuality or queering of heterosexual relationships. The majority of adults remain (apparently) heterosexual, even if they engage in serial relationships rather than lifelong monogamy. In Britain in 2007, 70 per cent of the population lived in heterosexual couple households (Office for National Statistics (ONS) 2008).

Sexual 'plasticity' for most heterosexuals has its limits; most accept their heterosexuality as given and natural. They may be happy to express liberal tolerance towards the homosexual other but continue to define them as other to their own sexuality. This is illustrated by Paul Johnson's (2005) study of heterosexual love. His participants, men and women, were mostly liberal in their attitudes and they saw 'love' as an emotion that could be experienced irrespective of gender and sexual orientation. When asked whether they could love someone of the same gender, however, they found that they could not imagine themselves engaging in a same-gender sexual relationship – and in some cases expressions of disgust, previously concealed beneath a veneer of tolerance, came to the surface. As Johnson argues: 'through a rejection of homosexuality as "outside" of themselves, heterosexuals establish an ontological validity for their own identities and ... as a consequence, their own intimate practices are naturalized' (Johnson 2005: 119).

At least now tolerance of sexual others is expected of heterosexuals. In terms of the social and legal position of gay men and lesbians, we have come a long way in a very short time. It was only in 1967 when male homosexuality was decriminalized in Britain and as recently as the late 1980s UK legislation barred local authorities from 'promoting' homosexuality as 'a pretended family relationship' through the infamous Section 28 of the Local Government Act 1988. Yet since the turn of the millennium we have seen not only the repeal of this legislation, but also the equalization of the heterosexual and homosexual age of consent, the introduction of civil partnerships for lesbians and gay men and the outlawing of discrimination on grounds of sexuality. Where as late as the 1980s lesbians could lose custody of their children, they now have access to infertility treatment and, along with gay men, have the right to foster and adopt children.

Progress, however, has its price in the heterosexualization of all sexual relationships. Gay and lesbian relationships are more accepted if long-term, monogamous and stable and if they buy into the dominant 'family values' of normative heterosexuality.[6] Increasingly claims to basic citizenship rights are based upon the heterosexual norm, on 'desiring sameness' (Richardson 2005b: 515ff.). While it may seem straightforwardly just and equitable that gay partnerships should gain the recognition granted to married heterosexual couples, such claims for rights buy into highly conventional lifestyles that not everyone – whether straight or gay – would want to endorse. Not only does this political strategy position heterosexuality as a standard to which to aspire (Rahman and Jackson 1997), but also, and importantly, it privileges sexual coupledom over all other relationships.[7] It also serves to redefine the boundaries of the normative, between those who live in couples and those – gay or straight – who do not live with a partner or indeed do not have one.

The demise of the critique of monogamy in mainstream feminist and gay politics marks a significant shift. During the 1970s, monogamy had been problematized as a linchpin of the patriarchal, heterosexual family (see e.g. Comer 1974; Red Collective 1978). It was seen as unhealthily individualistic, exclusive and as impoverishing broader social relationships. Lesbian feminists in particular were 'challenging the conventions of heterosexual models of sexual relationships *and* friendships, rethinking previously unquestioned priorities and risking new ways of thinking about and acting (or not acting) on feelings towards other women' (Bindel and Scanlon 1996: 69). This was part of the lesbian feminist commitment to women in general and critical thinking about the personal and political perils of putting all one's emotional energies into a single relationship to the detriment of other possible relationships, actual or potential. In the wake of the sex wars, with non-monogamy increasingly associated with libertarian feminism, there was a retreat from this radical position on the part of many political lesbians. Now some of the fiercest critics of 'heteropatriarchy', such as Celia Kitzinger and Sue Wilkinson (2004), argue for lesbian marriage as a way of undermining patriarchal heterosexuality by changing the meaning of marriage. Those still arguing for non-monogamy (Robinson 1997; Jackson and Scott 2003; or now more commonly 'polyamory' (Ritchie and Barker 2006; Haritaworn et al. 2008), remain a minority. The move away from questioning the privileging of couple relationships has blunted the critique of heterosexuality and is intimately connected with the pursuit of a rights agenda that seeks inclusion into pre-existing normative patterns of sexual and domestic life.

It would seem that while heterosexuality is not compulsory in quite the sense that it once was, it nonetheless remains institutionalized (Seidman 2009). The changes that have made it more possible for gay men and lesbians to lead tolerable lives, and for women to find some room for manoeuvre within heterosexual relations, have not dislodged the normative status of heterosexuality and have, in some respects at least, deradicalized sexual politics, in particular through the widespread acceptance that heterosexuality and homosexuality are innate states given by nature and in the acceptance of the monogamous couple – straight or not – as the model of the ideal sexual relationship.

Notes

1   This can also be said of later Foucauldian approaches.
2   Sue Wilkinson was and remains the regular editor of the journal; Celia Kitzinger joined her for this special issue and the two have co-authored many articles.
3   As will probably be clear, the concept of the imaginary being deployed here derives from Althusser's (1971) analysis of ideology, particularly that ideology constitutes our imaginary relation to our real conditions of existence.
4   The term 'meaning' is deliberately chosen in preference to such terms as 'the symbolic' or 'signification', because of their more specific theoretical connotations.
5   See the rapid responses to Ray Moynihan's (2003) critique of the concept of female sexual dysfunction in the *British Medical Journal* – especially from those who rushed to the defence of medical intervention.
6   An exuberant queer culture is permitted to flourish, provided it can be contained, commodified and marketed as a tourist spectacle.
7   It is interesting to note, though, that Parliament shrank away from defining civil partnership in sexual terms – there is no 'consummation' needed to confirm a partnership as existing. It seems no one, aside from a few unreconstructed right-wingers like Lord Tebbit, wanted to raise the spectre of gay sex in these debates (see Woo 2007).

CHAPTER 5

RISK, GOVERNANCE AND SURVEILLANCE: THE BOUNDARIES OF CHILDHOOD

One key site of contemporary tensions around sexuality is the state and status of childhood: although sex is now widely thought of as a fulfilling and life-enhancing activity, this applies only to adults. Just as sexuality is defined as a special area of life, so children are constructed as a special category of being; sexuality is seen as particularly problematic in relation to children and, in some respects, as inimical to childhood itself. This is probably most evident in the context of debates about sexual abuse, risk and danger, and also pervades discussion of sex education, teenage pregnancy, the consumption of popular culture by children and young people, and indeed the very nature of childhood itself. Childhood is frequently equated with a state of innocence, which is in turn conflated with sexual ignorance. This state of innocence is seen as being under threat, as potentially prefiguring the demise of childhood itself: 'To have to stand and wait as the charm, malleability, innocence and curiosity of children are degraded and then transmogrified into the lesser features of pseudo-adulthood is painful and embarrassing and, above all, sad' (Postman 1994: xiii).

Postman (1994) is expressing a widely aired concern that children are growing up too quickly without experiencing childhood to the full. Childhood is thus seen as being threatened by pressures towards early maturity, highlighting a fundamental contradiction in discourses around children and childhood: childhood is regarded as a natural state and yet also as perpetually at risk, requiring constant vigilance in order to protect, preserve and manage it. Thus risk anxiety helps to construct childhood and maintain its boundaries. The specific risks from which children must be protected serve to define the characteristics of childhood and the 'nature' of children themselves. Prominent among these are sexual 'ills', from the 'pernicious' consequences of sex in the media to the shadowy figure of the predatory paedophile.

Concerns about sexual threats to children's well-being highlight a number of contradictions within contemporary sexual culture. Erotic imagery is a ubiquitous feature of our cultural landscape, yet there is still the expectation that we should shield children from sexual knowledge – or more specifically knowledge that adults deem to be sexual. The effort required to keep children in sexual ignorance in turn engenders much agonizing about when and how to let them in on the 'secret'. Adults in general and parents in particular value openness about sexuality yet still find it difficult to discuss sexual matters with children (Botcherby and Scott 2004; Frankham 2006), while the conditions under which children are offered sex education in UK and US schools continue to be fraught with controversy (Levine 2002; Pilcher 2005). Attitudes to premarital and even casual sex have become more relaxed, but teenage sexuality, especially where it results in pregnancy, remains an object of major concern. There is immense public anxiety about paedophiles, which eclipses more common risks to children, while at the same time there is a failure to give children information that might protect them from sexual abuse.

The social construction of childhood

Sociologists have, for some decades, contested the notion that childhood is a natural state (Jackson 1982; Jenks 1996; Egan and Hawkes 2008a). They have also challenged the socialization paradigm, which positioned children as adults-in-waiting whose experiences were worthy of investigation only in so far as they shaped future adult lives (Thorne 1987). Developmental perspectives, however, remain prominent in everyday thinking and in both professional and public discourse. It is still taken for granted that the process of maturing from child to adolescent to adult unfolds as a series of naturally occurring stages, that there is a 'right age' at which children should develop certain competencies and acquire particular freedoms and responsibilities and this is particularly pertinent with regard to sexuality. Contemporary sociological approaches suggest that rather than viewing children as future adults in the making, we should focus upon children's own lives and activities. This entails a shift away from the idea of a child as 'becoming' an adult towards the notion of the 'being child', conceptualized as an active social agent (James et al. 1998). While such perspectives are essential in challenging adult-centred views, we should not forget that children's lives are largely bounded by adult surveillance. There is no free and autonomous realm of childhood outside the social relations in which childhood in general, and particular individual childhoods, are forged.

Here we are concerned with the ways in which sexuality figures in the construction and maintenance of the boundaries between children and adults. These boundaries are by no means clearly demarcated. While children are defined in relation to adults, there is no universal or unambiguous definition of what constitutes adulthood (see Jones and Bell 2000) and when, therefore, the child becomes an adult. Since childhood and adulthood are social and cultural constructs, the boundaries between them shift historically, contextually and across cultures. The construction of childhood needs to be understood at a number of different levels: the structural, the discursive, the situated and the subjective. Childhood is institutionalized through family, education and the state, resulting in dependence on adults and exclusion from full participation in adult society. Discursively, childhood has been constituted as an object of the scientific gaze through such disciplines as psychology, social work and education, which have claimed expertise in monitoring, categorizing and managing childhood and children (N. Rose 1989; Egan and Hawkes 2008b). These expert knowledges have in turn shaped commonsense thinking, so that we are all assumed to 'know' what a child is, to be able to comment on what constitutes a 'proper' childhood. The meaning of childhood is also negotiated through everyday situated interaction, where children themselves enter into the picture as active social agents with their own subjective sense of what being a child means. However, children's participation in constructing their everyday worlds takes place within the constraints set by their subordinate location in relation to adults.

Contemporary Western understandings of children and childhood, and particularly the idea that sexuality is antithetical to the well-being of children, have a history. The idea that childhood is a modern Western intervention was first proposed by the historian Philippe Ariès (1962). While his work prompted critical questioning of what we now take for granted about childhood, his contention that there was no concept of childhood in medieval Europe has been contested (see e.g. Shahar 1990). In claiming that medieval children, once past infancy, were treated simply as miniature adults, Ariès overstated his case. Children in medieval times *were* included into adult life far more than they are today, but it is clear that they were not regarded as exactly the same as adults. Ariès' own evidence indicates that children were seen as social subordinates within a patriarchal and feudal social order, that they were very much under the authority of the head of the household in which they lived and worked. Moreover childhood was regarded as a stage which prepared the young for later responsibilities, a period of moral and practical training for later life (Shahar 1990). Yet medieval childhood was not childhood as we know it today. In surveying historical debates, David Archard (1993) makes a useful distinction between the *concept* of childhood and specific *conceptions* of childhood. His argument suggests that while there has probably always been a *concept* of childhood, it is nonetheless the case that the current *conception* of childhood is the product of a lengthy process of historical transformation.

It was not until relatively late in this process, in the nineteenth century, when childhood came to be idealized as a state of innocence, that children could be thought of as beings in need of protection from adult 'facts of life'. The idea of the innocent child, which had its origins in late eighteenth-century Romanticism, differed radically from the earlier conception of the 'demonic' or 'dionysian' child (Skolnick 1973; Jenks 1996), tainted by original sin – and the carnal and the sinful have always been very closely entwined in the Christian imaginary. The innocent or 'apollonian' child (Jenks 1996) gained ground through the nineteenth century, popularized through Victorian sentimentalization. Once children were no longer seen as inherently sinful, it was possible to think of safeguarding them against temptation – and especially sexual temptation. Bourgeois Victorian standards of modesty and propriety also made this achievable. The shifts in the 'frontiers of shame' (Elias 1994) that had begun two centuries earlier (see Chapter 3), and which by the Victorian era had advanced further, made it possible to confine bourgeois children in an environment from which the sexual was carefully excluded.[1] These two historical processes – the emergence of the innocent child and the increasing concern with sexual propriety – gave rise to vocabularies of motive requiring adults to shield children from sexual knowledge and created the conditions that made it possible to keep children in ignorance.

From the late nineteenth century and into the twentieth century, new 'scientific' knowledge psychologized both childhood and sexuality, the former as a series of developmental stages and the latter as an attribute of the individual psyche. Thus it became possible to see sexuality as harmful not only to children's moral development but also to their psychological well-being. Childhood came to be an object of expert surveillance and of public and parental pedagogic projects which 'purport to safeguard it from physical, sexual and moral danger, to ensure its "normal development"' (Rose 1989: 121). During the first few decades of the twentieth century psychologists and educators, as a result of new ideas emerging from psychoanalysis and sexology, began to admit the possibility of children being sexual (Egan and Hawkes 2008b). This, however, made it all the more important that sexuality was regulated in order to ensure the inculcation of 'correct' sexual knowledge and guard against the emergence of precocious or inappropriate sexual interests. Thus the 'sexual child was discussable only in the context of the pathway to the properly sexual adult' (Egan and Hawkes 2008b: 461). Parents thus had to be instructed in the management of children's emergent sexuality and the imparting of sexual knowledge. Nonetheless, the presumption of innocence has persisted – along with the anxiety generated by awareness that children might not be as innocent as adults would wish them to be.

Surveillance of the sexual lives of children and young people occurred in the context of the prolongation of childhood, a consequence of the greater divide being created between childhood and adulthood and the extended period of education seen as necessary before maturity is attained. One significant indicator of the lengthening of childhood and the increasing concern for the moral (sexual) welfare of children, which also illustrates the significance of gender in these transformations, was the raising of the age of heterosexual 'consent'. The minimum legal age for marriage in England, and the age at which it became lawful for a man to have sex with a woman, had been set at 12 in the thirteenth century; this remained the case until 1875 when it was raised to 13, finally being raised to 16 in 1885. 'Consent' here is a gendered concept, implying that sex is something men do and women have done to them (with or without their consent): the law regulated men's conduct towards young women, not women's own conduct. The legislative changes in the nineteenth century were inspired by campaigns to protect young women from sexual predation (Gorham 1978; Walkowitz 1992), but were also indicative of changing understandings of the legal capacity to consent. In earlier centuries the ability to 'consent' was related to the age at which it was considered appropriate for a father's authority to give way to that of a husband, and had nothing to do with any idea of physical or emotional readiness for sex. By the late nineteenth century, as innocence and purity came to be redefined as (ideally) innate characteristics of children and women respectively, the capacity to consent did acknowledge that women above the age of 16 had at least some capacity for autonomous decision-making (see Waites 2005); the corollary was that those under 16 did not. Later the age of consent was recast in terms of developmental maturity, as part of the transition from childhood to adulthood. Today debates around 'under-age' sex continue to be framed within this developmental paradigm. Recent changes in English law have applied the concept of consent to young men as well as young women, and to heterosexual, homosexual and lesbian sex, making all those under 16 the focus of protection. Moreover, where young people are deemed to require additional protection, the age of consent has effectively been raised to 18 – for example, for prostitution and where a sexual relationship involves 'a breach of trust'.[2] Sex *per se* continues to be seen as constituting a risk to children and young people.

Risk anxiety: children and sexuality

Despite these historical continuities it can be argued that particular forms of risk anxiety are specific to the conditions of the late twentieth and early twenty-first centuries. We now live in a climate of heightened risk awareness coupled with a nostalgia for an imagined past in which children played safely throughout a carefree childhood. Recent social theory has conceptualized 'risk anxiety' as a social state engendered by an increasing lack of trust in both the project of modernity and expert knowledges (Giddens 1990; Beck 1992). As Giddens argues, it is not that day to day life is inherently more risky than was the case in prior eras. It is rather that, in conditions of modernity, for lay actors as well as for experts in specific fields, thinking in terms of risk and risk assessment is a more or less ever-present exercise.

(Giddens 1991: 123–124)

Whereas Beck and Giddens have concentrated primarily on the social consequences of technological change, we are suggesting that the anxieties specific to childhood are part of a general sense that the social world itself is becoming less stable and predictable. Of course, such fears have always surfaced in periods of rapid social change, but, in the past, social disorder was more often thought of as located within particular classes and communities and therefore as potentially containable even when perceived as threatening to more 'respectable' citizens. While some symptoms of social disorder continue to be associated with the rebarbative elements of an 'underclass' and the areas they inhabit, others are seen either as more ubiquitous or as less predictable, identifiable and locatable – as liable to disrupt social life at any time in any place. Perceived threats to children's well-being generally fall into the latter category, either as unpredictable (the actions of a murderous 'paedophile') or as ever-present and unavoidable (e.g. pressures towards sexualized consumption).

Children, then, are the object of a great deal of social concern. Increasing anxiety about risk has been superimposed upon an older 'protective discourse' (Thomson and Scott 1991) within which children are located as vulnerable innocents to be shielded from the dangers of the wider social (implicitly adult) world. The fusion of risk anxiety with protectiveness engenders a preoccupation with prevention (Scott and Freeman 1995; Green 1997), a need for constant vigilance in order to anticipate and guard against potential threats to children's well-being.

Existing empirical research on children and childhood, even where not addressed specifically to questions of risk and risk anxiety, also suggests that risk management might be central to an understanding of the social construction of childhood and the everyday experience of children (Scott et al. 1998; Jackson and Scott 1999; Backett-Milburn and Harden 2004). Ideas about children's competencies (or lack of them), their specific vulnerability and their (im)maturity, inform adult decisions about the degree of surveillance children require and the degree of autonomy they can be permitted. Risks to children are represented as inherently more grave than risks to adults: it is almost beyond debate that we should 'protect' children, that any potential risk to children should be taken more seriously than other risks. As adults we can decide to take risks, or to balance risk against pleasure, in our pursuit of sexual gratification. Children are rarely permitted to make their own assessment of risk; as adults we make these judgements on their behalf and from an adult perspective.

Managing and balancing these risks give rise to a number of key antinomies in relation to children and childhood, in particular contradictions between recognizing children's autonomy and the increasing emphasis on child protection, and the paradoxical perception of children as both at risk and as a potential threat to other children and to social order. These contradictions may be expressed as tensions between two conceptualizations of children, as active, knowing, autonomous individuals on the one hand and as passive, innocent dependants on the other. The old tension between the 'innocent' and the 'demonic' child still haunts our anxieties about children today.

Myths and monsters: the predatory paedophile

Of course there is a real sense in which sex does pose a threat to children – through the abusive actions of adults. As we have already suggested, parental risk anxiety often crystallizes around the threat of sexual violence from strangers, which is much rarer than the dangers posed by abusive fathers and other known males – and far less likely to cause the death of a child than accidents in the home or on the roads (see Green 1997; Scott et al. 1998; Levine 2002). The fear that children may be abducted, molested and murdered by a predatory pervert, however, seems to be firmly lodged in the public imagination. In our own research on children and risk anxiety, parents described this as their 'worst fear'; even those who were aware that it was statistically unlikely still felt the need to make every effort to guard against the possibility of it happening (Scott et al. 2000). As Judith Levine put it, 'if it happens to your baby, who cares about the statistics?' (Levine 2002: 26). Parents, and others, seem to find it difficult to keep this particular form of danger in perspective.

The events around which these fears are mobilized, which hit the headlines and provoke public outrage, are rare, but become significant because they serve to construct and reinforce the popular image of 'the paedophile' and engender campaigns to 'do something' to curb the activities of such monsters. In the USA, the rape and murder of a child by a man with a record of sex offences who lived across the street led to a successful campaign to change the law, so that the whereabouts of convicted sex offenders could be made public; this became known as Megan's Law. Attempts to introduce a similar law in the UK, following the murder of Sarah Payne in 2000, failed, but in the course of the campaign a Sunday tabloid, the *News of the World*, ran a 'name and shame' campaign, featuring photographs of 'known paedophiles'. The effect of such campaigns is to position the paedophile as a monster – distancing him from 'normal' men. While more liberal commentators recognize that most abusers of children are not strangers but often family members, the idea that there is an identifiable category of men known as paedophiles persists, and is recycled through countless news stories and television dramas. Only very rarely are parallels drawn between presumed perverse desires for children and the desires of 'normal' men. The popular discourses of sociobiology and evolutionary psychology tell us that what any red-blooded alpha male ought to find attractive is extreme youthful femininity. Of course there is nothing fixed or natural about this, rather it is the social construction of attractiveness that is in play here, but it should prompt us to question who qualifies as a child and whether desire for youthful innocence is more congruent with dominant sexual mores than is generally acknowledged. The pattern of older men desiring younger women, and adult men desiring children, has a great deal to do with gendered power dynamics. Yet when children are sexually abused, this is more often constructed as a desecration of innocence rather than as an abuse of power.

We are not discounting the real dangers facing children today and do not share the libertarian agenda of Frank Furedi (1997), who suggests that all concerns about risk are imaginings produced by the 'culture of fear'. However, we would seriously question the idea that sexuality *per se* endangers children's well-being, and suggest that the concomitant withholding of sexual knowledge from them may not promote their safety – certainly in so far as they are kept ignorant of forms of adult behaviour that might pose a threat and given vague warnings about strangers. The sexual component of such risks is rarely made explicit to children: the advice they are given, products of adult scripts and anxieties, is bounded by what cannot be said. This makes it extremely difficult to communicate to children the precise nature of the danger they are being warned about. Children are denied access to the 'full story' which informs adult understandings, because sex itself is often thought of as a risk to children (Jackson 1982; Stainton-Rogers and Stainton-Rogers 1992), and indeed to childhood itself.

Sexualization – the theft of childhood?

There are two distinct but often conflated notions of nature and the natural which are mobilized in relation to childhood. The first of these can be designated 'scientific nativism' (cf. Connell and Dowsett (1992) on sexuality). Here childhood is understood as a series of biologically ordained developmental stages, as in the socialization paradigm. The second form of nativism draws on understandings of a natural order in which children have their proper place. These give rise to different forms of anxiety: on the one hand, concerns about the consequences of perverting the 'normal' course of development and, on the other, fears of disrupting social order. Anxieties about teenage mothers, for example, draw on both sets of concerns, not only as signalling the loss of childhood innocence – premature sexual activity and premature entry into adulthood – but also as evidence of unruly and promiscuous teenagers becoming unfit mothers.

Fears for children tend to be expressed through the idiom of children 'robbed of their childhood'. Here there is general discomfort about loss of sexual innocence, pressures to be 'grown up', as well as more specific concerns about the hot-housing of child prodigies or children forced to take on adult responsibilities. Paradoxically worries about children's lack or loss of a 'proper' childhood are occurring in the context of social trends that appear to reinforce and prolong childhood dependency. While young people tend to be economically dependent for longer, they are more likely to assert their sexual independence earlier. Young children, on their own behalf (Martens et al. 2004), consume clothing, popular music videos and magazines which are seen by adults as overly sexualized and more are engaging in early sexual experimentation. Evidence of the sexualization of children is frequently represented as indicative of a more general social malaise, creating a climate in which the fears this evokes crystallize around particular stories of 'lost childhood'.

To take a specific example, in the 1990s there was a great deal of public interest in child beauty pageants. A key event was the murder, in Boulder, Colorado, in December 1996, of a star of the pageant circuit, 6-year-old JonBenét Ramsey. Coincidentally, the BBC had shown a documentary about this issue earlier the same year and rescreened it, with reference to the Ramsey murder, in 1998. In 2008, there was an update on the lives of the two children on whom the earlier documentary had focused. What fascinated the public then, and continues to fascinate now, was the image of small girls dressed up and sexualized as quasi-adult women. 'The film shocked many for its depiction of ruthless parents, and the kitsch sexualization of the children taking part' (*Woman's Hour*, 27 May 2008).[3] It is the sexualization of these girls which was and is particularly problematic – their make-up, their clothes, the routines they perform, their whole demeanour. In the *Radio Times*, Alison Graham (1996: 24) described a contestant as 'pretending a sexuality she should know nothing about'. The *Glasgow Herald* depicted JonBenét Ramsey's participation in the beauty pageant world as carrying 'a whiff of sexual exploitation and pornography'.

The media concentrated on what marked the 'difference' between these girls and 'normal' children, on their supposed lack of a 'proper' childhood. In other contexts, at the end of the twentieth century and the beginning of the twenty-first, the threat to childhood innocence was seen as more pervasive. Thus, for example, there have been concerns about girls' clothing becoming overly sexualized. In 2003, a British tabloid newspaper ran a campaign against the sale of sexy underwear, such as thongs and padded bras, to pre-teen girls (see Renold 2005). More recently, in 2007, the controversy re-emerged in the media around two events. First, the National Union of Teachers in the UK called for regulation of the 'inappropriate sexualization' of pre-pubescent children, citing such examples as supermarkets selling pole-dancing kits and lace lingerie for children. Second, the American Psychological Association published a report on the dangers of early sexualization for young girls. Once again media reportage, in tones of shock and horror, played up the sexualization of children who 'ought' to be innocent.

The idiom of lost childhood, while focused on girls, misses much of the gendered dimension of this sexualization. The sexualization of girlhood is neither novel nor exceptional. At the end of the 1940s Simone de Beauvoir commented that the average small girl was taught that 'in order to be pleasing she must be pretty as a picture' and encouraged to gain attention through 'childish coquetry' (Beauvoir [1949] 1972: 306). Moreover a number of commentators have drawn attention to the ways in which innocence itself is routinely sexualized (Ennew 1986; Kitzinger 1988; Kincaid 1998). Feminists in particular have emphasized the parallels between the sexualization of girlhood and the infantilization of female sexuality. For example, as Emma Renold (2005) points out, the same newspaper that spearheaded the 2003 campaign against sexy underwear for girls regularly features pictures of semi-nude models using props and poses resonant of childhood innocence. The adult woman represented as a schoolgirl has long been a staple image in soft pornography. Thus it is evident that the same cultural mores produce both the sexualization of girl children and the anxieties that this provokes. One way in which this is dealt with is by the 'othering' of the overly sexualized child, for example, as working class, in contrast to the 'demurely' dressed middle-class child, or as emblematic of 'American' excess in the case of the British media's portrayal of child beauty pageants.

Both public and parental anxieties, then, accrete around the issue of early sexual maturity which is seen as a particular threat to cherished ideals of childhood innocence. Paradoxically, despite the influence of psychoanalysis on commonsense ideas about sexuality more generally, the Freudian proposition that children are sexual beings has not taken root. The belief that children are, and should be, asexual persists. Those critical of the presumption of childhood asexuality tend to assert or imply that children *are* sexual beings. In our view debating whether or not children are sexual is irrelevant. Following the logic of our social constructionist position, children are neither inherently sexual nor inherently asexual: they are what it is possible for them be under specific social conditions. What is of more interest to us is how ideas about children's asexuality both reinforce and are reinforced by the social distribution of sexual knowledge, and how this in turn frames the ways in which they become sexual.

For adults only: the social distribution of sexual knowledge

Access to sexual knowledge is an important boundary marker between children and adults (Jackson 1982). This is evident, for example, in public debates about the 'nine o'clock watershed' through which television programming in Britain is divided between 'family' and 'adult' entertainment. Television has become a locus of parental anxiety about children's exposure to sex and violence (Buckingham 1994; Buckingham and Bragg 2004). Moreover, recent technological developments such as video and the Internet may mean that parents cannot always control the information their children are receiving. Parents are capable of being surprised and shocked by the sexual information available to their children, as evinced by the public debate in the 1990s on the content of magazines read by girls in their early teens (Jackson 1999).[4] Public anxiety about these magazines has usually focused on the possibility that they may be inciting young women to early sexual exploration in the pursuit of pleasure, thus denying young women's capacity for reflexive engagement with what they read (Frazer 1988; Buckingham and Bragg 2004). This issue is, of course, gendered: far less attention is paid to teenage boys' consumption of pornography.

While there may be cause for feminist concern in relation to the reinforcement of a heterosexual ideal in teenage magazines, they may also have value as a source of information about, and exploration of, sexuality often not available elsewhere (see Buckingham and Bragg 2004; Allen 2005). In her analysis of problem pages in girls' magazines in Australia and New Zealand, Sue Jackson (2005a) argues that such magazines offer permission to talk about sex, but that attempts to 'do' desire were frequently undone in the responses to the letters, especially if the desire in question was for another young woman. Sue Jackson (2005b) also found that, despite some recognition of sexual diversity, advice tended to reinforce the coital imperative and to emphasize risk and danger rather than pleasure.

Adults worry about access to sexual knowledge for children of all ages, particularly that they might learn too much too soon. Parents often appear willing to mandate teachers to undertake sex education on the assumption that they will be told the right things at the right time, just as they will learn addition before multiplication (Scott et al. 1997; Botcherby and Scott 2004). Yet when schools depart from these expectations, once again we are faced with scares about innocence corrupted. In the USA attention has focused on the reactionary and religious aspects of school-based sex education which have resulted in the widespread introduction of abstinence programmes – what Judith Levine (2002: 90ff.) refers to as 'no-sex education'. In the UK the picture is more complex and few educators would endorse the 'just say no' position. Since the 1950s, sex education in the UK, while always provoking controversy, has not followed a linear trajectory (Pilcher 2005); there have been periods of more liberal education followed by periods of greater restriction. Whatever form sex education has taken, the UK version has, for the most part, shared with the USA one notable absence: what Michele Fine has called 'the missing discourse of desire' (Fine 1988; Fine and McClelland 2006).

There was a time, though, when it might have been otherwise. The 1970s saw the introduction of condom machines into a number of schools for senior pupils and in the 1980s the UK Health Education Authority endorsed the publication and use in schools of a text entitled *Make it Happy* which discussed sexual pleasure, orgasm (male and female) and the possibility of gay and lesbian sex, drawing on the views of young people themselves (Cousins [1978] 1986). However, the end of the 1980s saw the introduction of the infamous Section 28 of the Local Government Act 1988, which sought to prevent the 'promotion' of homosexuality as a 'pretended family relationship' by local authorities, including schools (Stacey 1991; Weeks 1991; Epstein and Johnson 1998). Yet during the same period HIV/AIDS education was made compulsory. The politics of sex education at that time was characterized by a tension between moral conservatism and public health pragmatism (Thomson 1994). Concerns that sex education might encourage sexual activity led to some of the earlier liberalizing tendencies being reversed, yet the 'need' for more and better sex education was apparent and keeps returning to the agenda, each time provoking fresh controversies. There is a persistent conflict between trying to avoid the ill effects of sexual activity – STIs and teenage pregnancy – while not being seen to encourage or endorse early engagement with sex (Buston et al. 2001, 2002; Wight et al 2002), and schools that fail to strike the right balance can find their provision pilloried in the media (Epstein and Johnson 1998). Throughout the public debates a recurring theme has been parents' responsibility for sex education and the frequently aired opinion that sex education is better imparted in the home rather than the school; yet it has long been evident that parents are often neither a willing nor a reliable source of such information (Schofield 1965; Botcherby and Scott 2004; Frankham 2006).

Most recently, in 2008, a furore ensued as a result of a government initiative to include health and relationship education in the National Curriculum (in England and Wales) from age 5 onwards. The public and some areas of the media reacted as if 5 year olds were about to be inducted into the pleasures of the flesh rather than merely helped to understand their bodies and the differences between them. Commentators asserted that such information would confuse young children and that they would be told too much before they were ready. However, young children are often trying to make sense of the adult relationships that they see around them, as well as of their own experiences, while being excluded from much of the knowledge that would help them to accomplish this. Hence children have to struggle to make sense of a jigsaw puzzle of knowledge from which many pieces are missing and where they have no box with the whole picture on the lid (Jackson 1982; Thomson and Scott 1991). So how do they begin to put the pieces together? And how should we theorize the process by which children acquire sexual knowledge and become sexual actors?

Becoming sexual

The interactionist perspective that we are adopting provides an account of gendered and sexual subjectivity that stands in stark opposition to psychoanalysis (see Chapters 1 and 2). Psychoanalytic approaches see gender and sexuality as too closely entwined to be separated: both are subsumed under the single term 'sex'. In particular, the (gendered) objects of our desires are seen as crucially determining the sex (gender) we become: thus to be one sex is to desire the other. Moreover, since we are said to become 'sexed subjects' at an early stage in our life (albeit, after Lacan, as a precarious accomplishment), both sexual (gender) identification and 'object choice' are determined as soon as we move from infancy to childhood (see Chapter 2). Against this, Gagnon and Simon (1974) uncoupled gender and sexuality, accorded temporal priority to gender and insisted that children cannot become sexual without access to the sexual scripts through which acts, relationships and feelings (emotions and sensations) become sexually meaningful. To be clear about this, they are not saying that children are either sexual or asexual in any essential sense: only that sexual selfhood depends on being able to make sense of oneself as sexual. And, while children today may have far more resources available for sexual self-making than they did when *Sexual Conduct* was written, adults still attempt to police that availability. From this perspective, then, a gendered sense of self precedes our awareness of ourselves as sexual, and gender serves to frame and shape the process of becoming sexual.

Gagnon and Simon's account presupposes but does not explore the processes whereby gender is constructed. It is worth saying a little about this in order to tease out the ways in which gender and sexuality come to be interrelated at the level of subjective being. In doing so, we also provide a corrective to Gagnon and Simon's reliance on the now outmoded developmental language of socialization.[5] In one of the earliest and most thorough feminist critiques of the socialization paradigm, Liz Stanley and Sue Wise (1983) argued that it cannot explain those of us who rebel against conventional gender norms, for example, feminists, gay men and lesbians, and also that few women or men in actuality conform to rigid definitions of femininity and masculinity. Not only does the idea that we are socialized into 'gender roles' deny the variability and fluidity of gendered attributes and conduct, but also it fails to allow for agency and reflexivity in the ways in which gender is lived and continually negotiated. Stanley and Wise (1983) also challenge the dualistic opposition between 'the individual' and 'society' whereby socialization posits internal psychological mechanisms of 'internalization' but at the same time *what* is internalized is deemed to be determined by a society that exists separately from that individual. Some similar critiques were mounted from poststructuralist perspectives (e.g. Henriques et al. 1984; Davies 1989) and this led some to turn to psychoanalysis in order to avoid an overly mechanistic account of gendered subjectivity.

Our preference, though, is to follow this through from the interpretative sociological tradition that inspired Stanley and Wise and the pragmatist and interactionist tradition underpinning Gagnon and Simon's work – in particular the account of the self provided by G.H. Mead (1934). This, we would argue, provides a view of the self as a process that is as sophisticated as anything poststructuralists have since developed, which locates the self firmly in social context and which avoids the determinism and universalism of psychoanalysis (see Chapter 6).[6] In providing an outline of becoming gendered, we need not only to take account of the social significance and durability of the gender binary itself and the way that this is interwoven with the institutionalization of heterosexuality, but should also remain alert to the potential fluidity and variability of modes of becoming and being gendered and sexual.

The story begins with the initial act of gender attribution (Kessler and McKenna 1978; Kessler 1998) – the first act of social categorization that a child undergoes. As soon as it is born or, in this era of scanning technology, even earlier, it is identified as either a girl or a boy. It is only when a child becomes she or he, rather than 'it' that it can be seen as fully human – hence the immense anxiety when that identity is not immediately evident (Kessler 1998). But for gender to be 'evident' at least three distinct social processes are required: first, the act of recognition whereby the baby's genitals are read as a sign of its sex, second, the baby is reduced to its sex ('It's a girl'), and third, this reductive act effectively brings the child into being as gendered, as a little girl. This is an interactive process but one in which the child herself, as a newborn infant, is only a passive participant. In the formation of the self, in which gender becomes part of a child's own sense of who she is, she is an active participant.

This self begins to be formed early in life as a child learns to distinguish between self and other, to 'take the attitude of the other', to locate herself in relation to the others in her immediate circle and ultimately to social others in general (Mead's 'generalized other'). All this occurs in gendered terms, for these others are gendered and the child, in interacting with them, becomes able to locate herself or himself within a gendered social field. While the self is premised upon differentiation between self and others, this is quite a different view of the self–other relation from that posited by postmodern and Lacanian psychoanalytic theories. Not only is the self active in the process of coordinating action with others, but also the other is not positioned as oppositional to the self (see Stanley and Wise 1993). Rather than being constructed through repudiation of the other, the self is forged *in relation to* others, through being able to locate oneself within the social world of others. Moreover, while others are gendered, they do not need to occupy specific places in an Oedipal drama. There is, therefore, no need to assume, as psychoanalysis does, that the *mechanisms* of self-formation differ for boys and girls, simply that they acquire differently gendered selves through participating in gendered social interaction. Thus gendered selfhood emerges as variable, there is no single way of being a little boy or a little girl. Yet the incorrigibility of the taken-for-granted assumption that the world 'is populated by two sexes and only two sexes' (Garfinkel 1967: 122) bounds children's lives. The 'content' of gendered conduct and identity is immensely variable but the 'container' – the gender divide itself – is much less mutable (Delphy 1993). A child cannot, therefore, locate herself in a gendered social order without a sense of herself as gendered, without being able to make sense of self and others as embodied, gendered beings (Davies 1989). Once the basic reflexive capacities of self-formation have been set in motion within this binary frame, the self continues, throughout life, to evolve and change through social interaction by virtue of its constant reflexivity; it is not fixed by the 'traumas' of infancy. This reflexivity is also frequently mobilized through reconstructions of the past, as children and young, people strive to make sense of the present in terms of past experience (Mead 1929, 1932; Gagnon and Simon 1974).

As children grow older and begin to put together the jigsaw of sexual knowledge from the pieces made available to them, sexuality becomes entwined with their sense of gender – whether or not they become heterosexual – albeit in variable ways. Obviously we 'do not become sexual all at once' (Gagnon and Simon 1974: 27). Children are not only developing gendered selves, but also assimilating much from their social environment that is of potential sexual relevance. It is only the specifically erotic component of sexual scripts that adults attempt to conceal from children: other aspects of adult maps of sexuality impinge on children's self-understanding from an early age. For example, the sense children make of their own bodies is ordered by meanings deriving from adult sexual scripts and their conventions of modesty, decorum and morality. Adult sexual scripts also inform reactions to children playing 'sexual' games such as 'doctors and nurses' (which do not have the same meaning for children as they do for adults), reactions that typically vary from the punitive to the embarrassed. Frequently children do not understand adults' reactions (Frankham 2006), but they nonetheless learn that such activities are seen as 'bad' or 'dirty' and, if they wish to continue them, they must do so in secret.

Children are usually well aware that there are secrets that adults keep from them, that there are aspects of adult life from which they are excluded, and because they are active, interpreting beings they are often busy trying to make sense of adult evasions and half-truths. Adults, parents in particular, often fail to communicate directly with children about sex (Phelan 2007). Many parents say (and believe) that they are not being secretive, that they are answering children's questions and therefore providing them with the answers for which they are 'ready'. This common, reactive, approach often forecloses further questions and explanations (Frankham 2006) so that even where parents are not deliberately evasive, children may (at the time or later) interpret such responses as signalling that certain aspects of life are not open for discussion, are somehow taboo. A further consequence of this approach is that children's initial questions are often posed in terms of their origins (where they or babies come from) and thus the information they receive is framed in terms of reproduction and is thus heterosexually ordered – as is school sex education. Few parents (or teachers) are willing to discuss sexual pleasure with children, even when the latter's questions could raise this (see e.g. Frankham 2006: 241–242).

From parents and elsewhere children acquire a great deal of common-sense knowledge about the institution and practice of heterosexuality – about heterosexual love and marriage, about families, mothers and fathers – way before they are aware of the sexual activities these entail. Children also enact heterosexuality through play and, later, particularly as they approach puberty, through a more explicitly heterosexualized gendered interactions.[7] Emma Renold's research on 10 and 11 year olds in the UK illustrates how heterosexuality figures in the daily lives of these children, most of whom have received some basic sex education, though usually little beyond the mechanics of reproduction, and who are beginning to develop a sense of themselves as heterosexual actors. These children inhabit a world already divided by gender, where friendships across gender lines are difficult to sustain unless the parties are seen to be 'going out'. These early boyfriend–girlfriend relationships involve little physical intimacy but are nonetheless important features of social life and are markers of status for both boys and girls – especially the latter. Those who do not conform to this heterosexual culture are often stigmatized and bullied, especially girls who are seen as unattractive or boys who do not exhibit the markers of acceptable masculinity – who are likely to be labelled as 'gay' or 'benders'. Boys also engage in verbal and sometimes physical sexual harassment of girls (Renold 2002, 2005, 2006).

Even before they enter their teens, then, children have already begun to construct a provisional picture of a sexual world that is normatively heterosexual and in which sexuality is a source of both status and conflict. As more pieces of the jigsaw fall into place, their understanding of sexuality becomes more complete but remains provisional because it continues to be subject to change as they make sense of themselves as embodied sexual beings. This sense-making continues to be highly gendered. As Michael Kimmel (2005: 3) points out, gender 'is the dividing line along which sexual expression, desire and experience is organized', even allowing for the social changes that have brought women's and men's sexual lives closer together. For both young men and young women coming to terms with sexuality is achieved largely through drawing on the cultural scenarios available to them through (limited) formal sex education, the media and their peers. But even these sources may be gender-specific, for example, girls' reading of magazines and boys' use of pornography.

Such sources are also mediated through the interpersonal interaction with friends, which plays a vital role in collectively making sense of the sexual mores and practices deriving from generally available cultural scenarios. What is sometimes seen negatively from an adult perspective as 'peer pressure' plays a vital role in validating young people's own experience, making generally available sexual information personally meaningful and developing a sense of sexual competence (Allen 2005). But the influence of the peer group is double-edged: it can also regulate sexual identities and practices, stigmatizing those who are less conventional in terms of gender or sexuality, in particular through policing the boundaries of heteronormativity and local norms of heterosexual practice (Epstein and Johnson 1998; Phoenix et al. 2003; Chambers et al. 2004; Kimmel 2005).

Becoming sexual is not simply a matter of assimilating new knowledge and experience; it also involves retrospective reinterpretation as young people begin, in Gagnon and Simon's terms, to bring that past into greater congruity with their present understandings of themselves and their social world. It is for this reason that, for example, adult lesbians and gay men are able to tell a story of self in which they 'always knew' they were lesbian or gay, or that they always were but only later 'realized' that this was the case; this was often on the basis of feeling 'different' as children and, particularly, feeling they weren't quite normally (normatively) gendered. These accounts are not, as Vera Whisman says, simply reflections of their experience but are 'told to fit those experiences into a coherent ... story' (Whisman 1996: 181). Of course those who grow up to be heterosexual may also have felt themselves 'different' as children, but would not tell the same story. Heterosexuals are not called upon to account for their sexuality. They therefore do not feel it necessary to construct narratives explaining 'how I became a heterosexual' or 'how I knew I was heterosexual'; it is simply taken for granted. Since heterosexuality is the privileged norm, self-reflexivity about it is not integral to heterosexuals' emergent sexual selfhood. Indeed, Rebecca Phelan suggests that young heterosexuals may have only a fragmented picture of past sexual selves unless prompted into telling a story that links their childhood past with the present (Phelan 2007: 35).

Gender, however, remains central to young heterosexuals' sense of themselves as socially competent sexual actors and, conversely, heterosexual sexual competence helps to validate their sense of gendered selfhood. This is particularly important as young people struggle to leave the dependent status of childhood behind and make claims to autonomy and adulthood, since sexual and social maturity is gendered – and asymmetrical. For example, as Janet Holland and her colleagues found in investigating the experience of first heterosex, having sex is still understood as making a boy a man, but it does not make a girl a woman (Holland et al. 1996). There are other ways of validating manhood, such as through physical prowess, toughness and courage – all of which may help to safeguard a young man against the stigma of failed masculinity – but the spectre of homosexuality may nevertheless threaten the security of masculine identification. Michael Kimmel (2005: 35) argues that 'homophobia is a central organizing principle of our cultural definition of manhood', manifested through the critical gaze of other men – especially in adolescence when young men learn that their peers act as 'gender police' who constantly pose the threat of unmasking them as effeminate (Kimmel 2005: 36). Yet away from such scrutiny the mask of masculinity can and does slip – which is why researchers find that teenage boys appear far more 'macho' in group discussions than in face-to-face individual interviews (see, e.g. Phoenix et al. 2003). The sexual self is never a stable entity; it shifts with context as well as changing and evolving over time.

If being (hetero)sexually *active* confirms a masculine social identity, what confirms femininity is being sexually *attractive* to men. Young heterosexual women's sexual and gendered selfhood, however, is becoming more complex as they negotiate contradictory expectations. Their horizons are no longer limited to heterosexual domesticity, yet they still inhabit a highly heterosexualized social and cultural world where success in sexual relationships matters in terms of social esteem and self-worth. Here new sexual scripts are on offer, replacing the older goals of romance and marriage with aspirations towards sexual autonomy and experimentation. Magazines marketed to young women positively exhort them to take control of their own sexual pleasure, to 'discover' the potential of their bodies, to become proficient in new sexual skills. Yet the double standard of morality, although considerably eroded, has not disappeared altogether – and neither has sexual violence and coercion. As a result young women's desires, and their ability to manage a sexual project of the self, remain more constrained and more problematic than those of young men even when they stay within the bounds of normative heterosexuality (Holland et al. 1998; Phillips 2000; Tolman 2002). This is not to imply that they lack agency; they may actively seek to overturn barriers to sexual self-determination and to challenge gendered sexual conventions (Allen 2003, 2005). They are, however, faced with contradictory expectations: the contemporary sexual landscape would seem to require a high degree of self-reflexivity and indeed self-surveillance from young women as they attempt to avoid the pitfalls of deficiency (not being sexual enough) and excess (being too sexual).

Conclusion

In becoming sexual young people only gradually leave behind a childhood bounded by adult risk anxieties. In adolescence their lives continue to be shaped by adult fears and adult-imposed regulation while they are also encountering new risks as they try to find space to explore and develop their emerging sexualities. Risk anxiety in many respects defines the boundaries of childhood: becoming an adult involves a shift from being protected from sex to active management of sexual risk. The legacy of 'protection', however, brings with it certain costs, in particular an ambivalence surrounding sexuality. While sex is purportedly positive, pleasurable and fulfilling, its construction as inappropriate for children makes learning about it far from straightforward, and too often leaves a residue of negative associations deriving from past adult evasions and half-truths and consequent miscommunication, guilt and secrecy. The gendered and generational power relations that characterize the process of becoming sexual exacerbate these problems.

The sexualization of risk reflects historically and culturally specific constructions of both childhood and sexuality. Both are thought of as precious but in need of careful nurturance and containment in order to promote happy carefree childhoods and healthy (adult) sexual fulfilment. Indeed, the former is often seen as a precondition for the latter – a childhood free from the shadow of sexuality is thought necessary both to keep children safe and to secure their future sexual health and happiness.

Sexual risks to children, then, should be understood as integral to the social construction of childhood and sexuality, and as consequent upon the different levels at which that construction operates. Structurally, the sexual abuse and exploitation of children are made possible by hierarchies of gender and generation which render children relatively powerless and which shape adult male sexuality. Discursively children are constituted as vulnerable and sexually 'innocent' and sexuality is represented as a potent (adult) drive, which men in particular may be unable to control. Within these discourses it is deemed acceptable for men to be attracted to youth, vulnerability and innocence provided the object of desire is not too young, too vulnerable or too innocent. At the level of everyday interaction and practice, the boundaries between asexual childhood and sexual adulthood are constantly being tested by young people as they enter into consensual sexual relations. Here, too, the gendered meanings and power relations of sexuality are continually re-enacted and sometimes renegotiated or contested (Holland et al. 1998; Phillips 2000; Tolman 2002; Allen 2005). Subjectively asexual children must somehow become sexually aware adults through reworking the knowledge they already have, acquiring previously forbidden knowledge and reflexively reconstituting themselves as sexual beings. The emergent sexual self is never, however, fixed: it continues to be made and remade through the social, cultural and interpersonal contexts in which adult sexual lives are lived.[8]

Notes

1 Life for working-class children at this time was very different. Concern for the moral welfare of working-class children informed much Victorian philanthropic and reformist zeal – from the threats to propriety posed by children working 'semi-naked' in coal mines to the fear that overcrowded housing might lead to incest.
2 The Sexual Offences Act 2003, among other provisions, equalized the age of consent for men and women and for heterosexual and homosexual or lesbian sex. The 'breach of trust' provision applies when an older person is in a position of authority over or responsibility for a young person, for example, a teacher or youth worker (see Waites 2005).
3 See www.bbc.co.uk/radio4/womanshour/01/2008_22_tue.shtml (accessed 1 November 2008).
4 In Britain there was an attempt to legislate in relation to this type of content – to make it mandatory to print minimum recommended ages on the covers of the magazines. Since the 1990s the sexual content of such magazines has been reduced to make way for the ubiquitous celebrity gossip.
5 They were, however, hardly alone in this at the time: many feminist accounts of the acquisition of gender in the 1970s and early 1980s did the same.
6 Here we provide only a sketchy outline of Mead's approach and defer a more detailed discussion to Chapter 6.
7 Note that this is a social, not natural transition (Gagnon and Simon 1974; Thorne 1987), although children's perceptions of their own and others' bodies may play a part.
8 Ideas about childhood and sexuality are also culturally specific. The examples we have used pertain primarily to Britain. The peculiar anxieties about childhood and sexuality prevalent in Britain and the USA are not, for example, so evident in Scandinavian and Nordic countries. Even among Western societies, then, there are cultural differences in anxieties about and responses to sexual risks to children.

CHAPTER 6

THE SEXUAL SELF IN LATE MODERNITY

In Chapter 5 we argued that particular anxieties surrounding children's sexuality frame the ways in which they become sexual in late modern, Western societies. This is but one aspect of the wider tensions and antinomies characteristic of the contemporary sexual landscape within which we negotiate our sexual lives and reflexively construct our sexual selves. This is not a comfortably stable landscape, but one that often seems to be shifting beneath our feet and before our eyes as a result of rapid social change and the contradictions this throws up. It is a landscape saturated with sexual imagery yet also hedged in with all manner of cautions and prohibitions, in which the celebration of sexual freedom and diversity coexists with bigotry and exclusion. Here ordinary people's intimate sexual secrets can be revealed in detail on television chat shows or in the 'problem pages' of magazines, while few young people are able to discuss sexuality freely with their parents and heterosexual couples who engage in sex regularly can find themselves uneasy about communicating about their sexual desires to each other.

The diverse cultural scenarios available to us today do, however, provide copious resources for sexual self-fashioning and self-revelation through the circulation of sexual story-telling in popular mass media. Within these stories endless possibilities for sexual self-knowledge and self-improvement, for sexual choice and fulfilment jostle with diverse risks and anxieties, from fear of violence, disease and pregnancy to anxieties about not being 'fit' enough to compete in the sexual marketplace or not being proficient enough in one's sexual performance. To answer these anxieties there are the numerous products of the therapeutic culture – medical 'cures' for 'sexual dysfunction' and self-help books offering techniques for improving performance – which in turn add to the climate of excessive concern with the sexual and fuel the anxieties this creates.

In this chapter we focus on the selves produced within this shifting matrix of sexual possibilities. In the process we re-engage with the debates about late modernity discussed in Chapter 3 and further develop the approach to theorizing the self suggested in Chapter 5. In arguing for the continued salience of a broadly interactionist conceptualization of the sexual self, we draw on G.H. Mead's (1934) account of the self as located within the wider social relations through which it is constituted. This enables us to think about the ways in which sexuality has become a contested site of reflexive self-construction and gives us critical purchase on current theoretical debates on late modernity.

In returning to Mead we are invoking a conceptualization of self that dates back to the pragmatist philosophers and social psychologists of the early twentieth century,[1] and which later informed the development of interactionist sociology. Mead's work has suffered, in the interim, from oversimplification and distortion in innumerable sociology textbooks, which is perhaps why it is so often bypassed; for example, it does not receive a mention in many recent feminist works on the self (see e.g. Lupton 1998; Lawler 2000; Skeggs 2004). Now discussions of the self are more often framed in terms of the late modern 'project of the self' (Giddens 1991), Foucault's (1988) 'technologies of self' or Ricoeur's (1984, 1992) idea of self as narrative construction. Moreover the late modern concept of 'the self' coexists with other terms such as 'subjectivity', deriving from poststructuralist and postmodernist thought and the widely used 'identity'. These terms refer to our subjective being and sense of who we are, and all have been deployed in discussions of sexuality. A little conceptual and theoretical clarification is therefore in order before we proceed further.

Self/identity/subjectivity: conceptual and theoretical clarification

We have chosen to think in terms of self or subjectivity rather than identity because the latter is a more specific and less inclusive term. While identity is sometimes taken as synonymous with subjectivity or self, it is generally rather more narrowly conceived as our sense of who we are, which can be translated into labels with which we can identify ourselves or others, for example, as 'lesbian' or 'bisexual'. Identity can also imply a fixity about who one is, which is why, in part, it has been contested by queer theorists' insistence on destabilizing identity – though paradoxically 'queer' itself has in turn become an identity category. Furthermore, it does not account for those social categories that rarely become the basis of avowed identities but which might nonetheless be central to the self, such as heterosexuality. While gendered and sexual identities can be highly significant aspects of who we think we are and how we relate to others they do not encompass the whole of our subjective lives. Sexual subjectivity encompasses far more than identity: there are many aspects of the self that are not reducible to any identity or to the sum total of our identities.

The concepts of self and subjectivity refer more broadly to our subjective sense of ourselves, along with our inner thoughts and desires. While we have used these two terms synonymously at times, we recognize that they derive from different theoretical traditions which must, at this point, be disentangled. Subjectivity has generally been conceived in poststructuralist, postmodern and psychoanalytic terms as decentred, fluid or fractured – and not the product of conscious thought or agency. Subjectivity in this sense figured prominently in feminist theory in the 1980s and 1990s, and stood against humanist, modernist ideas of an essential unitary, fixed, rational subject (see e.g. Weedon, 1987; Flax, 1990a). The recent resurgence in sociological theorizing of the self, on the other hand, has posited a more coherent, conscious, reflexively fashioned, 'self-made self', with the emphasis on the self as 'project' (Giddens 1991, 1992) or as the object of 'technologies of the self' (Foucault 1988). In many accounts this self is historically specific, a product of the increasing individualism of the last few centuries. Self and subjectivity thus seem to be rather different phenomena – and sometimes an explicit distinction is made between them. Beverley Skeggs (2004), for example, distinguishes between the self as a 'coherent unity' and subjectivity 'which is not coherent and which we all live with in ways we do not often know' (Skeggs 2004: 191n.). In this kind of formulation a consciously constructed self is thought of as papering over the cracks of a fractured subjectivity underlying its carefully crafted surface. This is particularly pertinent to sexuality, since the influence of psychoanalysis often locates it as a subterranean force apt to bubble up through the cracks and disrupt the surface coherence of the conscious self.

We propose an alternative to this analytical split between conscious self and unconscious subjectivity, particularly its psychoanalytic underpinnings. It is here that Mead's conceptualization of the self is particularly useful since it encapsulates much of what is usually termed subjectivity, and thus bridges the divide between a self-consciously fabricated self and a less coherent, more fluid self. Mead's self is envisaged as process rather than structure and is hence neither unitary nor fixed. In this sense there is some congruence with poststructuralist ideas of 'subjectivity in process' (Weedon 1987) and postmodern critiques of the subject as 'a stable, reliable, integrative entity' (Flax 1990b: 8). This is not surprising, since part of the pragmatist project was to break with the Enlightenment conception of a transcendental self standing outside the social, and to replace it with a self very much embedded in everyday sociality. Conversely the idea of the self as socially located is what distinguishes this tradition from the later postmodern decentred and fragmentary subject, which is disembedded from the social, having no location from which any coherence can be established.

The postmodern subject might be seen as constituted *in* the social, but it is not *of* the social, participating in it and acting on it. As Dorothy

Smith (1999) argues, this is a subject whose being neither affects nor is affected by the social contexts in which everyday life goes on. Subjectivity is entirely the effect of language and discourse conceived as independent of the local production of meaning and of 'people's intentions to mean' (Smith 1999: 89–99). Moreover, this view of subjectivity cannot explain 'how individuals are endowed with the capabilities for independent reflection and action' (McNay 2000: 3). Moreover, it is difficult to see how anyone could act in the world with no sense of a coherent self. Even some of those sympathetic to postmodernism and psychoanalysis have critiqued an overly decentred notion of the subject. Jane Flax, for example, argues that we would slide into psychosis without a 'basic cohesion' within ourselves, which she locates in a core self which provides 'a sense of continuity of "going on being"' (Flax 1990b: 218–219). While a sense of oneself as having a past, present and potential future would certainly seem necessary to be able to act in the world at all, this does not have to be conceptualized as a core self or, in Flax's psychoanalytic terms, as 'deep subjectivity'. As one of us has argued previously:

> A better metaphor for the self as ongoing might be a complex, many stranded cord running through our lives, but one which does not necessarily stay the same since the threads that comprise it can be frayed or strengthened and are continually being spliced or woven in with other threads, remade over time. So, while we have a sense of our self as continuing, that self is never unchanging.
>
> (Jackson 2007: 7)

In keeping with this, and with Mead's perspective in mind, we would suggest that our 'going on being' derives from *social* experience, constructed and reconstructed through everyday social practices rather than being lodged deep in the psyche. Our sexual selves, for example, may be assembled from a disparate array of influences and experiences but they are given coherence through our ability to reconstruct a sexual self and sexual history as an ongoing reflexive process.

While reflexive selfhood makes possible a coherent 'narrative of self', it does not necessarily entail the heightened self-consciousness of the elaborated reflexive project of the self posited by Giddens (1991) as a product of modernity. Rather Mead's notion of reflexivity entails what it is to *be* social, to participate *in* the social. Reflexivity here is the capacity to engage in conversations with ourselves, see ourselves as subject and object in order to situate ourselves in relation to others. Without this capacity we would not be able to interact or cooperate with others and thus any sociality would be impossible. This we would read as a theoretical foundation for the idea of scripting – and Mead's thinking is one of the acknowledged influences on Gagnon and Simon's work (Gagnon 2004).

Reflexivity is central to intrapsychic scripting, to the 'internal conversations' through which we make sense of sexual feelings, desires and motivations and concoct sexual fantasies. Reflexivity as Mead envisaged it also, however, relates intrapsychic to interpersonal scripting and to cultural scenarios: sexual selfhood emerges from the play of reflexivity in interactions with others and from our understanding of cultural scenarios. Without the sociocultural resources that these levels of scripting make available to us, we would have no means of individual sense-making. Nor would we have any means of self-making, for the self depends on sociality: for Mead, the self cannot exist without the other (Mead 1934).

Reflexivity and the self

Reflexivity, or 'reflexiveness' as Mead called it,[2] is the ability to see oneself as both subject and object and is fundamental to our social being, to our active participation in social life. This idea of a reflexive self, in particular Mead's distinction between the 'I' and the 'me', is frequently misunderstood, largely because of repeated oversimplification in social theory textbooks. Thus the 'I' is frequently misrepresented as the individual part of the self and the 'me' as the social part. Or, as Anthony Giddens (1991) would have it, the 'me' is 'the identity – the social identity – of which the "I" becomes conscious in the course of psychological development' and the 'I' is 'the active, primitive will of the individual', its 'unsocialized part' (Giddens 1991: 52). In either case the 'I' is located as pre-social. Such misunderstandings miss a central point of Mead's thesis on the self: that the self is process not structure (Jenks 1996; Williams 2000; Crossley 2001).

In Mead's work there is no assumption of a primitive pre-social 'I'. Rather, the 'I' is only ever momentarily mobilized in dialogic, ongoing interplay with the 'me'. As Crossley (2001) argues, the relationship between them is not a spatial one, two separate parts of the whole, 'but a temporal and reflexive self-relationship of an agent who chases her own shadow' (Crossley 2001: 147). The 'I' is located in the being and doing of the present (or ongoing successive presents) and self-reflection always entails retrospection

> The 'I' of this moment is present in the 'me' of the next moment. There again, I can never turn around quick enough to catch myself ... It is in memory that the 'I' is constantly present in experience ... the 'I' in memory is there as the spokesman [*sic*] of the self of the second, the minute or the day ago. As given, it is a 'me', but it is a 'me' which was the 'I' at the earlier time. If you ask, then, where directly in your own experience the 'I' comes in, the answer is that it comes in as a historical figure. It is what you were a second ago that is the 'I' of the 'me'. It is another 'me' that has to take that role. You cannot get the

immediate response of the 'I' in the process. The 'I' is in a certain sense that with which we do identify ourselves. The getting of it into experience constitutes one of the problems of most of our conscious experience; it is not directly given in experience.

(Mead 1934: 174–175)

Not only is self-reflection temporal, but also to be/have a self is to have consciousness of self, which requires a memory of the past and a capacity to imagine possible futures in which we 'go on being'. As Mead says, 'we normally organize our memories along the string of the self' (Mead 1934: 135), and we strive to accomplish this, to create coherence, when fragments of unsituated memory come back to us. It is through remembering selves other than the situated self of the present social context that we prevent dissociation from the self (Mead 1934: 243–244). Remembering, as he tells us elsewhere (Mead 1964, 2002), is always accomplished from the perspective of the present, from the point of view of a socially situated self, a self engaged in the social activity of the present moment.

This is crucial for understanding how we construct and reconstruct our sexual biographies and our sense of sexual self. Most of us 'remember' incidents from childhood that we now see as sexual and are apt to interpret these as contributing to our present sense of our sexuality. But we are making that interpretation, as Gagnon and Simon (1974) point out, from the point of view of our adult sexuality and filtered through sexual scripts not available to us when we were children. Moreover, any memory, as Mead argues, is always reconstructed; the past is available to us only from the standpoint of the present since we cannot 'get back' the past self we once were:

> When one recalls his boyhood [*sic*] days, he cannot get into them as he was, without their relationship to what he has become; and if he could, that is if he could reproduce the experience as it then took place, he could not use it, for this would involve his not being in the present within which that use must take place.

(Mead 2002: 58)

The thread of the self, continually reconstructed through memory, is not strung in a straight line between past and present, but rather can be conceptualized as a spiral in which we circle round and back on ourselves, remembering and reworking past experiences as new ones evoke them. So when we think we have learnt from experience – perhaps recalling memories from past romantic relationships to guide present ones, or thinking we have 'been through this before' – we cannot get back to that earlier experience itself, but are always reviewing it from a new angle, a new present. Moreover we can never be sure that we remember actual events; those memories we have worked over often in making sense of where we are now may, in effect, be memories of memories, layers of reconstruction that have accreted over time.

This is not to say that the past is only a reconstruction; there is a material past that actually existed even if we can apprehend it only from the standpoint of the present (or cannot remember it at all). Mead does not consider the past to be *only* a symbolic reconstruction; it also provides the conditions for emergence of the present. This implies that the past may affect the present in ways that may not necessarily be consciously apprehended. New events or situations do not arise from nowhere, but are shaped (though not completely determined) by what has gone before.[3]

Thus far we have considered reflexivity primarily in terms of memory, where it comes into play in constructing a coherent sense of self. Reflexivity, however, is central to how the self comes into being in the first place and in carrying on everyday interaction. As we have argued in Chapter 5, the self is founded upon relations with others, and the dialogic interplay between the 'I' and 'me' is only possible because we can apprehend the world and ourselves from the point of view of the other. Since the self, according to Mead, arises in social experience and cannot exist without the other, it is fundamentally social and fundamental *to* sociality, to our collective ability to locate ourselves within the ongoing stream of sociality around us. Because of this responsiveness to interactional context the self is never finally fixed but can continually be modified according to context. We live with both the multiple selves called forth by differing social contexts and an evolving, continually reconstructed sense of self. The forms that selfhood takes, therefore, are in no way predetermined since they are contingent upon the social contexts we each inhabit. Yet because the self is continually shaped by our engagement in those social contexts, it can never be an entirely individual product.

One of the problems with the way in which reflexivity is used in much recent theorizing on modernity is that it is equated with individualization and framed in terms of freedom from social constraint. Undoubtedly social constraints do have material effects on the degree to which and the directions in which we exercise reflexivity, but a simple opposition between the collective (social) and the individual (reflexive) is inappropriate, even if the social is equated with the structural. Structures (such as patriarchal families and institutionalized heterosexuality) enable, albeit unevenly and unequally, as well as constrain – they make certain ways of acting, thinking and being possible as well as making others less possible. Furthermore, constraints (and enablements) do not come just from structures, but from the everyday business of interacting with others and also from the cultural resources we draw on in making sense of our social worlds. Once we see sociality as encompassing more than social structure and pay attention to the interactional, meaningful everyday aspects of sociality, reflexivity becomes not an individual quality opposed to the social, but a fundamental part of sociality.

To see reflexivity as symptomatic of freedom from constraint, as in Giddens (1991, 1992) and Beck and Beck-Gernsheim (2002), is problematic.[4] Feminist critics of variants of the individualization thesis have tended to focus on the uneven availability of the forms of reflexivity deemed characteristic of late modernity. For Lisa Adkins (2002), women in late modernity are subject to re-traditionalization as much as de-traditionalization and end up as 'reflexivity losers', while Beverley Skeggs (2003) focuses on classed aspects of reflexivity, suggesting that the middle classes have more resources from which to fashion the self as project. While we would not question the existence of such inequalities, from our perspective a lack of understanding of the social formation of reflexivity and its role in the maintenance of ongoing sociality marks these feminist critiques as much as the modernity theorists themselves. In particular, the equation of reflexivity with choice, privilege and freedom from constraint misses the sociality and relationality that are absolutely fundamental to the reflexive self.

Certainly social divisions and inequalities impact on our reflexive processes and the resources available to us for self-construction; if the self is social it cannot be otherwise. However, if reflexivity is fundamental to social being, it would seem impossible to argue that subordinate or marginalized groups are lacking in reflexive capacities. Indeed, taking Mead's conceptualization of reflexive selfhood as requiring the ability to imagine oneself from the other's perspective and anticipate the other's responses to oneself, then subordinates often need to be highly reflexive. To take the paradigmatic case, the master rarely needs to worry about what the slave might think of him and how that might impact on his future lines of action; the slave, in order to survive, has to be acutely aware of what her master thinks of her and might require of her. The same could be said of the historic position of women within traditional, patriarchal heterosexual relationships. Even in the absence of pronounced inequality, in the supposedly more democratic conditions of modern heterosexual relationships, women's responsibility for the care of others, where anticipating others' wants and needs becomes the stuff of everyday life, may also contribute to a heightened relational reflexivity. If men's freedom from having to be concerned with the localized business of maintaining their own bodies and spaces (D. Smith 1988) frees them to engage in certain forms of self-reflexivity, women's responsibility for maintaining others' bodies and places *constrains* them into other forms of reflexivity. Thus we are led to a very different picture of women's reflexive selfhood – one that locates women not as lacking reflexivity but as highly reflexive social actors.

Likewise, those marginalized from the heterosexual mainstream are not, as some theorists (*pace* Butler 1993) would have it, 'abject' subjects without a location from which to construct a sense of self. For example, gay men in the era before decriminalization may well have been highly vulnerable, but they were not lacking in subjectivity as the concept of abjection would imply. Rather they were *discreditable* subjects (Goffman 1963a), required to be highly reflexive in their presentation of self and management of information. Or to take a more contemporary example, lesbians in South Korea literally lead double lives, adopting secret names in an underground community of their 'own', in Goffman's terms, where no one knows each other's 'real' names. Under two names they move between two communities, requiring a highly attuned reflexivity to manage the transition between their two selves and two lives (see Woo 2007; Jackson et al. 2008; see also Park-Kim et al. 2006).

Reflexivity cannot exist outside, exceed or transcend the social, but it is possible, and consistent with Mead's theorization, to conceive of differing forms of reflexivity and reflexive selfhood engendered by particular social conditions and produced from differing social locations. We may then be able to move towards thinking about the varied forms of sexual selfhood available to us in late modernity. It is therefore worth considering how Mead's conceptualization of reflexive selfhood relates to the forms of self deemed typical of late modernity and to begin to think critically about the extent to which the latter are intrinsically modern (see also Jackson 2007, 2010).

Varying conditions for reflexive selfhood

Mead's reflexive self, then, is not the historically specific modernist self but, as Giddens (1991) himself notes, is a basic requirement for social competence. However, since in everyday life we constantly relate to others, this 'basic' social competence may nonetheless require a high degree of self-awareness. For women within traditional heterosexual relations, where life revolves around the work of care, it is likely to engender a sense of self defined in relation to others. Moreover, the work of care often includes 'feeding egos and tending wounds' (Bartky 1990: 99). Within heterosexual relations and elsewhere, as Anna Jónasdóttir (1994: 13) says, women are situated 'as "empowerers" of social existence – for men'. When women give researchers accounts of the ways in which they accede to men's sexual demands, are wary of asserting their own sexual preferences, fake orgasms and do the sexual and emotional work of keeping the relationship together (Duncombe and Marsden 1993, 1996; Roberts et al. 1995; Langford 1999; Tolman 2002), they betray not a lack of reflexivity but a highly attuned reflexive responsiveness to others. Women use reflexive skills relationally to bolster the selves of others: the emotion work and practical work they do on and for men simultaneously feeds into men's reflexive self-making. Men's sense of sexual competence may, therefore, require women's work.

We are all, women and men, likely to engage in another kind of reflexivity, which entails standing outside oneself in order to engage in self-judgement, self-justification or to make claims about oneself or one's actions. This is most likely to happen when one has done something unexpected, 'wrong' or non-normative – which must, in ethnomethodological terms, be made 'accountable' or intelligible. Thus, for example, heterosexuals rarely ask themselves why or how they 'got that way', whereas a lesbian or gay man might be expected to give such an accounting, and can usually tell a story of 'becoming' or 'having always been' gay or lesbian (Whisman 1996). Similarly someone in a heterosexual monogamous couple is less likely to be required to account for remaining 'faithful', but may well be asked to give an explanation for having 'an affair'. When called upon to account for ourselves, we reflexively bring order to the fluid self in process, seeking to tell (to ourselves and to others) a more coherent story of the self. This 'fixing' of the self, while accomplished through a different form of reflexivity from that required for routine interaction, may be only momentary, contingent, or strategic, something prompted by immediate circumstances. Where such a story of self comes to be retold over time, connected to an avowed identity and a broader vision of biographical continuity, it becomes associated with more elaborated practices of the self, such as Giddens' (1991) self as project – for example, a 'coming out' story linked to a lesbian or gay identity.

A further form of reflexivity is that occasioned by something unexpected happening *to* us. It is worth noting that Mead did not consider that we are continually or always consciously self-reflexive: much everyday social action and interaction becomes relatively habitual or routinized (Warde 1997). When we are confronted with novel situations, according to Mead, heightened reflexivity comes into play and thus reflexivity increases where there is more opportunity of meeting novelty. This is more likely to occur under conditions of social and cultural diversity and/or rapid social change. Here his work resonates with the work of theorists of late modernity, for whom the 'de-routinization of the mundane' breaks down the habitual 'into a cloud of possibilities to be thought about and negotiated' (Beck and Beck-Gernsheim 2002: 6).[5] There is, however, a disjuncture between this notion of self and that of Mead. For Mead (1934), the self, and the reflexivity that makes it possible, anchored in sociality whereas the late modernity theorists envisage the self as cast adrift from traditional cultural expectations, from habitual taken-for-granted ways of being. This can underestimate the extent to which 'the discourses we reflexively use to maintain self identity, the language of self awareness, [are] ... bound by its cultural situatedness' (Adams 2003: 229). We may be, as Giddens says, individually responsible for making sense of our experience, or as Beck would have it, putting together a do-it-yourself biography, but in so doing we 'still rely on common cultural forms' (Adams 2003: 229); how we construct a sense of sexual self depends on the cultural scenarios available to us.

In this respect, the Foucauldians, as has been argued elsewhere (Jackson 2007), are closer to the pragmatists than are the modernity theorists in that they see contemporary self-fashioning as deriving from wider cultural discourses rather than individual choice. The rise of confessional culture (Foucault [1978] 1981), the emergence of the 'psy' professions (N. Rose 1989) and the prevalence of therapeutic ideas in popular culture all shape the ways in which it is possible to think of and tell about the self. From a pragmatist or interactionist perspective these influences would be seen as cultural resources on which we draw in making sense of ourselves and the world, rather than, in poststructuralist terms, discourses in which we are positioned. Nonetheless, from either perspective, the selves we can envisage, and be, are always historically and culturally located. We can now begin to consider the forms of sexual selfhood available in late modernity, considering what is enabled and constrained by wider social conditions.

Resources for sexual selfhood

The cultural scenarios available in contemporary society have, as a result of modernity, become more complex, varied and diverse – thus increasing the range of resources for sexual self-making. It is this which can be seen as offering more 'choice' and more opportunities for reflexivity – but these choices and opportunities are bounded by the cultural resources available to us, which help shape what is thinkable and possible. The relationship between cultural scenarios and individual lives, however, is by no means direct: it is mediated through interpersonal scripting and through the reflexive 'conversations with oneself' of intrapsychic scripting, both of which are affected by our social location and individual biographies. Cultural resources are not all equally available to everyone. Some are widely accessible to the population at large through popular cultural products such as chat shows, self-help books and women's magazines. Others are more restricted in circulation, perhaps to academic or politicized audiences – such as the discourses of psychoanalytic or queer theory – or to those who can afford to pay them for them, such as the middle-class utilization of various forms of alternative therapy. It may well also be the case that material inequalities in conditions of life enable some to make elaborated use of available cultural resources while constraining such opportunities for others. This is particularly evident where the cultural props for the maintenance of sexual lifestyles and selves are commodified. Thus Rosemary Hennessy (2000) suggests that affluent queer lifestyles are constructed at the expense of those to whom such opportunities are denied and whose labour may well produce the commodities that become part of the ambience of queer spaces; for example, the personal 'style' required for queer self-presentation may rest on the sweated labour of those in other countries who have little opportunity to choose sexual or other lifestyles.

The cultural resources circulating within late modern societies vary between those that might be seen as progressive, such as feminist or queer discourses, and those that are more conservative, for example, those deriving from evolutionary psychology or fundamentalist Christianity. While new ways of thinking about sexual matters have filtered into popular culture, they often become reshaped as they come up against other cultural discourses. So, for example, feminist arguments for women's sexual autonomy and challenges to the double standard of morality are reconstructed in so-called 'raunch culture' in which women behave in ways once seen as possible only for men – engaging in casual sex, watching strip-shows and so on. Such manifestations of 'equal-opportunities' sexuality were not what was imagined by feminists seeking to reshape the normative practices of heterosexuality.

More conservative ideas about sexuality, particularly those endorsing the 'naturalness' of sexual and gender divisions, maintain a much stronger hold on the popular imagination than do challenges to such biological essentialism. This is particularly evident not only in the case of sociobiology and evolutionary psychology, but also, in more subtle and less obvious ways, in psychoanalysis. These cultural resources enable forms of sexual self-understanding that naturalize desires and practices and inhibit more radical exploration of sexual possibilities. To the extent that these are drawn upon in self-construction, they may serve to reinforce understandings of the sexual self as fixed.[6] The pervasiveness of biological essentialism in popular culture needs to be acknowledged as a corrective to those over-optimistic views of late modern intimate relations undergoing a queering process (e.g. Roseneil 2000). While there are signs of greater fluidity and variability in sexual scripts, lifestyles and practices, faith in 'nature' persists, exemplified by the popularization of certain supposed scientific 'discoveries', such as those focusing on gay brains and genes or the behaviour of our hominid ancestors (see Fausto-Sterling 2000; Jackson and Rees 2007). Accounts of the 'naturalness' of sexuality may be, from a sociological perspective, deeply flawed but *as* sociologists we should recognize that they constitute part of the social reality of many of the population.

Among the most compelling stories of human sexuality in circulation in contemporary culture are those offered by evolutionary psychology and psychoanalysis. These stories differ in crucial respects: in the complexity of their explanations, the degree to which they rely on biological explanations and in the audiences to which they appeal. What they have in common, however, is that both ground truth claims in retrospective reconstructions of the past, in the former case, the evolutionary past of the species, and in the latter case, the biographical past of individuals.

Evolutionary psychology

Sociobiology and its more recent incarnation as evolutionary psychology pervade every aspect of popular culture, in particular television programmes on animal and human sexual lives and self-help books, and have thus filtered into some of the most widely available sources of sexual self-making (see Jackson and Rees 2007; McCaughey 2008). What distinguishes evolutionary psychology as a particular form of evolutionary explanation is its almost exclusive focus on sexual selection as opposed to natural selection more broadly. The effect of this is to reduce all of human social life to heterosexual 'mate selection' and reproduction. The reasoning behind this is that those traits from our prehistoric past which have survived into the modern gene pool were those that were adaptive in terms of maximizing opportunities to produce offspring. In the competitive race to reproduce and pass on our genes, it is argued, women and men have different investments. It is seen to be in men's interests to spread their sperm as widely as possible, while women seek a long-term mate to protect themselves and their infants (see e.g. Diamond 1997; Dawkins [1976] 2006). This is said to explain, for example, men's philandering, their attraction to very young women and the propensity to rape. Accounts of physical evolution – how we developed opposable thumbs, large brains and the ability to walk upright – are based on reconstructions of the past rooted in traces as left by fossil records. Evolutionary psychology, however, reconstructs our behavioural past without any such direct evidence. Rather, it bases 'scientific' claims on observations about current sexual practices and preferences, which are then deemed, by virtue of their existence today, to have been adaptive in the distant past and therefore to have become fixed in 'human nature'. While this is obviously tautological, the ways in which it is presented in popular culture establish a comforting narrative which gels with commonsense representations of primitive 'man' and supports our desire to understand from whence we came (Jackson and Rees 2007; McCaughey 2008).

Evolutionary psychology provides an explanation of male sexual inconstancy, incontinence and aggression, which its proponents claim is more scientific and accurate than any social scientific account. One infamous example is Thornhill and Palmer's (2000) analysis of rape, which sees rape as common across many species and the inevitable outcome of the male competition to impregnate as many women as possible. They dismiss feminist and sociological accounts of rape (which see it as an outcome of social inequality between women and men) as failing to understand the powerful, innate sexual motivations underlying it. This is not only wrong, according to Thornhill and Palmer (2000), but also dangerous. It is important to understand that they are not justifying rape; rather they see their work as offering an objective explanation of men's behaviour, which can offer better strategies for combating rape than what they see as the 'misguided' politically motivated accounts of feminists and sociologists.

More generally, evolutionary psychologists do not see themselves as justifying the status quo but as explaining it. The problem for us is that they take the status quo as given, inevitable and as the foundation for their theory.

What happens when such explanations are taken up within popular culture is that they then become rationalizations and justifications of certain aspects of male sexual conduct. McCaughey (2008) provides numerous examples of this taken from media aimed at male audiences, from self-help books to men's magazines. For example, readers of *Men's Health* were told that men of all ages prefer 'young girls' because 'we were designed to get them pregnant and dominate their fertile years by keeping them that way' and tells them that once their 'first wife has lost the overt signals of reproductive viability', they will look for someone younger who 'still has them all' (quoted in McCaughey 2008: 4). Meanwhile popular self-help books offer similar accounts, though some advise men to control their primeval instincts, such as Jeff Hood's *The Silverback Gorilla Syndrome* (1999), which encourages men to get in touch with their 'inner gorilla' or 'Big G', who approaches every social situation with one of two questions: 'Fuck it?' or 'Kill it?' (in McCaughey 2008: 79). Women are not left out of this story; another genre of popular texts warns them about men's unfortunate natural proclivities. They are told that 'the primitive nature of every man is the innate desire to *bed any woman* who even *marginally* turns him on' (Smith and Doe 1998: 93, emphases in original, quoted in McCaughey 2008: 68).

McCaughey (2008) suggests that these popular versions of the 'caveman mystique' have a particular appeal to men in the context of the increasing erosion of traditional bases of male power and offer an explanation that resonates with how they see themselves. Evolutionary accounts do not remain confined to media representations but become part of everyday life, as 'images people have available to them in actionable scripts and narratives'. Drawing on Bourdieu's concept of habitus, she suggests that 'evolutionary narratives offer men a way to embody male sexuality' (McCaughey 2008: 66). In a sense this relates back to our own theoretical explanation where we suggest that cultural scenarios have consequences for everyday life in so far as they filter into interpersonal scripting and inform the reflexive intrapsychic processes through which we understand ourselves:

> [S]uch explanations, when offered by scientists, are part of the intersubjective cultural scenarios about sex that are current in the society, and such explanations when made by individuals are part of the 'why' of intrapsychic (what we say to ourselves) and interpersonal (what we say to others) sexual scripts.
>
> (Laumann and Gagnon 1995: 188)[7]

Thus evolutionary psychology has become a resource for sexual self-making, which may have particular appeal to men. It is, however, a totalizing and universalizing account of how men are, which allows for very little variability among them, minimal complexity in their motivations and limited opportunity for social change except to the degree that men can control their 'primitive biological urges'. In reducing male conduct to the urge to reproduce, the possibility of non-sexual motives for sex are ignored and the crucial distinction between sexual desire and the desire for sex disappears. This has potentially ironic consequences: a man who believes in his inner caveman may feel compelled to have sex to prove that he is a man. Rather than actually being motivated by an unstoppable urge, he is motivated by his belief in it. Thus we have the potential for the social construction of a supposedly evolved innate drive at the level of individual male subjectivity. Such is the expectation that men will always be eager for sex and 'forever functional' (Marshall and Katz 2002) throughout their lives that there is an immense market for the products of the pharmaceutical industry which seem to make this possible.

Psychoanalysis

Whereas evolutionary psychology represents a cultural scenario widely disseminated throughout Western popular culture, psychoanalytic narratives have a more limited audience. Certain psychoanalytic concepts such as drives, repression and Freudian slips may have become common currency in a diluted form, but the mobilization of psychoanalysis as a resource for telling stories of the self requires a degree of cultural capital, usually available only to highly educated people, and/or the economic capital to pay for the services of an analyst. Academic feminists constitute one section of the community which has the ability to draw on this particular resource in making sense of their sexuality. This has resulted in the production of accounts that give us access to their use of psychoanalysis in accounting for their own experiences – as well as their use of psychoanalytic theory to explain the sexuality of others.

The British feminists to whom psychoanalysis has particular appeal are, in the main, those who had affiliated with Marxist feminism during the late 1960s and the 1970s, and grappled with its limitations in relation to accounts of subjectivity and sexuality. As we explained in Chapter 2, these were the feminists who turned to structuralist and poststructuralist thought, including psychoanalysis, as a means of remedying Marxism's shortcomings. Not only was a political and theoretical trajectory being followed here, but also psychoanalysis was utilized in order to explain their personal experience, suggesting that it had considerable resonance for them. We suggest that the tendency to draw upon this narrative is related to the intersection between one's biography and one's location within a particular cultural, political and economic nexus. While we belong to this generation of feminists, and indeed were both engaged in Left politics, we have never found psychoanalysis to be in tune with our own biographies and subjectivities. Psychoanalysis is only one of the available resources on which it is possible to draw in constructing an account of ones sexual self and is not one that has universal appeal.

We can illustrate this with reference to the distance between our own understanding of heterosexual pleasure and that of one of the leading exponents of 'psychosocial' approaches to subjectivity, Wendy Hollway (see, e.g. Hollway and Jefferson 2000; Hollway 2006). In the context of the 1990s debates on heterosexuality, Hollway wrote a spirited and courageous defence of heterosex, explicitly informed by a psychoanalytic understanding of her own desires and pleasures. She talks of penetrative sex as signifying closeness because it 'breaches the separation from the other' and 'can allow early infantile desires for connectedness to be expressed and find temporary gratification' (Hollway 1993: 414). She talks of feeling 'safe, protected and loved' when wrapped in her lover's 'strong arms', which compensates for the pain of giving up the protection of 'parental arms'. The signifiers of this quest to return to the protection of intimacy, however, are gendered – she suggests the parallel for her partner is represented by her 'cradling breasts' (Hollway 1993: 414). Maternal breasts occupy a central place in the Kleinian framework on which Hollway draws, leading her to speculate that lesbians may 'get pleasure from what heterosexual women give up or displace: the chance of "having" another's breast as well as "being" that breast for another' (Hollway 1993: 415). While we appreciate that feelings of closeness and affection are often part of everyday interaction in sexual relationships, and a source of pleasure, we do not see that there is any need for recourse to psychoanalysis in order to account for this. Hollway's evocation of maternal breasts and parental protection as erotic has no such resonance for us. The erotic is a matter of definition and how such definitions are made depends on the specific scripts, discourses and scenarios on which we draw.

One of the key ways in which psychoanalysis is used is in the reconstruction of childhood experiences. An example is provided by Valerie Walkerdine (1990), who gives us access not only to a representation of her childhood, but also to a reconstruction actually achieved through psychoanalysis. In a piece written before she became so committed to psychoanalytic explanations, she writes of coming to terms with her ordinary childhood and suggests that 'caught in the threads of that ordinary life is the basis for understanding what my subjectivity might be about' (Walkerdine 1990: 162). She discusses the shift between herself as a delicate small child photographed when dressed as a bluebell fairy and photographs of her taken later, after she had gained weight. In a later essay she returns to the same memories and talks about her preference for the 'bluebell fairy' over the older 'fat child' and says that it is 'the mark of a set of moves made therapeutically' (Walkerdine 1990: 147–148) that she no longer found it necessary to hold on to the former image. She attributes her previous refusal to confront the fat image to the repression of aspects of herself she did not want to confront:

> Covered over, I suggest, was the fantasy of the angry child actively shouting out loud crying and screaming; the all consuming rapacious woman with a large (sexual) appetite.
>
> (Walkerdine 1990: 153)

In attributing unconscious motivations linked to fear of emerging sexuality to the fat child of her memories and family photographs, Walkerdine is clearly reconstructing the past to fit a psychoanalytically informed present. What is mentioned only in passing in this account is the 'active sexual and desiring adolescent' (Walkerdine 1990: 154). This is what William Simon (1996: 59ff.) refers to as the 'unremembered youth' of psychoanalysis. Psychoanalysis tends to project everything sexually significant in our subjectivities back onto childhood, thus avoiding the messy experimental stage when we do start to explore our own sexualities. This, Simon argues, relates to a curious absence of accounts of actual sexual practices in psychoanalytic writings in general and in Freud's work in particular, 'a nervous averting of attention from concrete details' (Simon 1996: 63). Thus while psychoanalysis does offer a resource for understanding sexual subjectivities, it seems to us an inadequate one, which fails to account for what actually happens to us sexually in the context of sexual practice.

Conclusion

Retrospective reinterpretations of the past – whether on an evolutionary or biographical timescale – cannot, we would argue, offer us the 'truth' of our sexualities. Instead such reconstructions should be understood as part of our active, reflexive sense-making, revealing the ways on which we draw on cultural resources to construct our sexual selves. Unlike psychoanalysis and evolutionary psychology, the interactionist account of sexuality and the pragmatist conception of self do not give us ready explanations of who we are or how we came to be as we are. What we are offering here is not a closed explanatory framework but rather a means of exploring, in a far more open way, how our sense of sexual selfhood is constituted through both biographical experience and our reflection back on that experience.

The idea of reflexive selfhood locates the self as always social and continually evolving as a result of its embeddedness in interactions with others within a wider social and cultural context. It therefore allows for historical, cultural and contextual variability in forms of sexual selfhood and the possibility of change. It might be objected that Mead's view of the self as reflexive and therefore cognitive (Mead 1934: 173) does not sit well with the complex emotions and inherent physicality of sexuality. He does not, however, dismiss emotions: rather he is suggesting that emotions cannot be called forth in response to other's reactions to us without the reflexive capacities entailed in having a self. Moreover, throughout *Mind, Self and Society* there are constant references to the body and to the ways in which reflexivity enables us to make sense of embodied experience. In Chapter 7 we will explore the embodied character of sexuality further, arguing that an interactionist perspective provides valuable tools for understanding the physicality of sexuality.

Notes

1. These included John Dewey and William James as well as Mead himself. Mead was influenced by both Dewey and James, the former in particular being influential in establishing his career. Of the pragmatists, Mead was the one whose thinking was most sociological.
2. Mead actually uses the words 'reflexive' and 'reflexiveness' only occasionally, but 'the turning back of the experience of the individual upon himself [*sic*]' (Mead 1934: 134), along with the idea that the self is both subject and object to itself are fundamental to his conception of mind, self and society.
3. The past does not always figure in Mead's work in terms of this symbolic reconstruction, but in other senses too. In his exegesis on Mead's (1929) essay on 'The Nature of the Past', David Maines (2001) distinguishes between the 'symbolically reconstructed past', 'the social structural past' (which provides the conditions of emergence for the present) and the 'implied objective past' (what is inferred to have happened for the present state of affairs to exist).
4. There are differences between Giddens and Beck and Beck-Gernsheim, particularly in relation to gender and sexual relations as well as their conceptualization of reflexivity and choice. To explore these, however, would take us away from our central argument. What is more important here is the ways in which they view the reflexive project of the self (Giddens) or the 'do-it-yourself biography' (Beck and Beck-Gernsheim) as products of late modern conditions in which we are freed from normative constraint and the constraining family and community ties.
5. Note that some of those associated with the early pragmatists also saw increased choice as an effect of modernization. For example, Cooley (1902) conceptualized choice as a river getting ever wider as it passes through history, requiring stronger and stronger swimming to survive.
6. Paradoxically, reflexivity, though fundamentally an ongoing process, can produce an understanding of self as fixed whether by our common evolutionary heritage or by the traumas each of us is said to experience in infancy. Such self-understandings, however, can nonetheless be seen as provisional in so far as they are always subject to modification through interaction and through new experiences.
7. Laumann and Gagnon (1995) make this point about a rather different form of scientific explanation, which relies on notions of 'drives' and 'instincts', but it is equally applicable to evolutionary psychology or any other form of biological explanation.

CHAPTER 7

EMBODIED PRACTICES AND SEXUAL PLEASURE

Sexuality is self-evidently embodied: 'having sex' obviously entails socially located bodies in interaction. Yet there is still surprisingly little sociological work on the bodily aspects of sexuality. Calls continue to be made for greater attention to be given to the lived, fleshy experience of embodiment, but these are more easily made than answered (see Morgan and Scott 1993). Within sociology on the one hand we have theories of the body and of the social construction of sexuality, which say little about embodied sexual practices, and on the other we have statistical data on who does what with whom and how often, but which tell us nothing about the processes involved. While some qualitative research attends to embodied experience and practice, elsewhere, amid ever more abstract theorizations of the body, embodied social actors disappear altogether.

In this chapter we consider how, as feminist sociologists, we might conceptualize the body as socially constructed without treating it as an abstraction floating free of the actualities of lived experience. In so doing we will argue that the interactionist approach that we have foregrounded throughout this book can offer a corrective to the rather abstract, asocial theorizations of the body deriving from corporeal feminisms, enabling us to 'embody gender without overwhelming the "sociality" of gender by "corporeality"' (Witz 2000: 7). It also provides an alternative to the over-reliance on the unconscious in feminist psychoanalytic approaches. Utilizing interactionism facilitates a conceptualization of sexual experience as socially mediated, and embodied sexual selves as reflexively constructed and reconstructed. In focusing, later in the chapter, on sexual pleasure we consider how desire and pleasure may be reflexively understood in the context of everyday/everynight sexual practices.[1] Taking orgasm as a paradigmatic case, we will argue that even this most individual, 'private', 'physical' experience is always also social, highlighting the gendering of orgasm within heterosexual practice.

In taking up this issue we recognize that there is a concern that, in giving attention to fleshy, sensate bodies, we will fall back into essentialism or even biologism, as if the only language we have to talk about actual, specific bodies is that of anatomy. Yet as sociologists we know, in other contexts, that experience is never simply given, but is interpreted, theorized and mediated through the meanings which are culturally available to us. Moreover, 'experiences' happen in social contexts and are made meaningful through social interactions within particular social locations. An adequate theorization of the body, then, should pay attention to bodies in interaction and bodies as socially located.

When sociologists began to attend to 'the body', this interest was in part motivated by a need to counter disembodied conceptualizations of social actors. There was a realization that social interaction is facilitated by bodily negotiations, that we recognize others through their bodies, that we categorize them by age, gender, ethnicity and class at least in part through bodily attributes, that this recognition itself requires a set of cultural competences through which we read the significance of appearance, dress, demeanour and deportment. These basic insights are well worth hanging on to, alongside the immense contribution that feminists have made to theorizing the body and to politicizing embodied social encounters.

The body has figured in feminist work, at least implicitly, since the beginning of the second wave. Feminists have challenged the reduction of women to their bodies associated with the historical equation of women with the body and men with the mind. We have critiqued and resisted sexual and medical objectification and all modes of thinking that naturalized women's subordination. Central to this has been the theorization of gender and sexual difference, which has given rise to recent debates between those seeking to find new ways of exploring women's embodied specificity and those who refuse to contemplate any account that risks reducing women's social being to pre-given bodily attributes or experiences. Alongside these theoretical preoccupations there have been activist campaigns calling for women's bodily self-determination, promoting reproductive rights and resisting male violence. Where theorists often seems to discuss bodies without any reference to the women whose bodies they are, activists have always kept actual embodied women in view.

The body has had a chequered history within sociological and feminist theory. An earlier language of social action and social actors made it possible to think of embodied individuals moving through time and space. Later Foucault had considerable influence on the study of the body, but his focus on governance and surveillance de-emphasized individual agency except in so far as it was engaged in resistance. Poststructuralism, postmodernism and much recent feminist and cultural theory have shifted attention away from an engagement with action and practice, indeed away from sociologically grounded theory in general and towards more philosophical conceptualizations of the body. Where context was central to early sociological theorizations of sexuality, now it is often lost sight of in favour of free-floating desire or sexual acts. It seems that the more we focus on the body, the more we lose sight of the context, and when the context comes into focus the body fades from view.

Sociological beginnings and feminist challenges

There are, and have long been, traditions in sociology, in particular interactionism and phenomenology, which do, implicitly at least, deal with embodied social actors. This is evident, for example, in Gagnon and Simon's (1974) emphasis on sexual *conduct* (see Chapter 1) and in Garfinkel's (1967) analysis of the embodied strategies used by the transsexual Agnes in order to pass as female. The best-known interactionist contribution to the sociology of the body is that of Goffman, whose acutely observed analyses of everyday social practices paid close attention to bodily interaction, including occasionally to gendered embodiment (Goffman 1979). Most of Goffman's work focused on the ways in which embodied actors positioned themselves in lifts or on buses, the bodily signals required by civil inattention, the deportment, deployment and adornment of bodies required for appropriate presentations of self and so on (see e.g. Goffman 1963b, 1969, 1971). Yet while embodied actors are ever present on Goffman's social stage, he was always concerned more with bodily action and performance than with the sensual, visceral body (just as he was concerned far more with the performative manifestations of self-reflexivity rather than the ongoing inner process of reflexive self-construction).

Giddens (1991) takes up and develops much of this and his greater emphasis on reflexivity and on bodies in time and space at first sight appears to offer a deeper understanding of embodied sociality. Yet the body still seems somehow separable from the self, it is monitored through reflexive self-construction but not fully part of the reflexive self.[2]

> The reflexivity of the self ... pervasively affects the body as well as psychic processes. The body is less and less an extrinsic 'given', functioning outside the internally referential systems of modernity, but becomes itself reflexively mobilized. What might appear as a wholesale movement towards the narcissistic cultivation of bodily appearance is in fact an expression of a concern lying much deeper actively to 'construct' and control the body.
>
> (Giddens 1991: 7)

Here the body is not so much a part of the reflexive project of the self as an object of that project, something to be worked upon. This conceptualization of embodiment perpetuates mind–body dualism in which the mind, or reflexive self, seeks to ' "construct" and control the body'. While rendering the body socially meaningful, Giddens' perspective still implicitly posits a pre-social body, rather like the drive reduction model of sexuality, which is constrained and modified by external social factors. Yet, conversely, Giddens also neglects the fleshy and sensual aspects of the body in favour of a more cognitively and reflexively managed body. This, it has been suggested, is an obstacle to the development of a fully embodied sociology. According to Shilling and Mellor (1996: 7), Giddens 'views people as, essentially, minds who happen to occupy bodies'. However, we do not share their diagnosis of the problem: that Giddens ignores 'embodied dispositions which lie beneath the reach of thought and reflexive control', nor their view that the sensual can somehow escape the social or lead people to reject it. Not only are we wary of looking to the unconscious every time we encounter something that is difficult to conceptualize within existing social theory, but also, as feminists, we are very aware of the dangers of positing sensual urges which prompt people to overturn social convention: think of the male mythology of uncontrollable desire and how it has been deployed in justifying rape.

Feminists have always been concerned to oppose the reduction of women to their bodies and the construction of women through the male gaze. One of the most fundamental challenges, at a theoretical level, was to the assumption that physical bodily differences between women and men could be taken as given. A great deal of debate has centred around the terms gender, sex and sexuality in an effort to wrest them away from the realm of biology. While there is a tradition of valorizing women's embodied specificity (Gatens 1982; Irigaray 1985; Braidotti 1994), what is more important from our own perspective is the more radical challenge to the idea that bodily differences are meaningful in themselves. One of the earliest contributions was that of Kessler and McKenna (1978). Building on Garfinkel's (1967) ethnomethodological study of Agnes, they unpicked the taken-for-granted assumption of men and women as biological categories, arguing that genitals are not meaningful in themselves but are culturally produced in the everyday doing of gender attribution, which entails a variety of cultural competences and complex interpretational processes (see also West and Zimmerman 1987; Fenstermaker and West 2002). In other words, what we take to be a self-evident, obvious, difference between women and men depends on socially meaningful gender categories that enable us to see genitals as signifying a social difference. Writing from a rather different, materialist feminist, perspective, Christine Delphy (1984) argued that sex 'has become a pertinent fact, hence a perceived category, because of the existence of gender'. Hence gender creates anatomical sex in that it 'transforms an anatomical difference (which is itself devoid of social implications) into a relevant distinction for social practice' (Delphy 1984: 144).

Somewhat later Judith Butler (1990a: 7) was to write: 'This construct called "sex" is as culturally constructed as gender; indeed, perhaps it was always already gender.' Echoing, though not acknowledging, earlier ethnomethodological insights, Butler questions the binary distinction between male and female, the assumption, as Garfinkel (1967) had put it, that there are two sexes and only two sexes. Like the ethnomethodologists Butler does not see the body as intelligible without the cultural construction of gender: 'Bodies cannot be said to have a signifiable existence prior to the mark of their gender' (Butler 1990a: 8). In *Gender Trouble* (1990a) gender is seen as performative in the sense that bodies become gendered through the continual performance of gender. Hence gender, rather than being part of our inner essence, is performative; to be feminine is to perform femininity, again resonating with Goffman (1969, 1979) and Garfinkel (1967). In *Bodies that Matter* (1993), Butler's approach shifts to linguistic performativity, to those forms of speech which, by their utterance, bring what they name into being. Performativity is effective because it is 'citational': it entails citing past practices, referring to existing conventions, reiterating known norms. In this sense the pronouncement 'It's a girl', made at an infant's birth, begins the process, as Butler puts it, of 'girling the girl' and 'this founding interpellation' is repeatedly reiterated (Butler 1993: 7–8). Sex is materialized, according to Butler, through a complex of such citational practices, which are both normative and regulative – and hence coercive and constraining (if never totally effective). In many respects what she is describing is what Kessler and McKenna (1978) called gender attribution.

Butler is sometimes seen as producing an overly abstract, disembodied theorization, but she is far less guilty of this than many others, since she does discuss the practices through which bodies are gendered. She also challenges those who misread her as implying that gender is something superficial and easily changed. She is not saying that gender is something you 'put on' in the morning and discard at will (see Butler 1993: x), but she is saying that the materiality of bodies is not given. For Butler materiality is an effect of power: sexed bodies are forcibly materialized through time. We share Butler's scepticism about any pre-given bodily materiality, and would agree that bodily materiality is in some sense produced through social and cultural processes. However, Butler's conceptualization of the process whereby gendered bodies are materialized is framed from within philosophical rather than sociological preoccupations. As a result, she misses what we would see as crucial elements of the *social* construction of gendered bodies. She reaches towards some notion of a socially ordered world in her deployment of the idea of the normative, even more evident in her more recent work (see Chapter 1), where 'the norm' is seen, rather as in sociologies of social structure, as external and constraining (cf. Dawe 1970), as having 'a status and effect that is independent of the actions governed by the norm' (Butler 2004: 42). She also notes that a norm 'renders the social field intelligible' (Butler 2004: 42). What she does not say is where such norms come from or how that intelligibility is produced through everyday interaction and social practice, enabling us to make sense of gendered bodies (see Chapter 4).

Although sexuality appears to be central to Butler's work, she devotes surprisingly little attention to it, focusing primarily on the normativity of heterosexuality. While she has a great deal to say about bodily practices that could potentially subvert gender, she says little about sexual practices: the sexual, erotic body is strangely silent in her work, discussed only in abstract, psychoanalytically grounded, theorizations of 'desire', which bear little relation to the actual, socially located embodied individuals who, in the everyday/everynight world, engage in sexual acts. Yet Butler does, at least, allow for social processes in the production of gendered and sexual bodies – which is more than can be said of some other theorizations drawing on psychoanalytic and Foucauldian traditions. This absence of the social is particularly evident in feminist theorizing that appropriates Foucault's sex/sexuality formulation rather than the concept of gender (see Chapter 1).

Elizabeth Grosz (1995a), for example, defines 'sex' as referring 'to the domain of sexual difference, to questions of the *morphologies of bodies*' (emphasis in original) as distinct from sexuality – erotic desires, pleasures and practices. She maintains that the term 'gender' is redundant because everything it designates is 'covered by the integration of and sometimes the discord between sexuality and sex' (Grosz 1995a: 213). Grosz's line of argument risks conflating social differences between women and men with bodily difference. This, as Anne Witz (2000: 8) points out, bequeaths us an impoverished concept of gender from which the social disappears.[3] A more sociologically informed analysis, as Witz goes on to elaborate, allows us to understand gender not as 'variations on the theme of "sex" but as a complex set of social relations which *defy* reduction to "sex", whether this is defined in naturalistic or social constructionist terms' (Witz 2000: 9, emphasis in original).[4] We feel it is important to retain a term capable of designating more than bodily sex differences and which is able to encompass the wider socially ordered character of male–female relations such as gendered divisions of labour. Such aspects of gender are not particularly relevant to the intellectual project of theorists such as Grosz and may, indeed, seem distant from bodies and sexuality. We, however, would wish to emphasize that all interaction is embodied *and* gendered and that sexual relations always occur within a nexus of wider social relations. This is particularly important in understanding the asymmetries and inequalities entailed in heterosexual sexual relations (Jackson and Scott 2004; Jackson 2006a).

The conflation and slippage between gender and sexuality, arising from appropriations of Foucault and also from psychoanalytic thought, pose another potential problem for feminist conceptualizations of the body.

Where women are concerned, the gendered body is often read as a sexual body, even by some feminists (see e.g. Coward 1984; McRobbie 1996). We should, however differentiate between the sexualization of women's bodies and women's own sexual desires, sensations and practices. A sexualized feminine body is a body disciplined into a sexually 'attractive' appearance and demeanour; this performance of sexual desirability is sometimes equated with 'female sexuality', which is thus reduced to 'the look' (Coward 1984). Sexualized femininity, however, may have little or nothing to do with autonomous desires and the practice of pleasure. We cannot read women's sexuality from how they look; we do not simply wear our sexuality on our sleeves or anywhere else. That feminists such as Coward (1984) and McRobbie (1996) can equate a performance of desirability and availability (clothes, make-up, styles of dancing, etc.) with 'female sexuality' and, in the case of McRobbie, see this as an assertion of sexual autonomy is surprising given that this is a very conventional and objectifying conceptualization of femininity.[5] A bodily performance that is readable as 'sexy' is not necessarily subjectively experienced as sexual.

Bodies are not meaningful in themselves: all of us are embodied within social contexts, which profoundly affect how we experience our own and others' bodies. Sexuality and sexual activity are very much about living bodies, what we do with them, what we feel through them, but are not just about bodies. In discussing the body, especially in relation to sexuality, it is very easy to forget that we are not just bodies, that the 'we' who inhabit these bodies are not reducible to the body. We must be wary of representing the body as uninhabited, of discussing embodied practices as if bodies existed without people. To borrow from Bryan Turner,[6] it would be ridiculous to say 'last night my body was in bed with my lover's body'; if we experience sex as involving only our bodies, this suggests a degree of distancing from the activity indicative of at best disinterest and at worst trauma. Sex entails embodied selves engaged in embodied social activity and embodied interaction. Here, as elsewhere, the body is inseparable from the totality of the self. If we forget this, foregrounding the body does not challenge body–mind dualism, but actually reinstates it. Moreover, this can be politically dangerous. If, for example, we speak of sexual violence as violence against 'women's bodies', it is as if the women themselves escape the consequences, thus negating their experience of an attack on their person and depoliticizing violence against women (qua women) (see Kappeler 1995).

Abstracting the body from the social can give the impression of a body with a life of its own and lead to a neglect of the everyday relations in which embodied individuals participate. Numerous critics of Foucault have noted a residual essentialism of the body in his work, especially in the first volume of *The History of Sexuality* (1978). Although Foucault is committed to the idea that the body is produced through discursive practices rather than given by nature, he nonetheless sees 'bodies and pleasures' as sites of resistance to power. Since sexuality is constituted through power, sexual desire and agency cannot escape power, yet bodies and pleasures become the touchstone of resistance, as if they lie outside the social (Fraser 1989). This gives rise to extravagant libertarian claims, in particular the idea that transgressive bodily acts are in themselves subversive and progressive (see e.g. Halperin 1995: 88ff.). The emphasis on bodies and pleasures can obscure forms of power other than those operating through the discursive constitution of sexuality. The classic example of this in Foucault's own work is the infamous passage where he characterizes an episode of what we would now see as child abuse as 'inconsequential bucolic pleasures' (Foucault 1981: 31; for a critique, see Plaza 1996). In today's world, the problem is manifested in an unwillingness, in some quarters, to acknowledge the pervasiveness and ubiquity of power within consensual heterosexual relations.

Lynn Segal's (1994) treatment of heterosexual pleasure, which we discussed in Chapter 4, exemplifies this problem in claiming that heterosex can threaten gender polarity. She goes on to say: 'In consensual sex, when bodies meet, the epiphany of that meeting – its threat and excitement – is surely that all the great dichotomies (activity/passivity, subject/object, heterosexual/homosexual) slide away' (Segal 1997: 86). It is as if these bodies are disconnected from the social locations and past biographies of those who inhabit them. We are less confident than Segal that vulnerability and loss of control, which both men and women may experience when in the throes of sexual passion, can transform gender relations. From our perspective embodied sexual sensations and practices cannot be understood as outside the social, interactional context in which they take place.

Sexual embodiment as social embodiment

If we understand sexual relations as social relations, then this necessitates thinking about the varied ways in which bodies and embodiment might figure in sexual encounters. First, the body can be an object of desire or of another's sexual acts; second, the embodied self is capable of sensual awareness of another – this is a self who sees, smells, touches; third, the embodied self also has the capacity to feel the emotions and sensations associated with erotic desire and sensual pleasure. The body in the first sense, the sexualized body, is often a passive body, looked at or acted upon. A sexual body implies more: a body in the second and third senses is a body both active and feeling. In all of these three senses a body can never be *just* a body abstracted from mind, self and social context.

In making these distinctions we are drawing on Gesa Lindemann's (1997) categories: the objectified, experiencing and experienced body. We rework these categories as objectified, sensory and sensate embodiment in order to emphasize social embodiment as process rather than structure in which the reflexive capacities of the self are implicated (Mead 1934). This facilitates a more nuanced understanding of the sociality of the body. Objectified embodiment refers to bodies as perceptible entities in physical and social space. In terms of sexuality this does not mean seeing bodies as sexual objects; rather it is to recognize that bodies can be perceived as objects of desire and can also be acted upon sexually. Sensory embodiment is the capacity to experience our surroundings through sight, hearing, taste, touch, which, in sexual terms, enables us to perceive another's embodiment as erotic. Sensate embodiment is the means through which we feel pleasure and pain, and more broadly experience our bodies as a part of our being – and, of course, a heightened awareness of our capacity to feel emotion and sensation is part of what defines a social situation as potentially sexual. Sensory and sensate embodiment together, therefore, constitute what might be called lived or experiential embodiment (cf. Williams and Bendelow 1998). Embodiment in all three senses has a physical materiality (a body will bleed when it is cut and can be seen to bleed and an embodied individual feels the pain of the wound and experiences that pain as her own), but embodiment is not simply a physical given: each aspect of it is always already social and intermeshed in complex relations of reciprocal effectivity with each other aspect.

Objectified embodiment, though materially 'there' in physical and social space, is not simply a natural state, but one marked by social place and history, coded by gender, class, context and happenstance rendering an embodied manifestation recognizable as a particular person or a member of a particular social category (e.g. as a man or a woman). As Nick Crossley notes, bodies 'are classified from birth and even before' and 'this process of categorization ... effects a "social magic"' (Crossley 2001: 151). This 'marking' of bodies is not simply symbolic – investing them with signifiers of, for example, class, gender and ethnicity – but also material in that social location and biographical events leave physical traces on bodies (e.g. effects of diet, environment, physical and emotional labour: Morgan and Scott 1993) as well as endowing us with a particular bodily hexis (Bourdieu 1992).

> As embodied beings we are 'reversible'. We not only perceive but are perceived: we can be seen, touched, heard, smelled and tasted. And, as a consequence, we can be classified according to our perceptible qualities, or at least according to those perceptible qualities deemed salient within the forms of classification that have been constructed historically within our societies.
>
> (Crossley 2001: 150–151)

This categorization and the recognition on which it is based are themselves a social act, an act of decoding that enables us to 'see' a particular body as someone we know or as classed raced, or gendered. Furthermore, our bodies can be objects to ourselves, which enables each person not only to see her/his body as object, but also to imagine how it is seen by another and envisage engagement with the embodied actions of others. Such self-reflexivity is a central premise of interactionism deriving from Mead (1934).

Here we are moving on to the second sense of embodiment, sensory embodiment, the capacity for sensory perception. But we do not perceive by physical sense alone: the work of perception is accomplished by an embodied *self*, someone who not only has 'sense organs' but also is capable of active, reflexive *sense-making* by virtue of her social being, social location and personal biography. For example, think of what is required to enable sensual perception of another as a lover. To 'see' another's (objectified) body as sexual requires interpretive work – even the simple identification of another as of a gender appropriate to our preferences is, as ethnomethodologists have demonstrated, a practical accomplishment (Garfinkel 1967; West and Zimmerman 1987). Further, to read another's body as desirable necessitates the mobilization of appropriate scripts and an ability to locate ourselves and the other within them (Gagnon and Simon 1974).

Finally, embodiment in our third sense, sensate embodiment, does not just produce sensations ready to be 'felt'; we interpret them and in so doing give them meaning. 'Feeling' requires a reflexive engagement with our own embodied state – whether immediate and conscious sense-making or a habitual recognition based on past experience. As Mead puts it, 'unordered sensuous content' only 'becomes experience when it is placed within the forms of understanding' (Mead 1964: 530); only then does it enter into the self's 'heritage of experience' (Mead 1934: 172). To feel desire and pleasure requires not just a sensate body, a body physically able to feel, but an embodied decoding of sensation (being caressed) and internal states (bodily signifiers of arousal) as sexually significant: 'the sources of arousal, passion or excitement (the recognition of a sexual possibility) ... derive from a complicated set of layered symbolic meanings' (Gagnon and Simon 1974: 23).

While objectified, sensory and sensate embodiment may be distinguished from each other analytically, in everyday sexual life they are inextricably intertwined and even more deeply embedded in the social. Objectified embodiment, while it is the mode through which we identify and experience bodies as having facticity, does not imply that bodies are simply there to be defined as sexual: how they are sexualized (for example, divided into erogenous zones) may well affect how bodily acts and sensations are perceived, ordered and experienced in the progress of a sexual encounter: which body parts are brought into play, which stimuli are interpreted as pleasure. Similarly the sexual experiences we have may then act back upon the way objectified embodiment is perceived. Thus, for instance, a woman's first sexual encounter with the penis may reorder her perception of the male body. Sensory and sensate embodiment – bodily sensual perception and feelings – are particularly closely linked through our lived embodiment. We can explore and thus experience another's body through our senses – sight, smell, touch while at the same time experiencing (feeling) sexual sensation in our own bodies. Thus the physical contact of sex involves, simultaneously, the sensory act of touching another's body and the sensate feeling of both our own touch and that of our lover/other. What makes this recognizable as erotic is first, as we have already indicated, each individual's understanding of embodied experience, and second, the interaction itself. Sexual interaction creates a potentially shared sense of erotic meaning,[7] a sense of a particular configuration of interacting bodies as erotic and thus the possibility of another level of reflexively embodied sexual meaning.

While this reflexive interplay is crucial to understanding our own experiences of the sexual and how they become felt and embodied, we must always be wary of presupposing these links when observing others' bodies. We cannot simply read off properties of another's lived (sensory and sensate) embodiment from their objectified embodiment, deduce what another person is feeling from the body we see e.g., an erect penis is conventionally read as an unproblematic signifier of male desire, but it may not have such meaning to the man experiencing it. A woman might be perceived as 'sexy', read as sexual, when she is not feeling sexual at all (Jackson and Scott 2001a); she may consciously project herself as sexy without feeling desire (Tolman 2002).

The view of embodiment being advanced here does not deny the physical materiality of bodies; rather it emphasizes that bodies are not meaningful in themselves. All of us are embodied within social contexts, which profoundly affect how we experience our own and others' bodies. Interpreting other bodies as sexual requires a set of culturally acquired competencies as does experiencing our own lived bodies as sexual. When we engage in sex with another person it is not about abstract bodies meeting in asocial space, but embodied social beings interacting in a social context, bringing with them a good deal of cultural and biographical baggage.

Pre-social and supra-social fictions

That sexuality is not a natural phenomenon has become almost axiomatic within critical academic thought, if not always in commonsense thinking. Sociologists have become used to contesting biological forms of essentialism, where sexuality is seen as an inherent property of the human organism and bodily sexual gratification as driven by biological imperatives. Here sexuality is conceptualized as *pre*-social, capable of modification by social mores but nonetheless as essentially prior to the social. Yet alongside this, there are other commonsense understandings of sexuality, whereby it is invested with magical, mystical and romantic properties, associated with ideas of transcendence, the belief that it can somehow raise us above the mundane realities of our quotidian existence. Sexuality becomes, in this sense, *supra*-social, beyond the social. In everyday terms these two frequently overlap, so that sex can paradoxically be seen both as an expression of humanity's animal nature and a means by which individuals can discover transcendental 'truths' about themselves.

Within social and cultural theory, pre-social conceptualizations of the sexual are routinely dismissed as essentialist. Supra-social imagery, however, is less easily contested. There are forms of theory that lend themselves to a view of desire itself as outside the social, as resistant to, and potentially subversive of, the social ordering of sexuality. For example in Lacanian psychoanalysis, desire, figured as a consequence of lack, is irreducible to need, in that it cannot be easily satisfied (see Rose 1982). In recent years Deleuzian thinking has to some extent displaced this notion with a reconceptualization of desire as 'positive, and associated with transformative production and experimentation' (Potts 2004: 18). Those who draw on such perspectives are by no means essentialists and are poles apart from those who view desire as a product of biological imperatives; rather, desire is here envisaged as in excess of the functional requirements of bodily and species needs and irreducible to physiological processes. It is in this idea of desire as potentially uncontainable by normative sexuality that we detect a *supra*-social imaginary that risks abstracting desire from both physical and social location. For Elizabeth Grosz (1995b), for example, desire is far more than an interaction between lovers or an exchange of physical intimacies:

> Erotic desire ... is a mode of surface contact with things and substances, with a world, that engenders and induces transformations, intensifications, a becoming something other. Not simply a rise and fall, a waxing and waning, but movement, processes, transformations. That is what constitutes the appeal and power of desire, its capacity to shake up, rearrange, reorganize the body's forms and substances, to make subject and body as such into something else, something other than what they are habitually ... desire need not, indeed commonly does not, culminate in sexual intercourse but in production ... the production of sensations never felt, alignments never thought energies never tapped, regions never known.

(Grosz 1995b: 294–295)

The appeal of this conceptualization of desire is that it resonates with feminists' investment in challenging the conventional sexual order and therefore championing forms of desire that push at the boundaries of normativity. Thus Annie Potts (2000) draws on Grosz's depiction of desire as a means of disrupting the mechanistic, end-driven model of the sexual encounter as a 'natural' sequence ending in orgasm. Potts (2000) takes 'the deconstructive implications of desire' as potentially destabilizing the meaning of sex and orgasm in pursuit of a different form of eroticism, in which orgasm is 'neither the target nor the non-target of sex' (Potts 2000: 70). We have some sympathy with this project and would also seek to de-privilege a monolithic notion of (hetero)sex, with orgasm as end point and high point (see Chapters 2 and 3). However, the notion of desire as a means through which this might be achieved is problematic in that desire, for us, cannot be envisaged as unmoored from the social: it will always be social and therefore meaningful, meaningful and therefore social. We would contend that locating desire as supra-social is no more tenable than positing instinctual drives as pre-social.

Embodied desires and practices cannot be disembedded from the social; if changing conceptualizations do help to effect change in embodied practices, it is as part of social life not as an escape from it (Cohen and Taylor 1978, 1992). There can be no 'revolutionary', 'productive', disruptive or subversive desire beyond the social. Human sexuality is not fixed, but it is both reproduced *and* transformed as an ongoing accomplishment of everyday practices within wider social relations.

The 'mystery' of the female orgasm

A common manifestation of supra-social thinking about the sexual, in both its commonsense and academic forms, is the assumption that women's pleasure is particularly mysterious, unknowable or unrepresentable. Women's orgasm has conventionally been seen as less physical than that of men and less susceptible to medical intervention (Clark 1993), a 'problem' currently bedevilling pharmaceutical companies in the race to find a female equivalent of Viagra. There is also a strong tradition of treating women's pleasure as mysterious and unrepresentable in psychoanalysis, perhaps the best-known example of which is Lacan's notion of a female *jouissance* beyond the phallus, beyond language, beyond – even – knowledge of those experiencing it. Yet, as Lacan himself seems to recognize understand, women's pleasure *is* commonly represented as in his own depiction of Bernini's statue of the medieval mystic, Teresa of Avila: 'You only have to go and look at Bernini's statue in Rome to understand immediately that she is coming, there is no doubt about it' (Lacan 1982: 147).[8]

Making connections between sexual and religious ecstasy is by no means peculiar to Lacan and frequently informs readings of Bernini's statue.[9] The reason why he and others can immediately see that she is coming is by interpreting a particular set of cultural insignia manifested not by a material embodied woman, but by a *statue*, a representation of a woman in a state of ecstasy: the head thrown back, the eyes closed, the lips parted, etc. What we have here are the conventions by which female ecstasy is represented, which may or may not bear any relation to women's embodied experience of orgasm. As we have cautioned earlier, we cannot read off the characteristics of sensory and sensate embodiment from the visible signs that constitute objectified embodiment even in the case of a material living person. Moreover, we should be wary of applying current constructions of sexuality to earlier representations, which might, in the context of their time, have had quite other meanings.

We would suggest that a sociological understanding of women's pleasure and its representation should recognize the ways in which representations enter into everyday interaction. Today's conventional depictions of women's pleasure and orgasm in many respects share a cultural history with Lacan's (1982) reading of Bernini, but now especially through the medium of film, combine sound effects with visual imagery.[10] These conventional representations have real effects – not least in that they provide women with everyday knowledge of how to fake an orgasm and perhaps how to have a convincingly 'authentic' one: how to signal an internal embodied event to a partner and how to understand a partner's responses as an orgasm. This performance, which is highly gendered, may be what makes an orgasm 'real' in sexual interaction.

The gendering of orgasm

We are interested then in the gendered meanings of orgasm, meanings which cannot be anything other than social. Even writers otherwise committed to an anti-essentialist stance often seem to assume, where arousal and orgasm are concerned, that meaning is inherent in bodily responses. Pasi Falk's (1994) discussion of pornography is a case in point. Male bodies, he tells us, evidentially signify arousal and pleasure through erection and ejaculation. Here the 'lack' of physical signs in women is represented as problematic: women's bodies simply cannot be read in the way male bodies can, hence the necessity for women in pornographic movies to 'act' desire and pleasure. Falk (1994) thus reduces male sexuality to an unproblematic bodily reflex – to which some theorists of masculinity and male sexuality might object. Emmanuel Reynaud (1983), for example, delivers an acerbic critique of the 'myth of the phallic orgasm'. 'Ejaculation in itself has little to do with sensual pleasure', he says, and more to do with concretizing men's power. For Reynaud (1983: 61), male sexuality is more a product of men's social location as the dominant gender than of their bodily capacities:

> Man is afraid of letting himself go. He does not abandon himself to his pleasure; he confines it within the limits of his penis ... he rarely lets himself be carried away by his own sensuality. He centres it on his penis without feeling that his whole body is totally sexualised.

(Reynaud 1983: 62)

While this may read as a rather essentializing account of masculinity, it does suggest that male desire and pleasure may be more problematic than Falk (1994) assumes. That such significance is accorded to a small quantity of body fluid – with the consequent equation of coming and 'cum' – is surely a consequence of its social definition rather than any essential properties. Susan Bordo (1999) offers an alternative explanation for the focus on female orgasm in representations of sex, one more in keeping with Reynaud's view that men are more concerned with demonstrating potency than pleasure. A man's virility is represented as control of both his own and his partner's sexual response: 'She's transported to another world; he's the pilot of the ship that takes her there' (Bordo 1999: 191).

While Bordo is critical of traditional representations of male sexuality, she nonetheless assumes that men's bodies unproblematically signify arousal, that arousal can simply be read off from the erect penis. She is not alone among feminist writers in reducing the meaning of male sexuality to physiological responses. It is not unusual for feminists to understand the conventional sequence of heterosex – dictated by his erection and his orgasm – as intrinsically male-defined rather than socially ordered; hence the assumption that the male definition of orgasm is somehow built into the male body. Describing models such as the Masters and Johnson sexual response cycle (arousal, plateau, orgasm, resolution), Annie Potts (2000: 61) comments: 'This tumescence and detumescence deemed to be characteristic of the "natural" course of sex is inevitably more consistent with a male (penis)-centred version of sexual experience.' Why should this be so? Certainly we should question the accepted syntax of heterosex – foreplay followed by penetration leading to (his) orgasm. But questioning the prioritization of penetration in this 'sexual sentence' (Scott and Freeman 1995) need not entail arguing that penetration *per se* is intrinsically 'male' or that it is simply about producing male orgasm. It is even more difficult to see why orgasm itself, or physiological responses preceding or following from it, are intrinsically male, somehow given by possession of a penis. The current masculine meanings associated with the 'sexual sentence', and orgasm itself, are not given by male sexual anatomy and physiology, but are the product of culturally ordered meanings embedded in particular social practices. The meanings of orgasm derive from social, not biological contexts.

To reiterate our earlier caveat, we are not denying the physicality of bodies. But physiologically the bodily responses which are understood to constitute orgasm are simply part of a reflex action, in themselves of no more social significance than any other reflex. Physical reflexes, including those associated with orgasm, happen in women's, as well as men's, bodies. Women, however, rarely describe orgasm in purely physical terms; it has become bound up with mystical ideas of ecstasy and transcendence and associated with the romantic trappings of love and intimacy (Roberts et al. 1995; Potts 2000). Women may thus unwittingly collude in the social definition of their orgasms as somehow more mysterious than those of men. This mystery is, then, a widely believed social fiction with real effects – and, to quote an old sociological maxim, if something is defined as real, it is real in its consequences (Thomas 1923).

Doing orgasm

Social definitions of male and female orgasm, then, have real consequences for everyday heterosexual practices. Qualitative research on the meanings of orgasm suggests, for example, that because women's orgasms are not deemed self-evident they are required to make a show of it, to produce a spectacular and noisy performance (Roberts et al. 1995; Potts 2000). Moreover, because orgasm is understood as the 'peak' of sexual experience (Potts 2000), its absence signifies a failed or incomplete sexual event, one which has not reached its proper conclusion: the sexual sentence has no full stop! In heterosexual intercourse, male orgasm is assumed to be virtually inevitable, whereas that of a woman requires male work and skill. Thus a woman's spectacular demonstration of orgasm affirms her partner's sexual expertise: 'The demand for noise ... indicates that heterosexuality becomes an economy in which the woman's orgasm is exchanged for the man's work' (Roberts et al. 1995: 528). Absence of orgasm in a woman may represent her own sexual 'failings', but may also reflect on her partner's 'flawed' technique, hence the pressure on her to reassure him, to provide evidence of her orgasm or, if necessary, to fake it. This is also an example of the embeddedness of sexual activity in everyday sociality: women's reassurance of their partners is part of the 'emotion work' of maintaining a heterosexual relationship (Duncombe and Marsden 1993, 1996) and conforms to the more general expectation that women will 'feed egos and tend wounds' (Bartky 1990).

There are a series of paradoxes here: the male performance ethic creates a demand that women enact a convincing performance of orgasm; the idea of women as passive recipients of male expertise requires an active use of 'their minds in order to perform (being) the body' (Roberts et al. 1995: 530). A woman's 'appreciation' of male sexual work requires considerable emotional labour to produce a performance that appears authentic and provides an appropriate affirmation of her partner's prowess.[11] Dealing with these paradoxes involves considerable interpretive work, reading a male partner's responses and producing a finely judged performance of orgasm. For, as Roberts et al. (1995) point out, an overly theatrical and extravagant display is likely to be read as faked; subtler performances are more convincing. They suggest that women are expert at this deception in that most women in their sample admitted faking it on occasion, while few of the men thought that they had ever been with a partner who had faked.

If a woman feels the need to reassure her male partner of the adequacy of his performance, that felt need will persist whether or not she 'really' experiences orgasm. Similar performances may thus accompany both 'faked' and 'authentic' orgasms. The cultural availability of these 'canonical orgasmic insignia' (DeNora 1997: 44) is what makes such performances possible and available to be read as 'authentic' orgasm. Tia DeNora is interested, as we are, in how cultural resources and various forms of representation 'actually "get into" and inform real lines of erotic conduct' (DeNora 1997: 44). The issue then becomes how orgasm is practically accomplished, how it is embodied, how it is manifested and reworked through social practice. This entails a reflexive process through which our embodied selves are continually constructed and reconstructed, through making sense of the social and cultural world available to us, in interaction with others.

If orgasm is a practical accomplishment in this sense, then at some stage we must acquire the cultural competencies that enable us to 'know' what it is, to 'recognize' it in ourselves and others. As we pointed out earlier, 'feeling' requires reflexive decoding of our own sensate embodiment. We would suggest that we have to learn to recognize an orgasm and also learn its cultural definitions. This resonates with one of the classics of the interactionist tradition, Howard Becker's study of marijuana users. Becker (1963) argues that while it is necessary to use marijuana 'properly' in order to get high, this is not sufficient and users must learn to relate their 'symptoms' not only to the action of the drug, but also to deem them comparable to the 'symptoms' experienced by other users and thus appropriate. This process is summed up neatly by one of Becker's respondents: 'I heard little remarks that were made by other people. Somebody said, "my legs are rubbery", I was very attentively listening for all these cues for what I was supposed to feel' (Becker 1963: 50). What Becker is suggesting is that users must learn to define the effects of drugs as pleasurable. Thus a three-stage process is involved: learning to use the drug, learning to perceive its effects and learning to define them as pleasurable. We would suggest that a similar process is entailed in learning to 'do' orgasm.

Orgasm, however, unlike getting high is not usually a collective experience; indeed there is a lack of everyday discussion of 'doing' sex and particularly of sexual pleasure. The most evident source from which it is possible to learn how to perceive its effects and come to define them as pleasurable is the media. As Susan Bordo points out, 'We learn what sexual arousal looks and sounds like from the movies, and – as with any other language – we pick up the grammar and syntax without being aware of it' (Bordo 1999: 65). These codes are highly conventionalized, learned by actors from other actors (Lewis 1997: 241), and become culturally available to us all as a means of 'making sense' of our own embodied sensations and of finding ways to communicate desire and pleasure in intimate interaction. There is some evidence that such images have long been drawn on, by young people, in learning to 'do sex' (Blumer 1933; Christian-Smith 1991; Thomson and Scott 1991; Illouz 1997; Allen 2005). Media representations of sex do not affect the lived body directly; their effects are mediated through the interactional contexts in which we 'do' sex and the reflexive processes whereby we interpret our own bodily responses and 'read' those of a lover. It is only then that cultural meanings of sex become part of our lived embodiment.

For orgasm to become a 'real' experience, for a simple reflex to be understood as an erotically significant event, requires far more than the technical know-how necessary to set off the appropriate physiological response. As Annie Potts' (2000) data suggest, the meanings of orgasm are extremely complex for both women and men, relying on particular interpretations of it as the ultimate or peak sexual experience. It is this which allows orgasm to become imbued with all manner of mystical and emotional meanings, which creates a space for the construction of specifically gendered understandings of what the experience *is*.

This raises the question of whether orgasm can be said to exist in the absence of such meanings. The obvious case here would be a child masturbating to 'orgasm' who does not have access to the meanings with which it is invested by adults. While the physical sensations may be homologous, they cannot be assumed to have the same significance. This is precisely because children are denied full access to adult means of making sense of the experience *as* orgasm; it is not that children are intrinsically asexual, but a result of the social organization of childhood and sexuality within contemporary culture (Jackson 1982; Jackson and Scott 1997, 1999, 2004). In so far as there are bodily links between these childhood and adult experiences, it is only because they are retrospectively reinterpreted as 'the same'.

We may remember sexual feelings and sensations associated with our own childhood activities, but this does not mean that we attached the same significance to them at the time, for in recalling our experiences we are interpreting them with the hindsight of adult knowledge (Jackson 1982: 70). Self-understanding can only ever be accomplished, as Mead says, from the perspective of the present. We cannot think ourselves back to the child we once were without taking the adult of the present moment back with us (Mead 1929, 1932); hence Gagnon and Simon's (1974) claim that our sexual pasts are shaped by the present (see Chapter 1).

Scripting or composing the sexual body

Orgasm is in many respects, in Gagnon and Simon's (1974) terms, scripted. But as we noted earlier (see Chapter 1), Gagnon and Simon themselves recognized that the term 'scripts' could be read too rigidly. The complex 'layered symbolic meanings', which they see as informing sexual conduct (Gagnon and Simon 1974: 23), come into play even in the most conventional erotic sequence (such as the 'sexual sentence'). Scripts, then, should not be understood as closed texts which lock us into predictable plots and roles, but something much more fluid and open, offering opportunities to improvise. Scripts are played with, not simply played out; they are open to renegotiation as we take cues from partners and make sense of what is happening to them, to us and between us. Gagnon and Simon's three interrelated dimensions of scripting (Gagnon 2004), 'cultural scenarios', interpersonal and intrapsychic come into play in making sense of our own embodied sexuality. Cultural scenarios provide us with recognized ways of 'doing sex',[12] interactionally shaped in each sexual encounter, reflexively mediated through our intrapsychic conversations with ourselves. These processes enable us to 'decode internal states', through which 'meaning is attributed to the interior of the body' (Gagnon and Simon 1974: 21) so that we are able to make sense of bodily states as sexually significant. Sexual feeling does not derive directly from the body, but must be actively interpreted before it becomes incorporated into our sensate embodiment as what arousal or orgasm 'feels like'.[13] Orgasm, then, is a cultural, interpersonal and intrapsychic construction and not the ultimate truth of sex.

The embodied sexual self, as we have described it, is provisional and always in process, engaged in sexual interaction in which meanings are emergent, negotiated and renegotiable – but always in the context of the actualities of social life. The advantage of this perspective is that it is non-deterministic, in that it allows for fluidity and agency, without assuming that we are free to do anything we please or to apply any number of an infinite array of meanings to erotic encounters. On the contrary, our practices and the meanings informing and emergent from them derive from the cultural resources we have to hand, from the social and cultural repertoires and vocabularies and the past biographical experience reflexively available to us in the present (Mead 1932). An interactionist perspective presupposes socially located bodies in interaction. Even when we are alone, however, we are still social beings (Mead 1934); hence solo sex, like sex with another, involves a reflexive process whereby cultural meanings and social knowledge, shaped and reshaped throughout our lives, guide both our minds (our fantasies) and our hands.

Thus sexual scripts, while always socially situated, are active compositions, not merely predefined guides for action. Elsewhere, extemporizing from DeNora's work on music and erotic agency, we have suggested an alternative metaphor: that of the composition of the sexual self and sexual embodiment (DeNora 1997; Jackson and Scott 2001b, 2007). The dual meaning of the verb 'to compose' and its associated nouns are suggestive of the active composition of narratives of embodied selfhood and the enactment of forms of bodily composure necessary for sexual interaction. The scripting or composition of sexual encounters shapes not only acts, but also how we make sense of what we feel and thus what we can make intelligible to ourselves as feeling – both emotion and sensation – and what we can therefore convey to others. The three forms of embodiment we outlined earlier in the chapter – objectified, sensory and sensate – are here brought into complex interplay. Engaging in sexual interaction entails reading, through our sensory embodiment, a partner's (or partners') embodied sexual composure – their objectified body – for imputed signs of their sensate embodiment. At the same time, we are objects of a similar process through which they are reading us. Through this interaction each participant can pick up cues for further improvisation. We cannot 'do sex' competently without this interactive process and the reflexivity this entails. Sexual embodiment requires that we compose ourselves bodily and construct an ongoing sense of embodied self within the intersubjective social space of the sexual encounter.

Bodily composure in its sexual and non-sexual forms is of course highly gendered. Iris Marion Young (1990), in her well-known phenomenological account of women's embodiment, argued that the typical female bodily comportment is a product of situatedness in the social environment and of the orientation of the body to the social world. Much of what Young (1990) identifies as the specificity of feminine embodiment is posited as consequential on women being objects of the male gaze and of men's actions. It could be said that just as a woman learns to 'throw like a girl', so she later learns to fake like a woman. However, this suggests that forms of sexual embodiment inevitably become fixed and habitual. There are of course forms of embodied selfhood which are pre-reflexive, as Mead (1934) recognizes: acquired habits of being, of bodily movement and deportment about which we no longer need to be reflexive (cf. Bourdieu's (1992) notion of bodily hexis). However, we would suggest that a fixed pre-reflexive bodily hexis may be less a characteristic of sexual embodiment, in that sexual comportment arises out of interaction and is therefore always subject to modification as a result of reflexive accommodation to a sexual partner or partners. Hence while sexual interaction in long-term couple relationships may become tacitly understood and habitual (see e.g. Duncombe and Marsden 1996), in any less routine sexual encounters, bodily contact and posture have to be negotiated anew in order to reach an accommodation to a different partner or situation.

The strength of the approach that we have advanced here is that it is applicable to routine forms of embodied sexual practice and to more unusual, less routine experiences and practices. It enables us to redirect attention to the everyday sociality (habitual or novel) in which bodily encounters take place and in which embodied experiences are negotiated. In its emphasis on the mundane, interactionism differs radically from traditions that emphasize the subversive power of desire and the destabilizing potential of sexual transgression. It also addresses aspects of sexual embodiment that have tended to fall between more abstract theorizations of the corporeal and empirical investigations of sexual conduct.[14] In making interaction central, the articulation between the cultural, interpersonal and subjective aspects of sexual embodiment can be explored without assuming deterministic lines of causation, while at the same time locating sexuality securely within the social. Because embodied, sensory and sensate experience takes place within the social, it is simultaneously corporeal *and* meaningful, physical *and* symbolic. By working through the example of orgasm we have endeavoured to show that sexual desire and pleasure, while always embodied, equally always entail interpretive interactional processes. Human sexual embodiment can be thought of neither as an abstract potentiality outside the social spaces where it is lived, nor as a mere assemblage of organs, orifices and orgasms.

Notes

1. The 'everyday/everynight' formulation derives from Dorothy Smith (1987).
2. Both Goffman and Giddens thus differ from Mead (1934), for whom the self is always both embodied and reflexive.
3. This disappearance of the social is a more general theoretical tendency within which the cultural is made to stand in for the social, leaving out of consideration both everyday practices and the material conditions under which they are accomplished.
4. In endorsing Witz's (2000) argument we are not engaging in sociological imperialism, but merely suggesting that particular forms of sociological understanding help to situate analyses of the body in the social relations of embodied interaction.
5. It should be noted that McRobbie is far less optimistic about opportunities for women's autonomy and 'empowerment' in her most recent work, McRobbie (2009).
6. This derives from a comment made in Bryan Turner's Plenary Address to the British Sociological Association's Medical Sociology Conference in the late 1980s. We are not aware of a published version of this.
7. A potentially shared sense of meaning because even in consensual heterosexual sex one partner may define interaction as erotic while the other might not, or may not invest it with the same form of eroticism. What might be understood by one as an overpowering physical need might be seen by the other as romantic passion.
8. For a particularly acerbic critique of Lacan's argument, see Luce Irigaray's 'Cosi Fan Tutti' (in Irigaray 1985) – see especially pp. 90–91 on Lacan's reading of the Bernini statue.
9. An example of this reading was offered by Simon Schama in his BBC2 television series, *The Power of Art* (2006). There is also a long psychoanalytic tradition of reading Bernini's sculpture in this way (see Macey 1988). This understanding is part of a very Western and Christian tradition. We cannot assume that all cultures share Western ideas about the transcendent and mystical meanings of sex.
10. Among the best-known versions is the scene from the film *When Harry Met Sally* (1989), in which Meg Ryan's character Sally demonstrates that orgasm can be convincingly faked. An earlier example is provided by Jane Fonda in

Barbarella (1968); the scene with the 'orgasmatron', a machine for producing orgasms, also represents a highly sexual woman as autonomously erotic only with the aid of a machine.

11 As Duncombe and Marsden (1996) point out, in long-term relationships women perform emotional work in sex in numerous ways, including pretending desire and acceding to unwanted sex.

12 An example would be conventionalized sequences of petting behaviour among adolescents; in our youth British teenagers followed a ten-point scale while North Americans favoured a four-stage baseball analogy.

13 Gagnon and Simon (1974: 23) discuss this in relation to the ways in which early adolescent feelings reported as 'anxiety, nausea, fear' later become re-recognized as sexual excitement.

14 Although, as Plummer (2003) notes, symbolic interactionists have recently neglected the embodied aspect of sexual (and other) interaction, G.H. Mead himself did pay considerable attention to human beings as embodied organisms.

CHAPTER 8

CONCLUDING THOUGHTS ON ORDINARY SEXUALITY

We began this book by mapping, in Chapters 1 and 2, the development of theories of sexuality since the 1970s and the debates they have engendered. As we pointed out, during this time much of the impetus for the study of sexuality as a social phenomenon has come from those with a political interest in challenging sexual convention, from feminist, lesbian, gay and, latterly, queer scholars. What has been collectively achieved in this time is considerable, not least in establishing the legitimacy of a field of study once deemed at best marginal to 'proper' sociological concerns and at worst disreputable.[1] The sociology of sexuality is now thriving, has led to an immense volume of research and theory and is taught in many British and North American universities. The political interests of those who built this academic enterprise have, however, shaped the development of the field in very particular directions. On the one hand, questioning heterosexual hegemony and championing those it excludes have led to a focus on sexual diversity, on *sexualities* (plural) and a fascination with novel and potentially subversive sexual lifestyles and practices. On the other hand, feminist challenges to male domination led to an emphasis on the most coercive, exploitative and violent aspects of contemporary sexuality. Those feminists who contested these preoccupations, from the 'sex wars' of the 1980s onward, set up a politics of 'pleasure' in opposition to a perceived discourse of 'danger' (Vance 1984) and thereby positioned themselves among those celebrating variety, 'outlaw' sexualities and the excitement of transgression (see Chapter 2).

This political history left a legacy of polarized priorities between those pursuing anti-violence and exploitation agendas on the one hand and defenders of pleasure and diversity on the other. We have always been uneasily positioned between these poles. We share in the conviction that combating sexual coercion and exploitation is as urgent a necessity as it ever was, but we also share in the desire for greater freedom to explore new forms of pleasure and see the continuing need to unsettle the taken-for-granted assumptions and practices underpinning institutionalized heterosexuality. We have, however, always been sceptical of the excessive weight accorded to sexuality within these debates. Sexuality, we have argued, should be seen neither as the root cause of women's subordination nor as a means of personal or social liberation. To take either stance neglects the multifarious ways in which sexuality is embedded in wider patterns of sociality.

What has always interested us most, and what has guided the trajectory of this book, is the ongoing, ordinary, everyday negotiation of conventional sexual lives.[2] This is not to say we are uninterested in sexual life beyond the unremarkable. Sociologists need, however, to understand more about the ordinary day-to-day patterns of sexual relations through which most people live their lives, not only to elucidate the taken-for-granted and habitual but also to appreciate why some forms of sexual diversity are tolerated, even celebrated, and others are not, why sexuality continues to be implicated in structured patterns of inequality and why sexual coercion and abuse remain such persistent problems. As feminists have long appreciated, the ordinary and routine give us clues to understanding the many forms and the persistence of sexual violence and exploitation, while a sensitivity to inequality, and oppression is essential to a critical analysis of the variability of sexual relations and practices. Neither normative nor transgressive practices should be exempt from critique; the defence of diversity should lead us not only to explore how the normative excludes its transgressive other but also to consider how all sexualities are negotiated and enacted within social contexts and can therefore be implicated in the perpetuation of inequalities and/or challenges to them. Only by knowing more about both normative and non-normative sexualities can we fully appreciate what is actually novel or subversive, how much is actually changing or remaining the same and thus map in more detail the topography of our shifting sexual landscape.

Sexual expression, whether highly conventional or extravagantly unconventional, is always embedded in wider patterns of sociality. This central insight of Gagnon and Simon's work has informed much of our argument. In keeping with this, we have argued that sexuality should be kept in proportion, not treated as a 'special' area of life or as a powerful force (whether dangerous or subversive) beyond the social. We therefore think it essential that we continue to emphasize the importance of locating sexuality within the everyday, as part of the fabric of routine day-to-day social life, as enmeshed with other, non-sexual aspects of life. Whatever the lure of the novel and unconventional, higher priority needs to be given to what goes on within less glamorous, more mundane sexual lives. The revival of interest in heterosexuality as something more than a norm against which other forms of sexuality are defined has been an important part of this (see Chapter 4). It is worth remembering, though, that even

CONCLUDING THOUGHTS ON ORDINARY SEXUALITY   163

those whose sexual practices place them well beyond the span of respectable heterosexuality do not spend all their time in sexual activity and must still engage in routine social life in order to survive (earning a living, doing the shopping) are also likely to sustain non-sexual relationships both within and outside their communities.

Sexuality, then, is only one area of social life and never the totality of our social being. In identifying sexuality in this way we make the case for retaining the concept of *sexuality* (singular) to denote a sphere of social life interconnected with all other aspects of the social, as well as the plural *sexualities*, which captures the variety and flexibility of sexual desires, practices and lifestyles. One problem we have identified with pluralizing sexuality is that it tends to lead to heterosexuality being seen as merely one practice or identity among many and can also position it as monolithic. There is variation *within* normative, everyday heterosexuality, as well as alternatives to it. Moreover, while some of those who live outside the heterosexual norm embrace dissident identities as central to their being, others are keen to emphasize the normality of their lifestyle (see e.g. Gabb 2004).

Most of us, whatever our individual sexualities, live ordinary everyday sexual lives. Ordinary everyday sexuality is obviously not the same for everyone. That it is structured both by the institutionalization of heterosexuality and by gender is well established. But if sexuality is part of wider social life, then class and ethnic variations require attention too. In sexual life, as elsewhere, the more privileged have more choices, more opportunities to explore different sexual lifestyles – and this has only just begun to be explored, notably in relation to lesbian and queer lifestyles more often than heterosexual ones (see e.g. Hennessy 2000; Taylor 2004); moreover the same sexual practices may be perceived differently by class (Skeggs 2003). Age and life-course variations are also part of the sexual landscape and, while young people's sexuality has received a great deal of attention – because it is so often defined as problematic – there is still far less work on older people's sexual lives, though this, too, is beginning to change.

The ordinary and the everyday is also, of course, subject to change and has changed in some very obvious ways since we first began to work on sexuality in the 1970s, so that what was once transgressive is now part of the norm. Heterosexual sex has been uncoupled from marriage and reproduction while homosexuality is undergoing normalization– or at least for those forms of homosexuality that themselves conform to certain conventions (Seidman 2005). We have cautioned against overestimating change at the expense of noting continuities – particularly the persistence of gender division – and against too celebratory an account of those transformations that have occurred, while noting the ways in which the boundaries of the normative are being redrawn and new tensions in sexual life are emerging (see Chapters 3 and 4). We would not deny that for women, lesbians and gay men, sexual life is less constrained than it once was, but neither should we ignore the problems that sexuality continues to pose for many of us in late modern societies.

One aspect of the social ordering of sexuality that continues to be thought of as particularly troubling is the boundary between childhood and adulthood. We chose to focus on childhood as an exemplar of the sexual antinomies pervading late modern life because here the status of sexuality as a 'special' area of life comes up against the idea of the child as a special category of person (see Chapter 5). This brings into sharp relief some of the contradictions inherent in contemporary constructions of sexuality: between sexuality as positive and fulfilling and also potentially dangerous; between a desire for sexual openness and the difficulties of communicating about sexuality; between the pervasiveness of sexual imagery and talk and the maintenance of secrecy and privacy. But there is another reason why childhood is important: if sexuality is socially constructed, then each of us, as sexual subjects, is a product of that society and, in part, of our passage through childhood on our way to becoming adult sexual actors. We have suggested that sexual selves are formed not only through childhood experiences and our later reflections back on them, but also by the contours of childhood itself, the boundaries between childhood and adulthood and the ways in which the regulation of sexuality and the social distribution of sexual knowledge shape those contours and police the boundaries.

The construction of the sexual self or subjectivity is among the most neglected aspects of sexuality, given scant attention by theorists other than those influenced by psychoanalysis. Psychoanalysis has always seemed to us to be insufficiently social and to place far too much emphasis on sexuality in the constitution of subjectivity. Yet many academics in the humanities and social sciences act as if there were no alternative. We are convinced that an alternative does exist, albeit one that requires further elaboration – and we have begun that task in Chapters 5 and 6. Taking our cue from Gagnon and Simon's conception of intrapsychic scripting and their insistence on the centrality of gender in the construction of individual sexualities, we have returned to the conceptualization of the social self developed by George Herbert Mead. This, we argue, is sufficiently sophisticated, nuanced and flexible to account for human agency, for variable ways of becoming and being gendered and sexual while nonetheless locating the self firmly within sociality.

This same perspective informs our final chapter on embodiment, surprisingly also under-theorized except by corporeal feminists and some postmodern thinkers. We suggest that the pragmatist and interactionist tradition offers a way of theorizing sexual embodiment that places it within the everyday/everynight world in which actual sexual encounters take place. Our development of this argument centres on the gendering of orgasm within heterosex, but we see its potential as broader than this, as a means of attending to all aspects of embodied sexual practice and

CONCLUDING THOUGHTS ON ORDINARY SEXUALITY 165

experience and the meanings these have for us. We should here remember another of Gagnon and Simon's guiding principles: that sexual conduct is socially meaningful and that the sense we make of embodied experience is always mediated through the scripts available to us.

Throughout, then, we have retained an emphasis on ordinary, mundane sexual experiences and argued that if theory is to do the analytical work we require of it, then it must have purchase on the empirically knowable world. We are aware, though, that the world we have been discussing is an exclusively Western one. One of the major challenges for the future is to begin to provincialize Western ideas (Burawoy 2005) while also being less parochial, to critically evaluate the applicability of Western theory to other contexts and to respond to work generated from other parts of the world. This is an ambitious project and beyond the scope of this book;[3] others, we know, have begun to think more globally about sexuality (Altman 2001; Binnie 2004). We would, however, like to conclude with some thoughts about the potential for, and pitfalls of, a more international perspective.

One danger attending attempts to internationalize the study of sexuality is that the confluence of Western ethnocentrism with the enticement of the different and unconventional can result in sexual practices elsewhere being explored primarily as exotically 'other'. It is already the case that Western scholars in the field of sexuality tend to know far more about sex tourism, prostitution and same sex desire in other parts of the globe than about the cultural diversity of conventional sexualities. There are, of course, vast swathes of the world where there is little opportunity to explore alternative sexual lifestyles, where lifestyle choices of any kind are limited by poverty and/or repressive regimes. Under such conditions sexuality has not been at the top of local activists' and scholars' agendas. Indeed, Western feminists have, in the past, often been criticized for focusing on something as 'trivial' as sexuality in the face of global inequality and injustice. Sexuality, however, is relevant to many of the more pressing issues facing poorer parts of the world. What has brought this to the fore is the challenge of HIV/AIDS, which has galvanized researchers into investigating local sexual mores and practices that contribute to HIV transmission or might be mobilized to inhibit its further spread (see e.g. Rivers et al. 1998 Campbell 2003). There are signs, too, that sexuality is beginning to be placed on the agenda by scholars in the field of development (see Cornwall et al. 2008).

There are also regions beyond the West where sexual life is not so constrained by extreme poverty or widespread disease, for example, in the wealthy modern societies of East Asia. Here social trends apparently similar to those of the West (women's flight from early marriage and domesticity, more sex outside marriage, greater visibility of queer sexualities) can easily be seen as part of a globalized late modernity, signalling in Castells' terms a possible 'end of patriarchalism' (Castells 2004). Quite apart from Castells' over-optimistic assessment of gender relations, it would be unwise to assume that 'our' modernity is everyone's or that what is happening to sexual lives in the East is an exact parallel of the West. There is research on everyday intimacy being produced from within East Asia, some of which reaches Western audiences, and in its attention to local conditions and cultures this could, if scholars here take note of it, add new dimensions to the theorizing of sexuality, social change and modernity.[4]

Everyday sexuality today has, like every other aspect of social life, been affected by movements of people and ideas around the globe. Sexual life is not necessarily tied to specific geographical locales and sexual relationships are not always confined within national borders. Representations and conceptualizations of sexuality also travel, though their meanings may change as they are dispersed far from their origins. New sexual scripts are emerging as part of these global encounters but, as with all scripts, access to them is not equally available, and neither is the opportunity to engage in transnational sexual encounters. The local, then, still matters and the extent to which most of us, most of the time conduct our sexual lives within immediate local contexts should not be forgotten. Theorizing sexuality as fully social, then, should involve taking account of the consequences of differing cultures, histories and social practices both globally and locally and considering how these impinge upon everyday, mundane sexual life, whether it is conventional or unconventional. The achievements of the last few decades notwithstanding, we are still only beginning to unravel the complexities of sexuality and our individual sexualities. The theory which we have drawn on and developed in this book, with its focus on the social and contextual meanings and practices of sexuality, is, we believe, more suited than many other 'Western' theories of sexuality to supporting comparative research and an understanding of ordinary, everyday sexual lives in globally diverse local contexts.

Notes

1. One of us was told, by colleagues, when teaching a new course on the sociology of sexuality, in the early 1980s, that it was 'merely pop sociology'; the other was similarly told that her research was 'not proper sociology' and even as late as the early 1990s was advised by a feminist colleague that continuing to work in this field was career suicide.
2. There has been a widespread tendency, in much recent sociology in general, to focus on the exotic and transgressive, which is now beginning to be rebalanced with more focus on the ordinary, mundane and routine (see e.g. Warde and Gronow 2001).
3. One of us has, however, begun to engage in cross-cultural work on sexuality (see Jackson et al. 2008).
4. For some examples of this work, see contributions to Jackson et al. (2008) and Khor and Kamano (2007).

REFERENCES

Acton, W. (1857) *The Functions and Disorders of the Reproductive Organs*. Philadelphia, PA: Lindsay & Blakiston.
Adams, M. (2003) The Reflexive Self and Culture: A Critique. *British Journal of Sociology* 54(2): 221–238.
Adams, P. (1989) Of Female Bondage, in T. Brennan (ed.) *Between Feminism and Psychoanalysis*. London: Routledge.
Adkins, L. (1995) *Gendered Work: Sexuality, Family and the Labour Market*. Milton Keynes: Open University Press.
Adkins, L. (2002) *Revisions: Gender and Sexuality in Late Modernity*. Buckingham: Open University Press.
Allen, L. (2003) Girls Want Sex, Boys Want Love: Resisting Dominant Discourses of (Hetero)sexuality. *Sexualities* 6(2): 215–236.
Allen, L. (2005) *Sexual Subjects: Young People, Sexuality and Education*. Basingstoke: Palgrave.
Althusser, L. (1971) Ideology and the Ideological State Apparatuses, in L. Althusser, *Lenin and Philosophy*. London: New Left Books.
Altman, D. (2001) *Global Sex*. Chicago, IL: University of Chicago Press.
Archard, D. (1993) *Children: Rights and Childhood*. London: Routledge.
Ariès, P. (1962) *Centuries of Childhood*. London: Cape.
Atkinson, P. and Housley, W. (2003) *Interactionism*. London: Sage.
Backett-Milburn, K. and Harden, J. (2004) How Children and their Families Negotiate Risk, Safety and Danger. *Childhood* 11(4): 429–447.
Bardeleben, H., Reinmann, B.W. and Schmidt, P. (1989) AIDS und das Problem eder prevention – Fakten und Fiction. *Sozialforschung* 29: 97–128.
Barnett, S. and Thomson, K. (1996) Portraying Sex: The Limits of Tolerance. In R. Jowell, J. Curtis, A. Park, L. Brooks and K. Thomson (eds) *British Social Attitudes: The 13th Report*, pp. 19–52, Aldershot: Dartmouth.
Barrett, M. (1980) *Women's Oppression Today*. London: Verso.
Barrett, M. (1991) *The Politics of Truth*. Stanford, CA: Stanford University Press.
Barrett, M. (1992) Words and Things: Materialism and Method in Contemporary Feminist Analysis, in M. Barrett and A. Phillips (eds) *Destabilizing Theory*. Cambridge: Polity.
Bartky, S. (1990) *Femininity and Domination*. London: Routledge.

Battersby, C. (1989) *Gender and Genius: Towards a Feminist Aesthetics*. London: Women's Press.
Bauman, Z. (1990) *Thinking Sociologically*. Oxford: Blackwell.
Beauvoir, S. de (1972) *The Second Sex*. Harmondsworth: Penguin.
Beck, U. (1992) *Risk Society: Towards a New Modernity*. London: Sage.
Beck, U. and Beck-Gernsheim, E. (2002) *Individualization*. London: Sage.
Becker, H. (1963) *Outsiders: Studies in the Sociology of Deviance*. London: Free Press of Glencoe.
Berger, P.L. and Luckmann, T. (1966) *The Social Construction of Reality*. London: Allen Lane.
Bindel, J. and Scanlon, J. (1996) Barking Back. *Trouble & Strife* 33: 68–72.
Binnie, J. (2004) *The Globalization of Sexuality*. London: Sage.
Black, P. (2004) *The Beauty Industry: Gender, Culture, Pleasure*. London: Routledge.
Bland, L. and Doan, L. (eds) (1998) *Sexology in Culture: Labelling Bodies and Desire*. Cambridge: Polity.
Blumer, H. (1933) *Movies and Conduct*. New York: Arno Press.
Blumer, H. (1969) *Symbolic Interactionism: Perspective and Methods*. Englewood Cliffs, NJ: Prentice Hall.
Bly, R. (1990) *Iron John: A Book about Men*. Reading, MA: Addison-Wesley.
Bordo, S. (1999) *The Male Body*. New York: Farrar, Straus & Giroux.
Botcherby, S. and Scott, S. (2004) *Parents as Sex Educators*. Report for Durham Education Authority.
Bourdieu, P. (1992) *The Logic of Practice*. Cambridge: Polity.
Braidotti, R. (1994) Feminism by Any Other Name: Interview. *Differences* 6(2–3): 27–61.
Brennan, T. (ed.) (1989) *Between Feminism and Psychoanalysis*. London: Routledge.
Brickell, C. (2006) The Sociological Construction of Gender and Sexuality. *Sociological Review* 54(1): 87–113.
Brownmiller, S. (1975) *Against Our Will: Men, Women and Rape*. London: Secker & Warburg.
Buckingham, D. (1994) Television and the Definition of Childhood, in B. Mayall (ed.) *Children's Childhoods*. London: Falmer.
Buckingham, D. and Bragg, S. (2004) *Young People, Sex and the Media: The Facts of Life?* Basingstoke: Palgrave.
Bunch, C. ([1975] 1997) Not for Lesbians Only. *Quest, A Feminist Quarterly* 2(2): 50–56. Reprinted in C. Ingraham and R. Hennessey (eds) *Materialist Feminism*. New York: Routledge.
Burawoy, M. (2005) Provincialising the Social Sciences, in G. Steinmetz (ed.) *The Politics of Method in the Human Sciences*. Durham, NC: Duke University Press.
Burke, K. (1945) *A Grammar of Motives*. Berkeley, CA: University of California Press.
Burke, K. (1950) *A Rhetoric of Motives*. Berkeley, CA: University of California Press.
Buston, K., Wight, D., Hart, G. and Scott, S. (2002) Implementation of a Teacher-Delivered Sex Education Programme: Obstacles and Facilitating Factors. *Health Education Research* 17(1): 59–72.
Buston, K., Wight, D. and Scott, S. (2001) Difficulty and Diversity: The Context and Practice of Sex Education. *British Journal of the Sociology of Education* 22(3): 353–368.

Butler, J. (1990a) *Gender Trouble: Feminism and the Subversion of Identity.* New York: Routledge.
Butler, J. (1990b) Gender Trouble, Feminist Theory and Psychoanalytic Discourse, in L. Nicholson (ed.) *Feminism/Postmodernism.* New York: Routledge.
Butler, J. (1991) Imitation and Gender Insubordination, in D. Fuss (ed.) *Inside Out.* New York: Routledge.
Butler, J. (1993) *Bodies that Matter.* New York: Routledge.
Butler, J. (2004) *Undoing Gender.* New York: Routledge.
Califia, P. (1981) Feminism and Sadomasochism. *Heresies* 12: 30–34.
Campbell, C. (2003) *Letting Them Die: Why HIV/AIDS Prevention Programmes Often Fail.* London: James Currey.
Cancian, F. (1990) *Love in America.* Cambridge: Cambridge University Press.
Carabine, J. (1996) Heterosexuality and Social Policy, in D. Richardson (ed.) *Theorising Heterosexuality.* Buckingham: Open University Press.
Castells, M. (2004) *The Power of Identity*, 2nd edn. Oxford: Blackwell.
Chambers, D., Tinknell, E. and Van Loon, J. (2004) Peer Regulation of Teenage Sexual Identities. *Gender and Education* 16(3): 397–415.
Chen Mei-Hua (2008) Sex and Work in Sex Work; Negotiating Sex and Work among Taiwanese Sex Workers, in S. Jackson, Liu Jieyu and Woo Juhyun (eds) *East Asian Sexualities: Modernity. Gender and New Sexual Cultures.* London: Zed.
Chesser, E. (1949) *Sexual Behaviour: Normal and Abnormal.* London: Medical Publications.
Chesser, E. (1965) *Married Love.* London: Jarrolds.
Christian-Smith, L. (1991) *Becoming a Woman through Romance.* Brighton: Falmer.
Clark, D. (1993) 'With My Body I Thee Worship': The Social Construction of Marital Sex Problems, in S. Scott and D.H.J. Morgan (eds) *Body Matters.* London: Falmer.
Cockburn, C. (1991) *In the Way of Women: Men's Resistance to Sex Equality in Organizations.* London: Macmillan.
Cohen, S. and Taylor, L. (1978) *Escape Attempts: The Theory and Practice of Resistance to Everyday Life.* Harmondsworth: Pelican.
Cohen, S. and Taylor, L. (1992) *Escape Attempts: The Theory and Practice of Resistance to Everyday Life*, 2nd edn. London: Routledge.
Comer, L. (1974) *Wedlocked Women.* Leeds: The Feminist Press.
Comfort, A. (1996) *The Joy of Sex.* London: Quartet.
Connell, R.W. (1995) *Masculinities.* Cambridge: Polity.
Connell, R.W. (2000) *The Men and the Boys.* Cambridge: Polity.
Connell, R.W. and Dowsett, G.W (1992) The Unclean Motion of the Generative Parts: Frameworks in Western Thought on Sexuality, in R.W. Connell and G.W. Dowsett (eds) *Rethinking Sex: Social Theory and Sexuality Research.* Melbourne: Melbourne University Press.
Cooley, C.H. (1902) *Human Nature and the Social Order.* New York: Scribner's.
Cornwell, A., Jolly, S. and Correa, S. (eds) (2008) *Development with a Body: Sexuality, Human Rights and Development.* London: Zed.
Cousins, J. ([1978] 1986) *Make it Happy: What Sex is All About.* Harmondsworth: Penguin.
Coward, R. (1984) *Female Desire.* London: Paladin.
Coward, R. and Ellis, J. (1977) *Language and Materialism.* London: Routledge & Kegan Paul.
Crossley, N. (2001) *The Social Body: Habit, Identity and Desire.* London: Sage.

Davidoff, L. and Hall, C. (1987) *Family Fortunes: Men and Women of the English Middle Class 1780–1850*. London: Hutchinson.
Davies, B. (1989) *Frogs and Snails and Feminist Tales*. Sydney: Allen and Unwin.
Davis, K. (1937) The Sociology of Prostitution. *American Sociological Review* 2: 744–755.
Dawe, A. (1970) The Two Sociologies. *British Journal of Sociology* 21(2): 207–218.
Dawkins, R. ([1976] 2006) *The Selfish Gene*. Oxford: Oxford University Press.
De Lauretis, T. (1994) Habit Changes. *Differences* 6(2–3): 296–313.
Delphy, C. (1984) *Close to Home: A Materialist Analysis of Women's Oppression*. London: Hutchinson.
Delphy, C. (1993) Rethinking Sex and Gender. *Women's Studies International Forum* 16(1): 1–9.
DeNora, T. (1997) Music and Erotic Agency: Sonic Resources and Socio-sexual Action, *Body and Society* 3(2): 43–65.
Denzin, N. (1992) *Symbolic Interactionism and Cultural Studies: The Politics of Interpretation*. Oxford: Blackwell.
Diamond, I. and Quinby, L. (eds) (1988) *Feminism and Foucault: Reflections on Resistance*. Boston, MA: Northeastern University Press.
Diamond, J. (1997) *Why is Sex Fun? The Evolution of Human Sexuality*. London: Weidenfeld & Nicolson.
Dollimore, J. (1991) *Sexual Dissidence*. Oxford: Oxford University Press.
Duchen, C. (ed.) (1987) *French Connections: Voices from the Women's Movement in France*. London: Hutchinson.
Duncombe, J. and Marsden, D. (1993) Love and Intimacy: The Gender Division of Emotion and Emotion Work. *Sociology* 27(2): 221–241.
Duncombe, J. and Marsden, D. (1996) Whose Orgasm Is This Anyway? 'Sex Work' in Long Term Relationships, in J. Weeks and J. Holland (eds) *Sexual Cultures: Communities and Intimacy*. London: Macmillan.
Dworkin, A. (1987) *Intercourse*. London: Secker & Warburg.
Egan, R.D. and Hawkes, G. (2008a) Imperiled and Perilous: Exploring the History of Childhood Sexuality. *Journal of Historical Sociology* 214: 355–367.
Egan, R.D. and Hawkes, G. (2008b) Developing the Sexual Child. *Journal of Historical Sociology* 21(4): 433–465.
Elias, N. ([1939] 1994) *The Civilizing Process*. Oxford: Blackwell.
Ennew, J. (1986) *The Sexual Exploitation of Children*. Cambridge: Polity.
Epstein, D. and Johnson, R. (1998) *Schooling Sexualities*. Buckingham: Open University Press.
Evans, D. (1993) *Sexual Citizenship: The Material Construction of Sexualities*. London: Routledge.
Evans, M. (2003) *Love: An Unromantic Discussion*. Cambridge: Polity.
Everingham, C. (1994) *Motherhood and Modernity: An Investigation into the Rational Dimension of Mothering*. Buckingham: Open University Press.
Falk, P. (1994) *The Consuming Body*. London: Sage.
Faraday, A. (1981) Liberating Lesbian Research, in K. Plummer (ed.) *The Making of the Modern Homosexual*. London: Hutchinson.
Fausto-Sterling, A. (2000) *Sexing the Body*, 2nd edn. New York: Basic Books.
Fenstermaker, S. and West, C. (2002) *Doing Gender, Doing Difference: Inequality, Power and Institutional Change*. London: Routledge.

Finch, J. and Summerfield, P. (1991) Social Reconstruction and the Emergence of Companionate Marriage, 1945–59, in D. Clark (ed.) *Marriage, Domestic Life and Social Change*. London: Routledge.

Fine, M. (1988) Sexuality, Schooling and Adolescent Females: The Missing Discourse of Desire. *Harvard Educational Review* 58(1): 29–51.

Fine, M. and McClelland, S. (2006) Sexuality Education and Desire: Still Missing after All These Years. *Harvard Educational Review* 76(3): 297–338.

Firestone, S. (1970) *The Dialectic of Sex*. London: Paladin.

Flax, J. (1990a) Postmodernism and Gender Relations in Feminist Theory, in L. Nicholson (ed.) *Feminism/Postmodernism*. London: Routledge.

Flax, J. (1990b) *Thinking Fragments: Psychoanalysis, Feminism and Postmodernism in the Contemporary West*. Berkeley, CA: University of California Press.

Ford, C. and Beach, F. (1952) *Patterns of Sexual Behavior*. New York: Harper & Bros.

Foucault, M. (1972) *The Archaeology of Knowledge*. London: Tavistock.

Foucault, M. ([1978] 1981) *The History of Sexuality, Volume One*. London: Pelican.

Foucault, M. (1979) *Discipline and Punish: The Birth of the Prison*. New York: Vintage.

Foucault, M. (1980) The Confessions of the Flesh: A Conversation with A. Grosrichard, G. Wajeman, J-A. Miller, G. Le Gaufey, D. Celasm, G. Miller, C. Millot, J. Livi and J. Miller, in C. Gordon (ed) *M. Foucault, Power/Knowledge*, Brighton: Harvester/Wheatsheaf.

Foucault, M. (1988) Technologies of the Self, in L.H. Martin, H. Gutman and P.H. Hutton (eds) *Technologies of the Self*. London: Tavistock.

Frankham, J. (2006) Sexual Antinomies and Parent/Child Sex Education: Learning from Foreclosure. *Sexualities* 9(2): 236–254.

Fraser, N. (1989) *Unruly Practices: Power, Discourse and Gender in Contemporary Social Theory*. Oxford: Polity.

Frazer, E. (1988) Teenage Girls Reading *Jackie*. *Media, Culture and Society* 9(4): 407–425.

Freud, S. (1905) Three Essays on Sexuality, in *The Standard Edition of the Complete Works of Sigmund Freud*, Volume 7. London: Hogarth Press.

Freud, S. (1925) Some Psychical Consequences of the Anatomical Distinction between the Sexes, in *The Standard Edition of the Complete Works of Sigmund Freud*, Volume 19. London: Hogarth Press

Freud, S. (1930) *Civilization and its Discontents*. London: Hogarth Press.

Freud, S. (1931) Female Sexuality, in *The Standard Edition of the Complete Works of Sigmund Freud*, Volume 21. London: Hogarth Press.

Freud, S. (1933) Femininity, in *The Standard Edition of the Complete Works of Sigmund Freud*, Volume 22. London: Hogarth Press.

Furedi, F. (1997) *Culture of Fear: Risk-Taking and the Morality of Low Expectation*. London: Cassell.

Fuss, D. (1991) Introduction, in D. Fuss (ed.) *Inside/Out: Lesbian Theories, Gay Theories*. New York: Routledge.

Gabb, J. (2004) Critical Differentials: Querying the Incongruities within Research on Lesbian Parent Families. *Sexualities* 7(2): 167–182.

Gagnon, J. (2004) *An Interpretation of Desire*. Chicago, IL: University of Chicago Press.

Gagnon, J. and Simon, W. ([1973] 1974) *Sexual Conduct*. London: Hutchinson.

Gagnon, J. and Simon, W. (2004) *Sexual Conduct*, 2nd edn. New Brunswick, NJ: AldineTransaction.
Gamson, J. and Moon, D. (2004) The Sociology of Sexualities: Queer and Beyond. *Annual Review of Sociology* 30: 47–64.
Garfinkel, H. (1967) *Studies in Ethnomethodology*. Englewood Cliffs, NJ: Prentice Hall.
Gatens, M. (1982) A Critique of the Sex/Gender Distinction, in J. Allen and P. Patton (eds) *Beyond Marxism?* Leichhardt, NSW: Intervention.
Gay Left Collective (1980) *Homosexuality Power and Politics*. London: Allison & Busby.
Giddens, A. (1990) *The Consequence of Modernity*. Cambridge: Polity.
Giddens, A. (1991) *Modernity and Self Identity*. Cambridge: Polity.
Giddens, A. (1992) *The Transformation of Intimacy*. Cambridge: Polity.
Goffman, E. (1963a) *Stigma: Notes on the Management of Spoiled Identity*. Englewood Cliffs, NJ: Prentice-Hall.
Goffman, E. (1963b) *Behaviour in Public Places*. New York: Free Press.
Goffman, E. (1969) *The Presentation of Self in Everyday Life*. London: Allen Lane.
Goffman, E. (1971) *Relations in Public: Microstudies of the Public Order*. London: Allen Lane.
Goffman, E. (1979) *Gender Advertisements*. London: Macmillan.
Gorer, G. (1971) *Sex and Marriage in Britain Today*. London: Nelson.
Gorham, D. (1978) The 'Maiden Tribute of Modern Babylon' Reconsidered: Child Prostitution and the Idea of Childhood in Late Victorian England. *Victorian Studies* 21: 353–379.
Gough, J. and Macnair, M. (1985) *Gay Liberation in the Eighties*. London: Pluto.
Graham, A. (1996) Made Up, Dressed Up and Fed Up (and She's Only Five). *Radio Times* 17 January–2 February: 22–24.
Gray, J. (1992) *Men are from Mars, Women are from Venus*. New York: HarperCollins.
Gray, J. (1996) *Mars and Venus in the Bedroom*. London: Vermillion.
Green, J. (1997) *Risk and Misfortune: The Social Construction of Accidents*. London: University College London Press.
Grosz, E. (1995a) Experimental Desire: Re-Thinking Queer Subjectivity, in E. Grosz *Space, Time and Perversion*. New York: Routledge.
Grosz, E. (1995b) Animal Sex, in E. Grosz and E. Probyn (eds) *Sexy Bodies*. New York: Routledge.
Guillaumin, C. (1995) *Racism, Sexism, Power and Ideology*. London: Routledge.
Hair, P. (1972) *Before the Bawdy Courts: Selections from the Church Court Records 1300–1800*. London: Paul Elek.
Hall, C. (1992) *White, Male and Middle Class: Explorations in Feminism and History*. London: Routledge.
Halperin, D.M. (1995) *Saint Foucault: Towards a Gay Hagiography*. Oxford: Oxford University Press.
Harding, S. (1988) Trends in Permissiveness, in R. Jowell, S. Witherspoon and L. Brook (eds) *British Social Attitudes: The 5th Report*, pp. 35–52. Aldershot: Dartmouth
Hardyment, C. (1983) *Dream Babies: Child Care from Locke to Spock*. London: Cape.
Haritaworn, J., Lin, C-J. and Klesse, C. (2008) Poly/logue: A Critical Introduction to Polyamory. *Sexualities* 9(5): 515–529.

Hawkes, G. (1996) *A Sociology of Sex and Sexuality*. Buckingham: Open University Press.
Hay, C.O., O'Brien, M. and Penna, S. (1994) Giddens, Modernity and Self-Identity: The 'Hollowing-Out' of Social Theory. *Arena* new series 2: 45–75.
Heath, A. and McMahon D. (1991) Consensus and Dissensus, in R. Jowell, L. Brook and B. Taylor (eds.) *British Social Attitudes: The 8th Report*, pp. 1–22. Aldershot: Dartmouth.
Heath, S. (1982) *The Sexual Fix*. London: Macmillan.
Hemmings, C. (2005) Telling Feminist Stories. *Feminist Theory* 6(2): 115–139.
Hennessy, R. (1995) Queer Visibility in Commodity Culture, in L. Nicholson and S. Seidman (eds) *Social Postmodernism*. Cambridge: Cambridge University Press.
Hennessy, R. (2000) *Profit and Pleasure: Sexual Identities in Late Capitalism*. New York: Routledge.
Henriques, J., Holloway, W., Venn, C. and Walkerdine, V. (1984) *Changing the Subject: Psychology, Social Regulation and Subjectivity*. London: Methuen.
Hertford, J. (1997) *A Pocket Guide to Sensational Sex*. New York: Carroll and Graf.
Hochschild, A. (1983) *The Managed Heart*. Berkeley, CA: University of California Press.
Holland, J., Ramazanoğlu, C., Scott, S., Sharpe, S. and Thomson, R. (1990) *'Don't Die of Ignorance' – I Nearly Died of Embarrassment: Condoms in Context*. London: Tufnell Press.
Holland, J., Ramazanoğlu, C., Sharpe, S. and Thomson, R. (1996) In the Same Boat? The Gendered (In)experience of First Heterosex, in D. Richardson (ed.) *Theorising Heterosexuality*. Buckingham: Open University Press.
Holland, J., Ramazanoğlu, C., Sharpe, S. and Thomson, R. (1998) *The Male in the Head*. London: Tufnell Press.
Hollibaugh, A. (1984) Desire for the Future: Radical Hope in Passion and Pleasure, in C. Vance (ed.) *Pleasure and Danger*. London: Routledge and Kegan Paul.
Hollway, W. (1993) Theorizing Heterosexuality: A Response. *Feminism and Psychology* 3(2): 412–417.
Hollway, W. (1996) Recognition and Heterosexual Desire, in D. Richardson, *Theorising Heterosexuality*. Buckingham: Open University Press.
Hollway, W. (2006) *The Capacity to Care: Gender and Ethical Subjectivity*. London: Routledge.
Hollway, W. and Jefferson, T. (2000) *Doing Qualitative Research Differently: Free Association, Narrative and the Interview Method*. London: Sage.
Hood, J. (1999) *The Silverback Gorilla Syndrome: Transforming Primitive Man*. Santa Fe, NM: Adventures in Spirit.
Illouz, E. (1997) *Consuming the Romantic Utopia*. Berkeley, CA: University of California Press.
Ingraham, C. (1996) The Heterosexual Imaginary, in S. Seidman (ed.) *Queer Theory/Sociology*. Oxford: Blackwell.
Ingraham, C. (1999) *White Weddings: Romancing Heterosexuality in Popular Culture*. London: Routledge.
Irigaray, L. (1985) *This Sex Which is Not One*. Ithaca, NY: Cornell University Press.
Irwin, S. (2005) *Reshaping Social Life*. London: Routledge.
Jackson, M. (1994) *The Real Facts of Life: Feminism and the Politics of Sexuality c.1850–1940*. London: Taylor and Francis.

Jackson, S. (1978a) *On the Social Construction of Female Sexuality*. London: Women's Research and Resources Centre.
Jackson, S. (1978b) The Social Context of Rape. *Women's Studies International Quarterly* 1(1): 27–38.
Jackson, S. (1978c) How to Make Babies: Sexism and Sex Education. *Women's Studies International Quarterly* 1(4): 341–352.
Jackson, S. (1982) *Childhood and Sexuality*. Oxford: Blackwell.
Jackson, S. (1995) Women and Heterosexual Love: Complicity, Resistance and Change, in L. Pearce and J. Stacey (eds) *Romance Revisited*. London: Lawrence & Wishart,
Jackson, S. (1996a) Heterosexuality and Feminist Theory, in D. Richardson (ed.) *Theorising Heterosexuality*. Buckingham: Open University Press.
Jackson, S. (1996b) Heterosexuality as a Problem for Feminist Theory, in L. Adkins and V. Merchant (eds) *Sexualizing the Social*. London: Macmillan.
Jackson, S. (1999) *Heterosexuality in Question*. London: Sage.
Jackson, S. (2001) Why a Materialist Feminism is *Still* Possible (and Necessary). *Women's Studies International Forum* 24(2–3): 283–293.
Jackson, S. (2006a) Gender, Sexuality and Heterosexuality: The Complexity (and Limits) of Heteronormativity. *Feminist Theory* 7(1): 105–121.
Jackson, S. (2006b) Heterosexuality, Sexuality and Gender: Re-thinking the Intersections, in D. Richardson, M. Casey and J. McLaughlin (eds) *Intersections between Feminist and Queer Theory*. London: Palgrave.
Jackson, S. (2007) The Sexual Self in Late Modernity, in M. Kimmel (ed.) *The Sexual Self: The Construction of Sexual Scripts*. Nashville, TN: Vanderbilt University Press.
Jackson, S. (2008) Ordinary Sex. *Sexualities* 11(1): 37–40.
Jackson, S. (2010) Self, Time and Narrative: Re-thinking the Contribution of G.H. Mead. *Life Writing* 7(2).
Jackson, S., Liu Jieyu and Woo Juhyun (eds) (2008) *East Asian Sexualities: Modernity, Gender and New Sexual Cultures*. London: Zed.
Jackson, S. and Rees, A. (2007) The Appalling Appeal of Nature: The Popular Influence of Evolutionary Psychology as a Problem for Sociology. *Sociology* 41(5): 917–930.
Jackson, S. and Scott, S. (1996) Sexual Skirmishes and Feminist Factions: Twenty-Five Years of Debate on Women and Sexuality, in S. Jackson and S. Scott (eds) *Feminism and Sexuality*. Edinburgh: Edinburgh University Press.
Jackson, S. and Scott, S. (1997) Gut Reactions to Matters of the Heart: Reflections on Rationality, Irrationality and Sexuality. *Sociological Review* 45(4): 551–575.
Jackson, S. and Scott, S. (1999) Risk Anxiety and the Social Construction of Childhood, in D. Lupton (ed.) *Risk and Sociocultural Theory: New Directions and Perspectives*. Cambridge: Cambridge University Press.
Jackson, S. and Scott, S. (2001a) Putting the Body's Feet on the Ground: Towards a Reconceptualisation of Gendered and Sexual Embodiment, in K. Backett-Milburn and L. McKie (eds) *Constructing Gendered Bodies*. London: Palgrave.
Jackson, S. and Scott, S. (2001b) Embodying Orgasm: Gendered Power Relations and Sexual Pleasure. *Women and Therapy* 24(1–2): 99–110.
Jackson, S. and Scott, S. (2003) Whatever Happened to Feminist Critiques of Monogamy?, in H. Graham, A. Kaloski, A. Neilson and E. Robertson (eds) *The Feminist Seventies*. York: Raw Nerve Books.

Jackson, S. and Scott, S. (2004) Sexual Antinomies in Late Modernity. *Sexualities* 7(2): 241–256.
Jackson, S. and Scott, S. (2007) Faking Like a Woman? Towards an Interpretive Theorization of Sexual Pleasure. *Body and Society* 13(2): 95–116.
Jackson, Sue (2005a) 'I'm 15 and Desperate for Sex': 'Doing' and 'Undoing' Desire in Letters to a Teenage Magazine. *Feminism and Psychology*, 15(3): 295–313.
Jackson, Sue (2005b) 'Dear Girlfriend ...': Constructions of Sexual Health Problems and Sexual Identities in Letters to a Teenage Magazine. *Sexualities* 8(3): 282–305.
James, A., Jenks, C. and Prout, A. (1998) *Theorizing Childhood*. Oxford: Blackwell.
James, N. (1989) Emotional Labour: Skill and Work in the Social Regulation of Feelings. *Sociological Review* 37: 15–42.
Jamieson, L. (1999) Intimacy Transformed? *Sociology* 33(3): 477–494.
Jeffreys, S. (ed.) (1987) *The Sexuality Debates*. New York: Routledge and Kegan Paul.
Jeffreys, S. (1990) *Anticlimax: A Feminist Critique of the Sexual Revolution*. London: Women's Press.
Jeffreys, S. (1994a) *The Lesbian Heresy: A Feminist Perspective on the Lesbian Sexual Revolution*. London: Women's Press.
Jeffreys, S. (1994b) The Queer Disappearance of Lesbian Sexuality in the Academy. *Women's Studies International Forum* 17(5): 459–472.
Jeffreys, S. (1997) The Queer Disappearance of Lesbians, in B. Mintz and E.D. Rothblum (eds) *Lesbians in Academia*. New York: Routledge.
Jenks, C. (1996) *Childhood*. London: Routledge.
Johnson, A., Mercer, C., Erens, B. et al. (2001) Sexual Behaviour in Britain: Partnerships, Practices, and HIV Risk Behaviours. *The Lancet* 358: 1835–1842.
Johnson, P. (2005) *Love, Heterosexuality and Society*. London: Routledge.
Jónasdóttir, A. (1994) *Why Women Are Oppressed*. Philadelphia, PA: Temple University Press.
Jones, G. and Bell, R. (2000) *Youth Policies in the UK: A Chronological* Map. Keele: University of Keele. Available at: www.keele.ac.uk/depts/so/youthchron/about/index.htm (accessed 12 October 2009).
Jordanova, L. (1989) *Sexual Visions: Images of Gender in Science and Medicine between the Eighteenth and Twentieth Centuries*. New York: Harvester Wheatsheaf.
Kappeler, S. (1995) *The Will to Violence: The Politics of Personal Behaviour*. Cambridge: Polity.
Katz, J.N. (1995) *The Invention of Heterosexuality*. New York: Dutton.
Kent, S.K. (1990) *Sex and Suffrage in Britain, 1860–1914*. London: Routledge.
Kessler, S.J. (1998) *Lessons from the Intersexed*. New Brunswick, NJ: Rutgers University Press.
Kessler, S.J. and McKenna, W. (1978) *Gender: An Ethnomethodological Approach*. New York: Wiley.
Khor, D. and Kamano, S. (eds) (2007) *'Lesbians' in East Asia: Diversity, Identities, and Resistance*. Binghampton, NY: Harrington Park Press.
Kimmel, M. (2005) *The Gender of Desire*. Albany, NY: State University of New York Press.
Kincaid, J. (1998) *Erotic Innocence: The Culture of Child Molesting*. Durham, NC: Duke University Press.

Kinsey, A.C., Pomeroy, W.H. and Martin, C.E. (1948) *Sexual Behaviour in the Human Male*. Philadelphia, PA: W.B. Saunders.
Kinsey, A.C., Pomeroy, W.H., Martin, C.E. and Gebhard, P.H. (1953) *Sexual Behaviour in the Human Female*. Philadelphia, PA: W.B. Saunders.
Kitzinger, C. (2005) 'Speaking as a Heterosexual': (How) Does Sexuality Matter for Talk-in-Interaction? *Research on Language and Social Interaction* 38(3): 221–265.
Kitzinger, C. and Wilkinson, S. (1992) Theorizing Heterosexuality, in S. Wilkinson and C. Kitzinger (eds) *Heterosexuality: A* Feminism and Psychology *Reader*. London: Sage.
Kitzinger, C. and Wilkinson, S. (2004) The Re-branding of Marriage: Why We Got Married Instead of Registering a Civil Partnership. *Feminism and Psychology* 14(1): 127–150.
Kitzinger, J. (1988) Defending Innocence: Ideologies of Childhood. *Feminist Review* 28: 77–87.
Koedt, A. (1972) The Myth of the Vaginal Orgasm, in A. Koedt (ed.) *Radical Feminism*. New York: Quadrangle.
Kollontai, A. (1972) *Sexual Relations and the Class Struggle/Love and the New Morality*, translated from the Russian by A. Holt. Bristol: Falling Wall Press.
Lacan, J. (1977) *Écrits: A Selection*. London: Tavistock.
Lacan, J. (1982) God and the *Jouissance* of the Woman, in J. Mitchell and J. Rose (eds) *Feminine Sexuality: Jacques Lacan and the Ecole Freuetienne* London: Macmillan.
Langford, W. (1995) The Subject of Love. Unpublished PhD thesis, University of Lancaster.
Langford, W. (1999) *Revolutions of the Heart*. London: Routledge.
Laqueur, T. (1990) *Making Sex: Body and Gender from the Greeks to Freud*. Cambridge, MA: Harvard University Press.
Lash, S. and Urry, J. (1987) *The End of Organized Capitalism*. Cambridge: Polity.
Laumann, E. and Gagnon, J. (1995) A Sociological Perspective on Sexual Action, in R. Parker and J. Gagnon (eds) *Conceiving Sexuality: Approaches to Sex Research in a Postmodern World*. New York: Routledge.
Laumann, E., Gagnon, J., Michael, R.T. and Michaels, S. (1994) *The Social Organization of Sexuality: Sexual Practices in the United States*. Chicago, IL: University of Chicago Press.
Lawler, S. (2000) *Mothering the Self: Mothers, Daughters, Subjects*. London: Routledge.
Leeds Revolutionary Feminists (1981) Political Lesbianism: The Case Against Heterosexuality, in Onlywomen Press Collective (eds) *Love Your Enemy: The Debate between Heterosexual Feminism and Political Lesbianism*. London: Onlywomen Press.
Leonard, D. and Adkins, L. (eds) (1996) *Sex in Question: French Materialist Feminism*. London: Taylor & Francis.
Levine, J. (2002) *Harmful to Minors: The Perils of Protecting Children from Sex*. Minneapolis, MN: University of Minnesota Press.
Lévi-Strauss, C. (1969) *The Elementary Structures of Kinship*. London: Eyre & Spottiswoode.
Lewis, J. (1997) 'How Did Your Condom Use Go Last Night, Daddy?' Sex Talk and Daily Life, in L. Segal (ed.) *New Sexual Agendas*. London: Macmillan.

Lewis, J., Clark, D. and Morgan, D. (1992) *'Whom God hath Joined Together'*: *The Work of Marriage Guidance*. London: Routledge.
Lindemann, G. (1997) The Body of Gender Difference, in K. Davis (ed.) *Embodied Practices: Feminist Perspectives on the Body*. London: Sage.
Liu Jieyu (2008) Sexualized Labour? 'White Collar Beauties' in Provincial China, in S. Jackson, Liu Jieyu and Woo Juhyun (eds) *East Asian Sexualities: Modernity, Gender and New Sexual Cultures*. London: Zed.
Lupton, D. (1998) *The Emotional Self: A Sociocultural Exploration*. London: Sage.
McCaughey, M. (2008) *The Caveman Mystique: Pop-Darwinism and the Debates over Sex, Violence, and Science*. London: Routledge.
McDonough, R. and Harrison, R. (1978) Patriarchy and Relations of Production, in A. Kuhn and A-M. Wolpe (eds) *Feminism and Materialism: Women and Modes of Production*. London: Routledge and Kegan Paul.
Macey, D. (1988) *Lacan in Contexts*. London: Verso.
McIntosh, M. (1968) The Homosexual Role. *Social Problems* 16(2): 182–192.
McIntosh, M. (1978) Who Needs Prostitutes? The Ideology of Male Sexual Needs, in C. Smart and B. Smart (eds) *Women, Sexuality and Social Control*. London: Routledge and Kegan Paul.
MacKinnon, C.A (1982) Feminism, Marxism, Method and the State: An Agenda for Theory. *Signs* 7(3): 515–544.
McNay, L. (2000) *Gender and Agency*. Cambridge: Polity.
McNay, L. (2003) Agency, Anticipation and Indeterminacy. *Feminist Theory* 4(2): 139–148.
McRobbie, A. (1996) *More!*: New Sexualities in Girls' and Women's Magazines, in J. Curran, D. Morley and V. Walkerdine (eds) *Cultural Studies and Communications*. London: Edward Arnold.
McRobbie, A. (2009) *The Aftermath of Feminism: Gender, Culture and Social Change*. London: Sage.
Maines, D. (2001) *The Faultline of Consciousness: A View of Interactionism in Sociology*. New York: Aldine de Gruyter.
Mangan, J. (1987) Social Darwinism and Upper-Class Education in Late Victorian and Edwardian Times, in J. Mangan and J. Walvin (eds) *Manliness and Morality: Middle-Class Masculinity in Britain and America, 1800–1940*. Manchester: Manchester University Press.
Mangan, J. and Walvin, J. (eds) (1987) *Manliness and Morality: Middle-Class Masculinity in Britain and America, 1800–1940*. Manchester: Manchester University Press.
Mansfield, P. and Collard, J. (1988) *The Beginning of the Rest of Your Life*. London: Macmillan.
Marcuse, H. (1956) *Eros and Civilization: A Philosophical Inquiry into Freud*. London: Routledge & Kegan Paul.
Marcuse, H. (1964) *One-Dimensional Man*. London: Routledge and Kegan Paul.
Marshall, B. (2002) 'Hard Science': Gendered Constructions of Sexual Dysfunction in the 'Viagra Age'. *Sexualities* 5(2): 131–158.
Marshall, B. (2006) The New Virility: Viagra, Male Aging and Sexual Function. *Sexualities* 9(3): 345–362.
Marshall, B. and Katz, S. (2002) 'Forever Functional': Sexual Fitness and the Ageing Male Body. *Body and Society* 8(4): 43–70.

Martens, L., Southerton, D. and Scott, S. (2004) Bringing Children (and Parents) into the Sociology of Consumption: Towards a Theoretical and Empirical Agenda. *Journal of Consumer Culture* 4(2): 155–182.

Martin, E. (1991) The Egg and the Sperm: How Science Has Constructed a Romance Based on Stereotypical Male-Female Roles. *Signs* 16(3): 485–501.

Masters, W.H. and Johnson, V. (1966) *Human Sexual Response*. Boston, MA: Little, Brown.

Masters, W.H., Johnson, V. and Kolodny, R. (1986) *On Sex and Human Loving*. Boston, MA: Little, Brown.

Matthewman, S. and Hoey, D. (2006) What Happened to Postmodernism? *Sociology* 40(3): 529–547.

Matza, D. (1969) *Becoming Deviant*. Englewood Cliffs, NJ: Prentice Hall.

Mead, G.H. (1929) The Nature of the Past, in J. Cross (ed.) *Essays in Honour of John Dewey*. New York: Henry Holt. Reprinted in A.J. Reck (ed.) *Mead: Selected Writings*. Indianapolis, IN: Bobbs-Merrill, 1964.

Mead, G.H. (1934) *Mind, Self and Society*. Chicago, IL: University of Chicago Press.

Mead, G.H. (1964) *On Social Psychology*. Chicago, IL: University of Chicago Press.

Mead, G.H. ([1932] 2002) *The Philosophy of the Present*. New York: Prometheus. (original 1932 publication, Chicago, IL: Open Court).

Millet, K. (1971) *Sexual Politics*. London: Rupert Hart-Davis.

Mills, C.W. (1940) Situated Actions and Vocabularies of Motive. *American Sociological Review* 5: 439–452.

Mills, C.W. (1970) *The Sociological Imagination*. Harmondsworth: Penguin.

Mitchell, J. (1975) *Psychoanalysis and Feminism*. Harmondsworth: Penguin.

Mitchell, J. (1982) Introduction I, in J. Mitchell and J. Rose (eds) *Feminine Sexuality: Jacques Lacan and the École Freudienne*. London: Macmillan.

Mitchell, J. and Rose, J. (eds) (1982) *Feminine Sexuality: Jacques Lacan and the École Freudienne*. London: Macmillan.

Morgan, D.H.J. and Scott, S. (1993) Bodies in a Social Landscape, in S. Scott and D.H.J. Morgan (eds) *Body Matters*. Basingstoke: Falmer.

Morrow, R. (2008) *Sex Research and Sex Therapy: A Sociological Critique of Masters and Johnson*. London: Routledge.

Moyniham, R. (2003) The Making of a Disease: Female Sexual Dysfunction. *British Medical Journal* 325 (4 January): 45–47.

Norwood, R. (1985) *Women Who Love Too Much*. New York: Pocket Books.

O'Brien, M. (1981) *The Politics of Reproduction*. Boston, MA: Routledge & Kegan Paul.

O'Connell Davidson, J. (1998) *Prostitution, Power and Freedom*. Cambridge: Polity.

O'Connell Davidson, J. (2002) The Rights and Wrongs of Prostitution. *Hypatia* 17(2): 84–98.

O'Connell Davidson, J. (2006) Will the Real Sex Slave Please Stand Up? *Feminist Review* 83: 4–22.

O'Faolain, J. and Martines, L. (1974) *Not In God's Image*. Glasgow: Collins/Fontana.

Office for National Statistics (ONS) (2008) *Social Trends 38*. London: ONS.

Oudshoorn, N. (1994) *Beyond the Natural Body: An Archeology of Sex Hormones*. London: Routledge.

Park-Kim, S.J., Lee-Kim, S.Y. and Kwon-Lee, E.J. (2006) The Lesbian Rights Movement and Feminism in South Korea, in D. Khor and S. Kamano (eds) *Lesbians' in East Asia: Diversity, Identities and Resistance*. Binghampton, NY: Harrington Park Press.
Phelan, R. (2007) In Search of Sexual Subjectivities: Exploring the Sociological Construction of Sexual Selves, in M. Kimmel (ed.) *The Sexual Self*. Nashville, TN: Vanderbilt University Press.
Phillips, L.M. (2000) *Flirting with Danger: Young Women's Reflections on Sexuality and Domination*. New York: New York University Press.
Phoenix, A., Frosh, S. and Pattman, R. (2003) Producing Contradictory Masculine Subject Positions: Narratives of Threat, Homophobia and Bullying in 11–14 Year Old Boys. *Journal of Social Issues* 59(1): 179–195.
Pilcher, J. (2005) School Sex Education: Policy and Practice in England 1970 to 2000. *Sex Education* 5(2): 153–170.
Plaza, M. (1996) Our Costs and their Benefits, in D. Leonard and L. Adkins (eds) *Sex in Question: French Materialist Feminism*. London: Taylor and Francis.
Plummer, K. (1975) *Sexual Stigma*. London: Routledge and Kegan Paul.
Plummer, K. (ed.) (1985) *Modern Homosexualities*. London: Routledge.
Plummer, K. (1995) *Telling Sexual Stories: Power, Change and Social Worlds*. London: Routledge.
Plummer, K. (2001) *Documents of Life 2: An Invitation to a Critical Humanism*, 2nd edn. London: Sage.
Plummer, K. (2003) Queers, Bodies and Postmodern Sexualities: A Note on Revisiting the "Sexual" in Symbolic Interactionism. *Qualitative Sociology* 26(4): 515–530.
Poovey, M. (1988) *Uneven Developments: The Ideological Work of Gender in Mid-Victorian England*. Chicago, IL: University of Chicago Press.
Poovey, M. (1989) *Uneven Developments: The Ideological Work of Gender in Mid-Victorian England*. London: Virago.
Postman, N. (1994) *The Disappearance of Childhood*. New York: Vintage.
Potts, A. (2000) Coming, Coming, Gone: A Feminist Deconstruction of Heterosexual Orgasm. *Sexualities* 3(1): 55–76.
Potts, A. (2002) *The Science/Fiction of Sex*. London: Routledge.
Potts, A. (2004) Deleuze on Viagra (Or, What Can a 'Viagra-Body' Do?). *Body and Society* 10(1): 17–36.
Potts, A., Gavey, N., Grace, V.M. and Vares, T. (2003) The Downside of Viagra: Women's Experiences and Concerns. *Sociology of Health and Illness* 25(7): 697–719.
Poulantzas, N. (1978) *State, Power and Socialism*. London: New Left Books.
Quaife, G.R. (1979) *Wanton Wenches and Wayward Wives*. London: Croom Helm.
Questions Féministes Collective (1981) Variations on a Common Theme, in E. Marks and I. de Courtivron (eds) *New French Feminisms: An Anthology*. Brighton: Harvester.
Radicalesbians (1972) The Woman-Identified Woman, in K. Jay and A. Young (eds) *Out of the Closets: Voices of Gay Liberation*. New York: Pyramid.
Rahman, M. and Jackson, S. (1997) Liberty, Equality and Sexuality: Essentialism and the Discourse of Rights. *Journal of Gender Studies* 6(2): 117–129.
Ramazanoğlu, C. (ed.) (1993) *Up Against Foucault: Explorations of Some Tensions between Foucault and Feminism*. London: Routledge.

Red Collective ([1973] 1978) *The Politics of Sexuality in Capitalism*. London: Red Collective/Publications Distribution Cooperative.
Reich, W. (1951) *The Sexual Revolution*. London: Vision Press.
Renold, E. (2002) Presumed Innocence: (Hetero) sexual, Heterosexist and Homophobic Harassment among Primary School Girls and Boys. *Childhood* 9(4): 415–434.
Renold, E. (2005) *Girls, Boys and Junior Sexualities*. London: Routledge Falmer.
Renold, E. (2006) 'They Won't Let Us Play … Unless You're Going Out with One of Them': Girls, Boys and Butler's 'Heterosexual Matrix' in the Primary Years. *British Journal of the Sociology of Education* 27(4): 489–509.
Reynaud, E. (1983) *Holy Virility: The Social Construction of Masculinity*. London: Pluto.
Rich, A. (1980) Compulsory Heterosexuality and Lesbian Existence. *Signs* 5(4): 631–660.
Richards, M.P. and Elliott, B.J. (1991) Sex and Marriage in the 1960s and 1970s, in D. Clark (ed.) *Marriage, Domestic Life and Social Change*. London: Routledge.
Richardson, D. (1993) *Women, Motherhood and Childrearing*. London: Macmillan.
Richardson, D. (ed.) (1996) *Theorising Heterosexuality: Telling it Straight*. Buckingham: Open University Press.
Richardson, D. (2000) *Rethinking Sexuality*. London: Sage.
Richardson, D. (2004) Locating Sexualities: From Here to Normality. *Sexualities* 7(4): 391–411.
Richardson, D. (2005a) Claiming Citizenship: Sexuality, Citizenship and Lesbian Feminist Theory, in C. Ingraham (ed.) *Thinking Straight: The Power, the Promise and the Paradox of Heterosexuality*. New York: Routledge.
Richardson, D. (2005b) Desiring Sameness? The Rise of a Neoliberal Politics of Normalisation. *Antipode* 37(3): 515–535.
Ricoeur, P. (1984) *Time and Narrative*. Chicago, IL: University of Chicago Press.
Ricoeur, P. (1992) *Oneself as Another*. Chicago, IL: University of Chicago Press.
Ritchie, A. and Barker, M. (2006) 'There Aren't Words for What We Do or How We Feel So We Have to Make Them Up': Constructing Polyamorous Languages in a Culture of Compulsory Monogamy'. *Sexualities* 9(5): 584–601.
Rivers, K. Aggleton, P., Scott, S et al. 1998 'Gender Relations, Sexual Communication and the Female Condom', **Critical Public Health** 8:4 Autumn 1998.
Roberts, C., Kippax, S., Waldby, C. and Crawford, J. (1995) Faking It: The Story of 'Ohh!'. *Women's Studies International Forum* 18(5–6): 523–532.
Robinson, V. (1996) Heterosexuality and Masculinity: Theorising Male Power or the Wounded Male Psyche?, in D. Richardson (ed.) *Theorising Heterosexuality*. Buckingham: Open University Press.
Robinson, V. (1997) My Baby Just Cares for Me: Feminism, Heterosexuality and Non-Monogamy. *Journal of Gender Studies* 6(2): 143–158.
Rose, J. (1982) Introduction II, in J. Mitchell and J. Rose (eds) *Feminine Sexuality*. London: Macmillan.
Rose, J. (1986) *Sexuality in the Field of Vision*. London: Verso.
Rose, N. (1989) *Governing the Soul*. London: Routledge.
Roseneil, S. (2000) Queer Frameworks and Queer Tendencies: Towards an Understanding of Postmodern Transformations of Sexuality. *Sociological Research Online*. Available at: 5(3) www.socresonline.org.uk/5/3/roseneil.html (accessed 3 September 2009).

Roseneil, S. and Budgeon, S. (2004) Cultures of Intimacy and Care Beyond 'The Family': Personal Life and Social Change in the Early 21st Century. *Current Sociology* 52(2): 135–159.
Rubin, G. (1975) The Traffic in Women: Notes on the 'Political Economy' of Sex, in R. Reiter (ed.) *Toward an Anthropology of Women*. New York: Monthly Review Press.
Rubin, G. (1984) Thinking Sex: Notes for a Radical Theory of the Politics of Sexuality, in C. Vance (ed.) *Pleasure and Danger*. London: Routledge and Kegan Paul.
Rubin, L. (1983) *Intimate Strangers*. New York: Harper & Row.
Schiebinger, L. (1989) *The Mind Has No Sex? Women in the Origins of Modern Science*. Cambridge, MA: Harvard University Press.
Schofield, M. (1965) *The Sexual Behaviour of Young People*. London: Longman.
Schofield, M. (1973) *The Sexual Behaviour of Young Adults*. London: Allen Lane.
Schrager, C.D. (1993) Questioning the Promise of Self-Help: A Reading of *Women Who Love Too Much*. *Feminist Studies* 1: 31–192.
Schutz, A. (1972) *The Phenomenology of the Social World*. London: Heinemann.
Scott, M.B. and Lyman, S.M. (1968) Accounts. *American Sociological Review* 33(1): 46–62.
Scott, S. and Freeman, R. (1995) Prevention as a Problem of Modernity: The Example of HIV and AIDS, in J. Gabe (ed.) *Medicine, Health and Risk: Sociological Approaches*. Oxford: Blackwell.
Scott, S., Jackson, S. and Backett-Milburn, K. (1998) Swings and Roundabouts: Risk Anxiety and the Everyday Worlds of Children. *Sociology* 32(4): 689–705.
Scott, S., Jackson, S., Backett-Milburn, K. and Harden, J. (2000) *The Impact of Risk and Parental Risk Anxiety on the Everyday Worlds of Children*. ESRC research report. Available at: www.esrcsocietytoday.ac.uk/ESRCInfoCentre.
Scott, S., Wight, D. and Buston, K. (1997) Innocence and Ignorance: Professionals' and Pupils' Discourses of Sex Education. Paper presented at the Scottish Medical Sociology Conference, Kinloch, Rannoch.
Sedgwick, E. (1990) *The Epistemology of the Closet*. Berkeley, CA: University of California Press.
Sedgwick, E. (1991) *The Epistemology of the Closet*. Hemel Hempstead: Harvester Wheatsheaf.
Segal, L. (1994) *Straight Sex: The Politics of Pleasure*. London: Virago.
Segal, L. (1997) Feminist Sexual Politics and the Heterosexual Predicament, in L. Segal (ed.) *New Sexual Agendas*. London: Macmillan.
Seidman, S. (1991) *Romantic Longings: Love in America 1830–1980*. New York: Routledge.
Seidman, S. (1997) *Difference Troubles: Queering Social Theory and Sexual Politics*. Cambridge: Cambridge University Press.
Seidman, S. (2002) *Beyond the Closet*. New York: Routledge.
Seidman, S. (2005) From Polluted Homosexual to the Normal Gay: Changing Patterns of Sexual Regulation in America, in C. Ingraham (ed.) *Thinking Straight: The Power, the Promise and the Paradox of Heterosexuality*. New York: Routledge.
Seidman, S. (2009) Critique of Compulsory Heterosexuality. *Sexuality Research and Social Policy: Journal of NSRC* 6(1): 18–28.
Shahar, S. (1990) *Childhood in the Middle Ages*. London: Routledge.

Shilling, C. and Mellor, P. (1996) Embodiment, Structuration Theory and Modernity: Mind-Body Dualism and the Repression of Sensuality. *Body and Society* 2(4): 1–15.
Simon, W. (1996) *Postmodern Sexualities*. New York: Routledge.
Simon, W. and Gagnon, J. (1986) Sexual Scripts: Permanence and Change. *Archives of Sexual Behavior* 15(2): 97–120.
Skeggs, B. (1997) *Formations of Class and Gender: Becoming Respectable*. London: Sage.
Skeggs, B. (2003) Becoming Repellent: The Limits of Propriety. Plenary Address to the British Sociological Association Annual Conference, University of York, 20 April.
Skeggs, B. (2004) *Class, Self, Culture*. London: Routledge.
Skolnick, A. (1973) *The Intimate Environment: Exploring Marriage and the Family*. Boston, MA: Beacon.
Slater, E. and Woodside, M. (1951) *Patterns of Marriage: A Study of Marriage Relationships in the Urban Working Classes*. London: Cassell.
Smart, C. (ed.) (1992) *Regulating Womanhood: Historical Essays on Marriage, Motherhood and Sexuality*. London: Routledge.
Smart, C. (1996) Collusion, Collaboration and Confession: On Moving beyond the Heterosexuality Debate, in D. Richardson (ed.) *Theorising Heterosexuality*. Buckingham: Open University Press.
Smith and Doe (1998) *What Men Don't Want Women to Know: The Secrets, the Lies, the Unspoken Truth*. New York: St Martin's Press.
Smith, A-M. (1997) The Good Homosexual and the Dangerous Queer: Resisting the 'New Homophobia', in L. Segal (ed.) *New Sexual Agendas*. London: Macmillan.
Smith, D.E. (1987) *The Everyday World as Problematic: A Feminist Sociology*. Boston, MA: Northeastern University Press.
Smith, D.E. (1988) *The Everyday World as Problematic*. Milton Keynes: Open University Press.
Smith, D.E. (1999) *Writing the Social*. Toronto: University of Toronto Press.
Stacey, J. (1991) Promoting Normality: Section 28 and the Regulation of Sexuality, In S. Franklin, C. Lury and J. Stacey (eds) *Off Centre: Feminism and Cultural Studies*. London: HarperCollins.
Stacey, J. (1996) *In the Name of the Family: Rethinking Family Values in the Postmodern Age*. Boston, MA: Beacon.
Stacey, J. (2004) Cruising to Familyland: Gay Hypergamy and Rainbow Kinship. *Current Sociology* 52(2): 181–197.
Stainton Rogers, R. and Stainton Rogers, W. (1992) *Stories of Childhood: Shifting Agendas of Child Concern*. Hemel Hempstead: Harvester Wheatsheaf.
Stanley, L. (1984) Should 'Sex' Really be 'Gender' or 'Gender' Really be 'Sex'?, in R. Anderson and W. Sharrock (eds) *Applied Sociology*. London: Allen and Unwin.
Stanley, L. (1995) *Sex Surveyed: From Mass-Observation's 'Little Kinsey' to the National Survey and the Hite Reports*. London: Taylor and Francis.
Stanley, L. and Wise, S. (1983) *Breaking Out: Feminist Consciousness and Feminist Research*. London: Routledge.
Stanley, L. and Wise, S. (1993) *Breaking Out Again*. London: Routledge.
Taylor, F.W. (1911) *Principles of Scientific Management*. New York: Harper and Bros.

Taylor, Y. (2004) Negotiation and Navigation: An Exploration of the Spaces/Places of Working-class Lesbians. *Sociological Research Online* (9)1. Available at: www.socresonline.org.uk/9/1/taylor.html (accessed 3 September 2009)
Thomas, W.I. (1923) *The Unadjusted Girl.* Boston, MA: Little, Brown.
Thomson, R. (1994) Moral Rhetoric and Public Health Pragmatism: The Recent Politics of Sex Education. *Feminist Review* 48: 40–60.
Thomson, R. and Scott, S. (1991) *Learning about Sex.* London: Tufnell Press.
Thorne, B. (1987) Revisioning Women and Social Change: Where are the Children? *Gender and Society* 1(1): 85–109.
Thornhill, R. and Palmer, C. (2000) *A Natural History of Rape: Biological Bases of Sexual Coercion.* Cambridge, MA: MIT Press.
Tolman, D. (2002) *Dilemmas of Desire.* Cambridge, MA: Harvard University Press.
Vance, C.S. (ed.) (1984) *Pleasure and Danger.* London: Routledge.
VanEvery, J. (1996) Heterosexuality and Domestic Life, in D. Richardson (ed.) *Theorising Heterosexuality.* Buckingham: Open University Press.
Waites, M. (2005) *The Age of Consent: Young People, Sexuality and Citizenship.* Basingstoke: Palgrave.
Walby, S. (1986) *Patriarchy at Work.* Cambridge: Polity.
Walby, S. (1990) *Theorizing Patriarchy.* Oxford: Blackwell.
Walkerdine, V. (1990) *Schoolgirl Fictions.* London: Verso.
Walkowitz, J.R. (1992) *City of Dreadful Delight.* London: Virago.
Warde, A. (1997) *Consumption, Food and Taste: Culinary Antinomies and Commodity Culture.* London: Sage.
Warde, A and Gronow, J. (eds) (2001) *Ordinary Consumption.* London: Routledge.
Weedon, C. (1987) *Feminist Practices and Poststructuralist Theory.* Oxford: Blackwell.
Weeks, J. (1981), *Sex, Politics and Society: The Regulation of Sexuality since 1800.* London: Longman.
Weeks. J. (1989) *Sex. Politics and Society: The Regulation of Sexuality since 1800*, 2nd edn. London: Longman.
Weeks, J. (1991) Pretended Family Relationships, in D. Clark (ed.) *Marriage, Domestic Life and Social Change.* London: Routledge.
Weeks, J. (2007) *The World We Have Won: The Remaking of Erotic and Intimate Life.* London: Routledge.
Weeks, J., Plummer, K. and McIntosh, M. (1981) The Homosexual Role Revisited, in K. Plummer (ed.) *The Making of the Modern Homosexual.* London: Hutchinson.
Wellings, K., Field, J., Johnson, A. and Wadsworth, J. (1994) *Sexual Behaviour in Britain: The National Survey of Sexual Attitudes and Lifestyles.* London: Penguin.
West, C. and Zimmerman, D. (1987) Doing Gender. *Gender and Society* 1(2): 125–151.
Whisman, V. (1996) *Queer by Choice.* New York: Routledge.
Whittier, D. and Simon, W. (2001) The Fuzzy Matrix of 'My Type' in Intrapsychic Sexual Scripting. *Sexualities* (4)2: 139–165.
Wight, D. (1996) Beyond the Predatory Male: The Diversity of Young Glaswegian Men's Discourses to Describe Heterosexuality, in L. Adkins and V. Merchant (eds), *Sexualizing the Social.* London: Macmillan.
Wight, D., Raab, G.M., Henderson, M. et al. (2002) Limits of Teacher Delivered Sex Education: Interim Behavioural Outcomes from a Randomised Trial. *British Medical Journal* 324: 1430–1435.

Wilkinson, S. and Kitzinger, C. (eds) (1993) *Heterosexuality: A Feminism and Psychology Reader*. London: Sage.

Williams, R. (2000) *Making Identity Matter: Identity, Society and Social Interaction*. Durham: sociologypress.

Williams, S.J. and Bendelow G. (1998) *The Lived Body: Sociological Themes, Embodied Issues*. London: Routledge.

Wilson, E. (1993) Is Transgression Transgressive?, in J. Bristow and A. Wilson (eds) *Activating Theory*. London: Lawrence & Wishart.

Wilson, T.P. (1971) Normative and Interpretive Paradigms in Sociology, in J. Douglas (ed.) *Understanding Everyday Life: Towards the Reconstruction of Sociological Knowledge*. London: Routledge and Kegan Paul.

Wilton, T. (1996) Which One's the Man? The Heterosexualisation of Lesbian Sex, in D. Richardson (ed.) *Theorising Heterosexuality*. Buckingham: Open University Press.

Wittig, M. (1980) The Straight Mind. *Feminist Issues* 1(1): 103–111.

Wittig, M. (1982) The Category of Sex. *Feminist Issues* 2(2): 63–68.

Wittig, M. (1992) *The Straight Mind and Other Essays*. Hemel Hempstead: Harvester Wheatsheaf.

Witz, A. (2000) Whose Body Matters? Feminist Sociology and the Corporeal Turn in Sociology and Feminism. *Body and Society* 6(2): 1–24.

Woo, J. (2007) Sexual Stories Go to Westminster: Narratives of Sexual Citizens/Outsiders in Britain. Unpublished PhD thesis, University of York.

Young, I.M. (1990) Throwing Like a Girl, in I.M. Young, *Throwing Like a Girl and Other Essays in Feminist Philosophy and Social Theory*. Bloomington, IN: Indiana University Press.

INDEX

aims, this book's 3
Althusser, L., feminism 32
asymmetry, gender 93–4

Barrett, Michèle
   feminism 32, 38–40
   interactionism 38–40
Bauman, Z., male sexuality 58
becoming sexual 113–19
   see also childhood
   gender attribution 113–15
   heterosexuality 115–18
   Mead, G.H. 114–15
   risk anxiety 118–19
boundaries, childhood 101–20
Butler, Judith
   gender attribution 143–4
   heterosexuality 80
   queer theory 20–1

case for sociality of sexuality 1–4
cataloguing sexual behaviour
   conceptualizing sexuality 6–9
   Davis, Kingsley 8
   Kinsey, Alfred 6–7
   prostitution 8
childhood 101–20
   see also becoming sexual
   boundaries 101–20
   concepts/conceptions 102–5
   consent, age of 105
   governance 101–20
   paedophilia issues 107–8
   risk 101–20

   risk anxiety 105–7, 118–19
   sexualization 108–10
   social construction of 102–5
   social ordering of sexuality 165
   surveillance 101–20
children and sexuality, risk anxiety 105–7, 118–19
class
   gender 86–90
   heterosexuality 86–90
   sexuality 86–90
composing the sexual body
   embodied practices 157–60
   sexual pleasure 157–60
concepts/conceptions, childhood 102–5
conceptual slippages
   gender 82–6
   heterosexuality 82–6
   sexuality 82–6
conceptualizing sexuality 5–23
   cataloguing sexual behaviour 6–9
   Foucault 16–19
   history overview 5–6
   psychoanalysis 9–11
   queer theory 19–23
   social constructionism 11–19
   social constructionism reorientation 16–19
consent, age of 105
Crossley, Nick, embodied practices 147
cultural context, sexuality 50–6

Davis, Kingsley
  cataloguing sexual behaviour 8
  prostitution 8
definitional difficulties
  gender 82–6
  heterosexuality 82–6
  sexuality 82–6
dimensions
  gender 86–90
  heterosexuality 86–90
  sexuality 86–90
discursive meanings
  gender 90–4
  heterosexuality 90–4
  sexuality 90–4
drive reduction model, sexuality 8, 11
dysfunction, sexual 65, 68–9
education, sexual *see* sexual knowledge

Elias, N., historical context 53
embodied practices
  composing the sexual body 157–60
  doing orgasm 155–7
  feminist challenges 142–7
  gender attribution 143–5
  gendering of orgasm 152–4
  'mystery' of female orgasm 152–5
  objectified embodiment 147–9
  pre-social fictions 150–2
  scripting the sexual body 157–60
  sensate embodiment 149
  sensory embodiment 149
  sexual embodiment as social embodiment 147–50
  sexual pleasure 140–61
  sociological beginnings 142–7
  supra-social fictions 150–2
emotional entanglement 69–71
Enlightenment 56–7
erotic desire, Grosz, Elizabeth 150–2
'eroticization of sex' 61–3, 96
evolutionary psychology
  Gagnon, John 135
  Laumann, E. 135
  sexual self 133–5

faking orgasm 155–7
'fallacy of misplaced scale'
  feminism 45–9

Rubin, Gayle 45
Faraday, Annabel
  feminism 42–4
  interactionism 42–4
feminism 24–49
  Althusser, L. 32
  Barrett, Michèle 32, 38–40
  challenges 24–5
  competing positions 25–6
  culture 31–6
  'fallacy of misplaced scale' 45–9
  Faraday, Annabel 42–4
  Foucault, M. 35–6
  French materialist feminists 28–9
  gender vs. sexuality 25–6
  interactionism 36–45
  Lacan, Jacques 33–4
  Leeds Revolutionary Feminists 27
  Marxism 29, 31–3
  McIntosh, Mary 38
  Mitchell, Juliet 33
  psychoanalysis 32–5
  Rubin, Gayle 45
  sex, views of 47–9
  social structural analysis 26–31
  structural approaches 30–1
  subjectivity 31–6
  tensions 25
  Walby, Sylvia 40–1
Feminism and Psychology, heterosexuality 78–9
feminist challenges
  embodied practices 142–7
  sexual pleasure 142–7
feminist critiques, heterosexuality 77–82
flexible sex 66–9
Foucault, M.
  feminism 35–6
  historical context 54
  homosexuality 17–18
  repression 17–18, 46–7
  social constructionism reorientation 16–19
French materialist feminists, feminism 28–9
Freud, Sigmund, psychoanalysis 9–11
Fuss, Diana, queer theory 22

Gagnon, John
  evolutionary psychology 135

INDEX

social constructionism 12–16, 18–19
gender
 asymmetry 93–4
 class 86–90
 conceptual slippages 82–6
 definitional difficulties 82–6
 dimensions 86–90
 discursive meanings 90–4
 everyday interaction 92–4
 interactional meanings 90–4
 interconnections 86–90
 vs. sexuality 2, 25–6
 and sexuality 145–6
 social change 95–100
 sociality of the self 94–5
 structural dimension 86–90
gender attribution
 becoming sexual 113–15
 Butler, Judith 144–5
 embodied practices 143–5
 sexual pleasure 143–5
Gender Trouble, heterosexuality 80
gendering of orgasm 153–5
Giddens, A.
 reflexivity 142–3
 risk anxiety 105–6
governance, childhood 101–20
Grosz, Elizabeth, erotic desire 150–2

heterosexuality 74–100
 becoming sexual 115–18
 Butler, Judith 80
 class 86–90
 conceptual slippages 82–6
 definitional difficulties 82–6
 dimensions 86–90
 discursive meanings 90–4
 everyday interaction 92–4
 Feminism and Psychology 78–9
 feminist critiques 77–82
 Gender Trouble 80
 Ingraham, Chrys 81–2
 interactional meanings 90–4
 interconnections 86–90
 Kitzinger, Celia 78–9
 queer critiques 77–82
 questioning 75–7
 Segal, Lynne 78–9
 social change 95–100
 sociality of the self 94–5
 Straight Sex 78–9
 structural dimension 86–90
 Wilkinson, Sue 78–9
historical context, sexuality 50–6
history overview, conceptualizing sexuality 5–6
HIV/AIDS 166
homosexuality, Foucault, M. 17–18

identity, conceptual/theoretical clarification 122–5
Ingraham, Chrys, heterosexuality 81–2
interactional meanings
 gender 90–4
 heterosexuality 90–4
 sexuality 90–4
interactionism
 Barrett, Michèle 38–40
 Faraday, Annabel 42–4
 feminism 36–45
 social constructionism 11–16
 Walby, Sylvia 40–1
interconnections
 gender 86–90
 heterosexuality 86–90
 sexuality 86–90
internationalizing the study of sexuality 166–7
intimacy rationalization 69–71

Jackson, S., sexual self 124

Kinsey, Alfred
 cataloguing sexual behaviour 6–7
 social factors, sexuality 7
Kitzinger, Celia, heterosexuality 78–9
knowledge, sexual *see* sexual knowledge

Lacan, Jacques, feminism 33–4
late modernity, sexual self in 121–39
Laumann, E., evolutionary psychology 135
Leeds Revolutionary Feminists, feminism 27
liberalization
 sexual attitudes 71–2
 sexual regulation 71–2
 trends 71–2

male passions, controlling 58–60

male sexuality, Reynaud, Emmanuel 153–4
Marxism, feminism 29, 31–3
McIntosh, Mary, feminism 38
Mead, G.H.
   becoming sexual 114–15
   reflexivity ('reflexiveness') 125–6
   sexual self 122
   sociality of the self 94
medicalization of sex 60–1, 97–8
Mitchell, Juliet, feminism 33
'mystery' of female orgasm 152–5

objectified embodiment, embodied practices 147–9
Oedipus complex, psychoanalysis 10–11
ordinary sexuality, concluding thoughts 162–7
orgasm
   doing 155–7
   faking 155–7
   gendering of 153–5
   'mystery' of female 152–5
   Reynaud, Emmanuel 153–4
overview, this book's 3–4

paedophilia issues 107–8
penis envy, psychoanalysis 10–11
phenomenology, social constructionism 11–12
'plastic sexuality' 96–9
pre-social fictions
   embodied practices 150–2
   sexual pleasure 150–2
prostitution
   cataloguing sexual behaviour 8
   Davis, Kingsley 8
psychoanalysis
   conceptualizing sexuality 9–11
   feminism 32–5
   Freud, Sigmund 9–11
   Oedipus complex 10–11
   penis envy 10–11
   queer theory 20–1
   sexual self 135–7
   Walkerdine, Valerie 136–7
psychology, evolutionary *see* evolutionary psychology

queer critiques, heterosexuality 77–82

queer theory
   Butler, Judith 20–1
   conceptualizing sexuality 19–23
   Fuss, Diana 22
   psychoanalysis 20–1

rationalization, intimacy 69–71
rationalizing sex 56–8
reflexivity
   Giddens, A. 142–3
   Mead, G.H. 125–6
   self 124–31
   types 129–31
   varying conditions 129–31
repression, Foucault, M. 17–18, 46–7
Reynaud, Emmanuel
   male sexuality 153–4
   orgasm 153–4
risk, childhood 101–20
risk anxiety
   becoming sexual 118–19
   children and sexuality 105–7, 118–19
Rubin, Gayle
   'fallacy of misplaced scale' 45
   feminism 45
   structural approaches 30–1

scripting the sexual body
   embodied practices 157–60
   sexual pleasure 157–60
Segal, Lynne, heterosexuality 78–9
self
   see also sexual self
   conceptual/theoretical clarification 122–5
sensate embodiment, embodied practices 149
sensory embodiment, embodied practices 149
sex
   defining 7–8
   medicalization 60–1, 97–8
   rationalizing 56–8
   views of, feminist 47–9
sexual attitudes, liberalization 71–2
sexual embodiment as social embodiment 147–50
sexual knowledge, social distribution 110–12
sexual pleasure

composing the sexual body 157–60
doing orgasm 155–7
embodied practices 140–61
feminist challenges 142–7
gender attribution 143–5
gendering of orgasm 153–5
'mystery' of female orgasm 152–5
pre-social fictions 150–2
scripting the sexual body 157–60
sociological beginnings 142–7
supra-social fictions 150–2
sexual regulation, liberalization 71–2
sexual self
  conceptual/theoretical clarification 122–5
  evolutionary psychology 133–5
  Jackson, S. 124
  late modernity 121–39
  Mead, G.H. 122
  psychoanalysis 135–7
  reflexivity 124–31
  resources 131–3
sexuality
  class 86–90
  conceptual slippages 82–6
  cultural context 50–6
  defining 1–2
  definitional difficulties 82–6
  dimensions 86–90
  discursive meanings 90–4
  drive reduction model 8, 11
  everyday interaction 92–4
  vs. gender 2, 25–6
  and gender 145–6
  historical context 50–6
  interactional meanings 90–4
  interconnections 86–90
  internationalizing the study of 166–7
  ordinary sexuality 162–7
  'plastic sexuality' 96
  pluralizing 164
  social change 95–100
  social ordering of 164–5
  sociality of the self 94–5
  structural dimension 86–90
  terminology 2
  views of 1–3, 50–6
sexualization, childhood 108–10
'sexualization of love' 61–3, 96

Simon, William, social constructionism 12–16, 18–19
social change
  gender 95–100
  heterosexuality 95–100
  sexuality 95–100
social construction of childhood 102–5
social constructionism
  conceptualizing sexuality 11–19
  emergence 11–16
  Foucault, M. 16–19
  Gagnon, John 12–16, 18–19
  interactionism 11–16
  phenomenology 11–12
  reorientation 16–19
  Simon, William 12–16, 18–19
social distribution, sexual knowledge 110–12
social embodiment as sexual embodiment 147–50
social factors, sexuality, Kinsey, Alfred 7
social ordering of sexuality 164–5
social structural analysis, feminism 26–31
sociality of the self
  gender 94–5
  heterosexuality 94–5
  Mead, G.H. 94
  sexuality 94–5
sociological beginnings
  embodied practices 142–7
  sexual pleasure 142–7
Straight Sex, heterosexuality 78–9
structural approaches
  feminism 30–1
  Rubin, Gayle 30–1
structural dimension
  gender 86–90
  heterosexuality 86–90
  sexuality 86–90
subjectivity, conceptual/theoretical clarification 122–5
supra-social fictions
  embodied practices 150–2
  sexual pleasure 150–2
surveillance, childhood 101–20

Taylorized sex 60–9
terminology, sexuality 2

Viagra 65, 68–9

Walby, Sylvia
   feminism 40–1
   interactionism 40–1

Walkerdine, Valerie
   psychoanalysis 136–7
   sexual self 136–7
Wilkinson, Sue
   heterosexuality 78–9